ETS® TOEFL.ITP

Official Guide
TO THE
TOEFL® ITP
TEST

Official Guide TO THE *TOEFL* *ITP* TEST

Korean Language Edition Copyright © 2014 by YBM

Copyright © 2014 Educational Testing Service, Princeton, New Jersey, U.S.A. and exclusively distributed in the Republic of Korea by YBM. ETS has granted YBM the non-exclusive right to translate this publication into Korean. All other rights reserved to ETS.

Original: Official Guide to the *TOEFL* *ITP* Test
By Educational Testing Service (ETS)
ISBN 978-0-88685-416-4

ETS, the ETS logo and TOEFL are registered trademarks of Educational Testing Service (ETS) in the United States and other countries, and used under license in the Republic of Korea by YBM. TOEFL ITP is a trademark of ETS in the Republic of Korea, and used under license by YBM.

Official Guide
TO THE
TOEFL *ITP* TEST

발행인	오재환
발행처	**YBM**

저자	Educational Testing Service (ETS)
편집	신재미
마케팅	김광희, 구태종, 정연철, 강승훈, 고영노
디자인	김혜경

초판인쇄	2014년 9월 5일
7쇄 발행	2018년11월20일

등록일자	1964년 3월 28일
등록번호	제 1-214호
주소	서울시 종로구 종로 104
전화	(02) 2000-0515[구입문의] / (02) 2000-0503[내용문의]
팩스	(02) 2285-1523
홈페이지	www.ybmbooks.com

ISBN 978-89-17-22269-2

ETS® TOEFL.ITP

Official Guide

TO THE
TOEFL® ITP
TEST

YBM

CONTENTS

INTRODUCING THE *TOEFL® ITP* TEST

Introducing the
TOEFL® ITP Test

이 책은 TOEFL ITP(TOEFL Institutional Testing Program)의 안내서이다. 수험자들은 이 책으로 TOEFL ITP 시험을 준비하면서 대학이나 대학원 과정에서 필요한 학습 능력을 기르고 영어 학습의 목표도 성취하게 된다.

*TOEFL® ITP*의 개요

TOEFL ITP(기관토플)는 기관에서 실시하는 PBT 방식의 영어 평가 시험이다. 전 세계 47개국 2,500여개 기관에서 연간 60만명 이상이 응시하고 있으며, 특히 400여개의 명성 있는 미국 대학 및 기관에서 국제교환학생 선발 등을 위해 활용 중이다.

Placement	교양 영어를 효과적으로 운영하기 위한 신입생들의 수준별 영어 능력 측정
Progress monitoring	교내 영어 프로그램 또는 어학 연수 전후의 영어 능력 향상도 확인
Exiting	영어 프로그램 수료 시 학생들의 영어 능력 평가
Admissions to short-term, non-degree programs in English-speaking countries	영어권 국가에서의 단기 또는 비학위 과정의 교환 학생 선발
Admissions to undergraduate and graduate degree programs in non-English speaking countries	비영어권 국가에서의 대학 신입생 또는 대학원생 선발
Admissions and placement in collaborative international degree programs	복수 학위 과정의 입학 및 반배정 평가
Scholarship programs	장학생 선발

해당 기관에서 원하는 시험 날짜나 장소를 지정해 TOEFL ITP를 실시할 수 있으며, 성적표에는 각 영역 점수와 총점이 표시된다. 기관별 최저 점수 기준은 해당 기관에 직접 문의하여 확인해야 한다. TOEFL ITP 점수는 2년간 유효하지만, 일반적으로 시험을 실시한 기관에서만 유효하다.

TOEFL® *ITP*의 구성

TOEFL ITP는 듣기(Listening Comprehension)와 문법(Structure and Written Expression), 읽기(Reading Comprehension)의 3개 영역으로 구성된다. 모든 문제는 객관식이며, 시험 시간은 약 2시간이다.

영역	문항 수	소요 시간	점수
듣기(Listening Comprehension)	50	35분	31-68
문법(Structure and Written Expression)	40	25분	31-68
읽기(Reading Comprehension)	50	55분	31-67
총점(TOTAL)	140	115분	310-677

SECTION 1 - 듣기(LISTENING COMPREHENSION)

듣기 영역은 짧은 대화와 긴 대화, 담화의 세 파트로 구성된다. 이 영역에서는 녹음 대화 및 지문을 듣고 문제를 풀게 되는데, 이 대화와 지문에는 구어체 영어에서 흔히 사용되는 어휘와 관용어구, 문법 구조가 포함된다.

SECTION 2 - 문법(STRUCTURE AND WRITTEN EXPRESSION)

문법 영역은 문어체 영어의 구조 및 문법 요소에 대한 지식을 측정하는 문장으로 구성된다. 이 문장들에는 다양한 주제가 포함되어 있어서 특정 분야의 학생이라고 더 유리하지는 않다. 만약 주제가 특정 국가와 관련이 있다면, 미국이나 캐나다의 문화, 예술 및 문학과 관련이 있을 수 있다. 하지만, 이런 맥락의 지식을 알지 못해도 문장 구조나 문법 문제를 풀 수 있도록 되어 있다.

SECTION 3 - 읽기(READING COMPREHENSION)

읽기 영역은 지문과 그 부속 문제로 구성된다. 지문을 읽고 주제와 중요한 세부 사항을 묻는 문제를 풀게 된다. 특정 정보 추론, 전후 문단 추론, 어휘, 지시 대상 찾기 등의 문제도 출제된다.

TOEFL® *ITP*의 주제

TOEFL ITP에서는 학업과 관련이 있는 주제, 즉 교실이나 캠퍼스 등 교육 환경에 적절한 주제를 다룬다.

1. 학업 관련 주제 (Academic Topics)
- **예술** _ 미술, 공예, 연극, 무용, 건축학, 문학, 음악, 영화, 사진
- **인문** _ 역사, 정치학, 행정, 철학, 법학
- **생명과학** _ 생물, 고생물학, 생화학, 동물 행동학, 생태학, 해부학, 생리학, 유전학, 보건학, 농학, 식물학
- **자연 과학** _ 지질학, 천문학, 화학, 지구과학, 공학, 기상학, 에너지학, 응용 과학, 해양학, 물리학
- **사회 과학** _ 인류학, 사회학, 교육학, 지리학, 고고학, 심리학, 경제학, 경영학, 행정학, 마케팅, 언론정보학

2. 캠퍼스 생활 관련 주제(Campus-Life Topics)
  - **교실** _ 수업 일정, 수업 준비, 도서관 이용 방법, 과제(논문, 프레젠테이션, 독서), 교수, 학업, 견학
  - **캠퍼스 행정** _ 등록, 기숙사, 유학, 인턴십, 학칙
  - **특별 활동** _ 동아리, 사교 행사

3. 일반 주제(General Topics)
  - **비즈니스** _ 경영, 연구실, 공문서, 규정
  - **환경** _ 날씨, 자연, 기후, 환경
  - **음식** _ 음식 종류, 식당, 식사 계획
  - **의사 소통** _ 우편, 이메일, 전화, 메시지, 정보 요청
  - **미디어** _ TV, 신문, 인터넷
  - **비품** _ 설명서, 장비
  - **개인** _ 가족, 친구, 건강, 감정, 외모, 일상사
  - **계획** _ 행사, 초대, 일정
  - **구매** _ 의류, 쇼핑, 은행 업무, 돈
  - **레크리에이션** _ 스포츠, 게임, 음악회, 연극, 예술, 도서, 사진, 음악, 모임, 강의
  - **교통 수단** _ 여행, 운전, 주차, 대중 교통, 여행 예약
  - **직장** _ 입사 지원, 교내 취업, 근무 일정

교재의 구성

이 책에는 TOEFL ITP의 지시 사항, 연습 문제 및 영어 구사 능력을 향상시킬 수 있는 전략 등이 수록되어 있다.

  - **Chapter 1** _ TOEFL ITP의 개요, 점수 환산법, 성적표
  - **Chapter 2, 3, 4** _ TOEFL ITP의 각 파트별 문제 유형, 연습 문제
  - **Chapter 5, 6** _ TOEFL ITP 시험 문제 2회분
  - **Chapter 7** _ TOEFL ITP와 관련하여 자주 묻는 질문 및 답변
  - **정답 및 해설** _ 정확한 해석과 알찬 해설

TOEFL® *ITP* 점수 환산 (SCORE SCALES)

이 책에는 각 영역별 점수가 제공되며, 총점을 환산해 볼 수 있다.

영역	점수
듣기(Listening Comprehension)	31-68
문법(Structure and Written Expression)	31-68
읽기(Reading Comprehension)	31-67
총점(TOTAL)	310-677

TOEFL® ITP 성적표 (SCORE REPORT)

TOEFL.ITP
Quality Beyond Measure.

TOEFL® ITP Official Score Report

Student Name: HONG GIL DONG

Student Number: 001235*******

Date of Birth: 1985-02-28   **Gender:** Male

Test Date: 2014-11-23

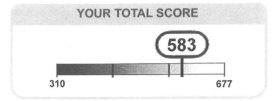

YOUR TOTAL SCORE

583

310   677

Listening Comprehension

Test takers who score between 64 and 68 may have the following strengths:

64

31   68

CEFR Level **C1**

- Can understand a wide range of demanding, longer texts, and recognize implicit meaning.
- Can express him/herself fluently and spontaneously without much obvious searching for expressions.
- Can use language flexibly and effectively for social, academic and professional purposes.
- Can produce clear, well-structured, detailed text on complex subjects, showing controlled use of organizational patterns, connectors and cohesive devices.

Structure and Written Expression

Test takers who score between 53 and 63 may have the following strengths:

56

31   68

CEFR Level **B2**

- Can understand the main ideas of complex text on both concrete and abstract topics, including technical discussions in his/her field of specialization.
- Can interact with a degree of fluency and spontaneity that makes regular interaction with native speakers quite possible without strain for either party.
- Can produce clear, detailed text on a wide range of subjects and explain a viewpoint on a topical issue giving the advantages and disadvantages of various options.

Reading Comprehension

Test takers who score between 48 and 55 may have the following strengths:

55

31   67

CEFR Level **B1**

- Can understand the main points of clear standard input on familiar matters regularly encountered in work, school, leisure, etc.
- Can deal with most situations likely to arise whilst travelling in an area where the language is spoken.
- Can produce simple connected text on topics which are familiar or of personal interest.
- Can describe experiences and events, dreams, hopes and ambitions and briefly give reasons and explanations for opinions and plans.

776467

100621-100621 • S1013E500 • Printed in U.S.A. • I.N. 776467

How to Interpret Your Score Report

The *TOEFL® ITP* test measures the English proficiency of test takers whose native language is not English and assesses their ability to use the language in an academic setting.

TOEFL ITP scores can be used to make placement decisions, to monitor progress, and to inform end-of-course decisions. TOEFL ITP scores can also be used for admissions to programs and institutions where English is not the dominant language of instruction. Learn more at *www.ets.org/toefl_itp/use*.

The TOEFL ITP score report provides both section and total scores.

Sections	Scaled Scores
Listening Comprehension	31–68
Structure and Written Expression	31–68
Reading Comprehension	31–67
Total Score	310–677

The section scores are based on the number of correctly answered test questions, converted to a scaled score between 31 and 68 (or 67 for Reading Comprehension). The total score is calculated by adding the three section scaled scores, multiplying the sum by 10, and then dividing by 3. For example, if the scaled score for Listening Comprehension is 60, Structure and Written Expression is 60, and Reading Comprehension is 60, the total score is (60+60+60)*10/3 = 600.

To help you interpret the scores, a mapping of TOEFL ITP scores to the Common European Framework of Reference (CEFR) was conducted in 2011. Results of this study provide the minimum TOEFL ITP score for four of the levels defined in the CEFR (A2, B1, B2, C1).

In addition, The TOEFL ITP Program offers test takers the option to obtain certificates of achievement indicating the CEFR level that corresponds to their TOEFL ITP scores: a Gold certificate for scores at the C1 level, a Silver certificate for the B2 level, and a Bronze certificate for the B1 level.

TOEFL ITP scores are valid for two years. Because language proficiency may change in a relatively short period of time, scores that are more than two years old cannot be reported or verified.

Alternate Form

TOEFL ITP Examinee Score Report

Name: HONG GIL DONG   Student Number: 001235

DOB: 02/28/1985   Sex: M   Degree: Times Taken TOEFL:

Native Country: Other
Native Language: Other

Purpose:

Scaled Scores: Listening Comprehension: 64   Test Date: 11/23/2014
                            Structure & Written Expression: 56

ETS TOEFL.ITP   Reading Comprehension: 55
                            Total Score: 583   **Student's File Copy**
The face of this document has a security background. The back contains a watermark. Hold at an angle to view.   **Do Not Copy**

The *TOEFL* *ITP* Assessment Series is designed to be used for placement, progress monitoring,
and exit purposes. *TOEFL* *ITP* scores can also be used for admissions to programs and institutions
where English is not the dominant language of instruction for content courses. Learn more at
www.ets.org/toefl_itp/use.

98151-16573 • FB413R200 • Printed in U.S.A.   I.N. 770462

CHAPTER 2

LISTENING COMPREHENSION SECTION

Listening Comprehension Section

Listening Comprehension 영역에서는 강의실, 교실, 도서관, 기숙사, 사무실, 카페테리아, 오락 시설이나 기타 공공 장소에서 듣게 되는 전형적인 대화나 담화가 다뤄지며, 구어체 영어(Spoken English)의 이해력을 측정한다.

Listening Comprehension 영역의 개요

Listening Comprehension 영역에서 시험 시간은 40분으로, 총 50문항(3파트)가 출제된다.

영어권 대학과, 전문대학, 기타 교육 기관에서 공부하는 학생들에게는 당연히 학교 강의를 이해하는 영어 능력이 필요하다. 그렇지만, 학생들에게는 사무실, 도서관, 카페테리아, 레크리에이션 센터 등에서 친구, 행정직원들, 교수들과 의사소통할 수 있는 능력도 필요하다. TOEFL IPT에서는 다른 유형의 듣기 과제를 통해서, 학업적인 주제와 학업이 아닌 일반적인 주제를 포함해서 학생들이 처해 있는 이런 다양한 대화 및 환경을 반영하고 있다.

교실 및 개인적인 대화 상황에서 논의 중인 주제를 이해하는 것뿐만 아니라 그 주제의 세부사항을 이해하는 것이 중요하다. 하지만, 다른 화자들의 목적과 태도를 인지하고 들은 정보를 바탕으로 추론하는 것도 중요하다. TOEFL IPT에서는 이렇게 각기 다른 듣기 능력을 측정하는 문제들이 출제된다.

Listening Comprehension 영역의 구성

Listening Comprehension 영역은 짧은 대화(Short Conversations)와 긴 대화(Extended Conversations), 짧은 담화(Short Talks)의 세 파트로 구성된다. 대화나 담화를 듣고 한 개 이상의 질문에 알맞은 대답을 고르면 된다. 대화나 담화는 한 번만 들려주며, 객관식 문제(4지 선다형)로 출제된다. 대화나 담화 및 질문은 시험 문제지에 인쇄되어 있지 않으며, 시험 문제지에는 4개의 보기만 나와 있다.

▶ PART A: 짧은 대화

Part A는 짧은 대화 30개로 구성된다. 들려주는 대화문은 두 사람이 한 번씩 주고 받는 대화로, 대화문에 이어 화자의 말이나 의도를 묻는 질문이 나온다. 여기서는 전형적인 대학 캠퍼스 생활과 관련된 주제가 다뤄진다. 예를 들어, 책을 도서관에 반납하거나 숙제를 끝마치거나 버스를 타는 등의 주제가 출제된다. 또한, 화자들이 대화하는 목적도 많이 다르다. 예를 들어, 행사를 설명하거나 조언을 하거나 초대를 하는 등의 목적에서 나누는 대화가 출제된다.

▷ 문제 유형

주제 및 중요한 세부 사항 파악, 화자의 말을 듣고 추론하는 문제, 관용 표현이나 대화의 목적을 묻는 문제가 출제된다.

유형 1. 주제 및 요지 파악

대화의 요지를 파악하는 문제가 출제되는데, 들려주는 대화에 요지가 명확히 언급되지 않는 경우도 있다.

질문 유형

- **What does the man/woman mean?**
  남자/여자는 무엇을 의미하는가?

- **What does the woman/man say about X?**
  여자/남자는 X에 대해 뭐라고 말하는가?

유형 2. 추론하기

대화에서 명백히 언급되지 않는 정보를 추론하는 유형으로, 두 사람의 대화에서 연관성을 추론해야 하는 경우도 있다.

질문 유형

- **What does the woman/man imply?**
  여자/남자가 암시하는 것은 무엇인가?

- **What does the man/woman imply about X?**
  남자/여자가 X에 대해 암시하는 것은 무엇인가?

- **What can be inferred about the woman/man?**
  여자/남자에 관해 추론할 수 있는 것은 무엇인가?

- **What does the man/woman imply that X should do?**
  남자/여자는 X가 어떻게 해야 한다고 암시하는가?

- **What can be inferred from the conversation?**
  대화에서 추론할 수 있는 것은 무엇인가?

- **What can be inferred about the speakers?**
  화자들에 대해 추론할 수 있는 것은 무엇인가?

유형 3. 조언 및 제안하기

한 화자가 다른 화자에게 제안한 사항을 파악하는 유형으로, 대화에서 제안 사항이 명백히 언급되지 않는 경우도 있다.

질문 유형

· What does the woman/man suggest the man/woman do?

  여자/남자가 남자/여자에게 제안하는 것은 무엇인가?

· What advice does the woman/man give to the man/woman?

  여자/남자가 남자/여자에게 충고하는 것은 무엇인가?

유형 4. 미래에 할 일 예측하기

화자가 다음에 할 일을 묻는 문제이다.

질문 유형

· What will the woman/man probably do (next)?

  여자/남자가 (다음에) 할 것 같은 일은 무엇인가?

유형 5. 어휘

흔히 사용되는 관용 표현의 의미를 묻는 문제이다

질문 유형

· What does the man/woman mean?

  남자/여자가 의미하는 것은 무엇인가?

▶ PARTS B AND C: 긴 대화 및 짧은 담화
(EXTENDED CONVERSATIONS AND SHORT TALKS)

PART B는 긴 대화 2개로 구성된다. 주로 대학 캠퍼스에서 이뤄지는 대화가 출제되며, 대학생들의 일상 생활에 관련된 다양한 주제가 다뤄진다. 교수에게 수업 관련 정보를 문의하는 학생, 과제에 대해 조언하는 교수, 또는 구술 발표를 준비하는 두 학생 간의 대화가 출제된다.

Part C는 화자 특히 교수가 주도하는 담화 3개로 구성된다. 주로 강의실이나 교실처럼 교내 담화가 많지만, 박물관이나 미술관처럼 교외의 장소에서 이뤄지는 담화도 출제된다. 담화는 대학 생활에 관한 내용으로, 예술, 인문학, 생명과학, 사회과학 등의 분야가 출제된다.

Part B와 C에서는 약 2분 정도 길이의 대화나 담화를 듣고, 화자가 언급한 내용이나 암시한 내용을 묻는 3~5개의 문제를 풀게 된다. 주제나 요지, 중요한 세부 사항, 화자의 목적이나 정체를 묻는 문제가 출제된다.

▷ 문제 유형

유형 1. 주제 및 요지 파악

대화나 담화의 주제 및 목적을 파악하는 문제가 출제되는데, 들려주는 지문에 주제나 목적이 직접적으로 언급되지 않는 경우도 있다.

질문 유형

- **What are the speakers mainly discussing?**
  화자들은 주로 무엇에 관해 이야기하고 있는가?

- **What is the professor mainly discussing?**
  교수는 주로 무엇에 관해 이야기하고 있는가?

- **What is the conversation/lecture mainly about?**
  대화/강의는 주로 무엇에 관한 것인가?

- **What is the purpose of the lecture/conversation?**
  강의/대화의 목적은 무엇인가?

- **Why does the man/woman go to speak to the professor?**
  남자/여자가 교수에게 말하러 가는 이유는 무엇인가?

유형 2. 세부 사항 파악

대화나 담화에 언급된 세부 사항을 이해하는 능력을 측정한다. 주어진 제안, 조언, 지시 사항, 주의 사항, 주요 어구나 표현의 의미 등을 묻는다. 담화나 대화에 언급된 2개 이상의 세부 사항을 연계하거나 추론해야 하는 경우도 있다.

질문 유형

· Why does the professor mention X?
교수가 X에 대해 언급한 이유는 무엇인가?

· According to the professor, what was the result of X?
교수에 따르면 X의 결과는 무엇이었는가?

· What does the student imply about X?
학생이 X에 대해 암시하는 것은 무엇인가?

· What will the student/professor probably do (next)?
학생/교수가 (다음에) 할 것 같은 일은 무엇인가?

Listening Comprehension 영역의 전략

· 짧은 대화를 들을 때는 화자의 강세 및 억양에 주의해 들으면 화자의 의도를 파악하는 데 도움이 된다.
· 긴 대화를 들을 때는 질문에 대답한 화자의 응답에 주의해 들으면 구체적인 세부사항을 파악하는 데 도움이 된다.
· 긴 대화나 짧은 담화를 들을 때는 교수가 소개하는 새로운 단어나 개념에 주의해 듣는다.
· 화자가 언급하거나 암시한 것을 바탕으로 정답을 고른다.

▶ 듣기 능력을 향상시키는 방법

학교 생활이나 일반 생활을 잘 하려면 듣기 실력이 중요하다. 듣기 실력을 향상시키는 최선의 방법은 다양한 정보가 포함된 강의, 토론, 뉴스 보도 등 다른 종류의 지문을 듣는 것이다.

영화나 TV를 시청하거나 라디오를 듣는 것도 듣기 실력을 향상시키는 좋은 방법이다. 강의나 프레젠테이션을 녹화한 것도 유용하며, 인터넷에서도 훌륭한 듣기 자료를 찾을 수 있다.

▷ 기본 사항 듣기

- 매일 영어를 듣거나 읽어서 어휘력을 기른다.
- 화자의 스타일이나 말솜씨에 신경 쓰지 말고 말하는 내용이나 흐름에 관심을 갖는다.
- 화자의 말에 집중해서 들으면서 화자가 다음에 할 말을 예상한다.
- 예를 들어, '교수가 하는 말의 요지는 무엇인가?(What is the main idea that the professor is communicating?)' 처럼 대화나 담화를 들으면서 스스로에게 질문해 본다.
- 대화나 담화를 들으면서 '요지', '주요 사항', '세부 사항' 등을 표시한다.
- 강의나 담화를 들으면서 중요 요소의 개요를 잡아 간단히 요약한다.

▷ 세부 사항 듣기

- 화자가 말하고자 하는 의도를 생각한다. 강연이나 대화의 목적은 무엇인가?, 화자는 사과를 하고 있는가, 불평을 하고 있는가, 아니면 제안을 하고 있는가?
- 화자의 어투에 주의한다. 격식을 차린 어투인가, 아니면 격식을 차리지 않은 어투인가?, 화자의 목소리가 차분한가 아니면 감정이 들어가 있는가?
- 화자의 어조는 어떠한가?
- 화자가 얼마나 확신하는지 주의해 듣는다. 화자는 얼마나 확신에 차서 말하고 있는가?
- TV나 영화를 시청하면서, 강세나 억양에 주의해 듣는다.
- 강의를 들으면서 어떤 식으로 이야기가 전개되는지 생각한다. 소개, 요지, 예제, 결론이나 요약을 암시하는 말에 유의해 듣는다. first, for instance, next, finally 등의 표현에서 강의의 진행 단계를 짐작할 수 있다.
- 원인/결과, 비교/대조 등 가능한 관계를 파악한다. however, on the other hand와 in addition 등의 어구는 관계를 나타낸다.
- 정보들 간의 관계나 연관성을 나타내는 말을 듣는다.
- 다음에 어떤 정보나 아이디어가 나올지 예상하면서 듣는다.
- 들으면서 또는 다 들은 후에 논의된 내용의 개요를 작성한다.

LISTENING COMPREHENSION PRACTICE

Practice Set 1 **SHORT CONVERSATIONS**   해설 p.152

Directions: Now you will hear some short conversations between two people. After each conversation, you will hear a question about the conversation. The conversations and questions will not be repeated. After you hear a question, read the four possible answers in your test book and choose the best answer. Then, on your answer sheet, find the number of the question and fill in the space that corresponds to the letter of the answer you have chosen.

Here is an example.

On the recording, you hear: **Sample Answer**

In your test book, you read: (A) He does not like the painting either.

(B) He does not know how to paint.

(C) He does not have any paintings.

(D) He does not know what to do.

You learn from the conversation that neither the man nor the woman likes the painting. The best answer to the question "What does the man mean?" is (A), "He does not like the painting either." Therefore, the correct choice is (A).

1. (A) A two-bedroom apartment may be too expensive.
    (B) The woman should not move off campus.
    (C) The woman should pay the rent by check.
    (D) The university has a list of rental properties.

2. (A) Talk to Dr. Boyd about an assignment
    (B) Return their books to the library
    (C) Meet Dr. Boyd at the library
    (D) Make an appointment with their teacher on Friday

3. (A) The transportation for the trip is free.
    (B) The class did not enjoy going on the field trip.
    (C) Some people may not go on the trip.
    (D) Everyone in the class has paid the fee.

4. (A) The woman should avoid getting cold.
    (B) It is easy to get sick in cold weather.
    (C) The woman should get more rest.
    (D) Dressing warmly can prevent illness.

5. (A) The woman should get another job.
    (B) He will not have to wait much longer.
    (C) The woman was mistaken.
    (D) He was waiting in the wrong place.

6. (A) He is probably nearby.
    (B) He should pick up his things.
    (C) He broke his racket.
    (D) He might be playing tennis right now.

7. (A) Watch the clock carefully during the final exam
   (B) Pick up their papers on the twelfth
   (C) Finish their assignment early
   (D) Discuss their topics after class

8. (A) She was not able to organize it.
   (B) Its location has been changed.
   (C) It has been rescheduled.
   (D) She does not know anything about it.

9. (A) The man is mistaken.
   (B) The error will be corrected.
   (C) She did not know about the problem.
   (D) Grades were sent late.

10. (A) Stay home and prepare for his exams
    (B) Attend the concert after his exams are over
    (C) Ask the woman to study with him
    (D) Go to the concert with the woman

PRACTICE SET CONTINUES ON THE NEXT PAGE.

Directions: Now you will hear a longer conversation. After the conversation, you will hear several questions. The conversation and questions will not be repeated.

After you hear a question, read the four possible answers in your test book and choose the best answer. Then, on your answer sheet, find the number of the question and fill in the space that corresponds to the letter of the answer you have chosen.

Remember, you are **not** allowed to take notes or write in your book.

1. (A) To get help in finding a new college
    (B) To change his major
    (C) To fill out an application for college
    (D) To find out how to change dormitories

2. (A) A small school does not offer a wide range of courses.
    (B) His tuition will not be refunded.
    (C) Changing majors involves a lot of paperwork.
    (D) He may not be able to transfer all his credits.

3. (A) He does not like his professors.
    (B) His classes are too difficult.
    (C) He cannot transfer his credits from his previous school.
    (D) He does not get along with his roommate.

4. (A) The registrar's office
    (B) The admissions office
    (C) The housing office
    (D) The math department

해설 p.158

Directions: Now you will hear a short talk. After the talk, you will hear some questions. The talk and the questions will not be repeated.

After you hear a question, read the four possible answers in your test book and choose the best answer. Then, on your answer sheet, find the number of the question and fill in the space that corresponds to the letter of the answer you have chosen.

Here is an example.

On the recording, you hear:

Sample Answer

Now listen to a sample question.

In your test book, you read:
(A) To demonstrate the latest use of computer graphics
(B) To discuss the possibility of an economic depression
(C) To explain the workings of the brain
(D) To dramatize a famous mystery story

The best answer to the question "What is the main purpose of the program?" is (C), "To explain the workings of the brain." Therefore, the correct choice is (C).

Now listen to another sample question.

Sample Answer

In your test book, you read:
(A) It is required of all science majors.
(B) It will never be shown again.
(C) It can help viewers improve their memory skills.
(D) It will help with course work.

The best answer to the question "Why does the speaker recommend watching the program?" is (D), "It will help with course work." Therefore, the correct choice is (D).

Remember, you are **not** allowed to take notes or write in your book.

1. (A) The properties of quartz crystals
    (B) A method of identifying minerals
    (C) The life of Friedrich Mohs
    (D) A famous collection of minerals

2. (A) Its estimated value
    (B) Its crystalline structure
    (C) Its chemical composition
    (D) Its relative hardness

3. (A) Collect some minerals as homework
    (B) Identify the tools he is using
    (C) Apply the information given in the talk
    (D) Pass their papers to the front of the room

4. (A) When it is scratched in different directions
    (B) When greater pressure is applied
    (C) When its surface is scratched too frequently
    (D) When the tester uses the wrong tools

CHAPTER 3

STRUCTURE AND WRITTEN EXPRESSION SECTION

Structure and Written Expression Section

Structure and Written Expression 영역에서는 문어체 영어에 적절한 언어 능력을 측정한다. 특히 대학 환경에서 의사를 명확히 전달하려면 올바른 문법과 어법을 알아야 한다.

Structure and Written Expression 영역의 개요

Structure and Written Expression 영역에서 시험 시간은 25분으로 총 40문항의 문제가 두 가지 유형으로 출제된다. 이 영역에서는 간단한 문법 시험을 치른다기 보다는 학술적인 글쓰기 능력을 간접적으로 평가한다.

Structure and Written Expression 영역의 구성

▶ 구문 문제 (STRUCTURE)

구문 문제에서는 문법적으로 완벽한 문장을 완성하는 능력을 측정하며, 다양한 학문 분야에서 발췌한 문장이 출제된다. 빈칸을 포함한 문장과 보기가 4개 제시되며, 보기는 한 단어 이상으로 되어 있다. 주어진 문장이 완벽한 문장이 되도록 빈칸에 들어갈 알맞은 보기를 고르면 된다.

구문 문제에서는 문법적으로 완벽한 문장을 만들기 위해 필요한 문장의 구성 요소에 대해서 다룬다. 특히 절이나 구 등의 문장 구성 요소에 초점을 둔 문제가 출제되는 데, 주로 규칙 동사와 불규칙 동사, 주어와 동사의 수 일치, 명사 · 형용사 · 부사의 형태와 어법, 비교, 어순, 대명사 · 전치사 · 관사 · 접속사 어법 등을 묻는다.

▶ 표현력 문제 (WRITTEN EXPRESSION)

표현력 문제에서는 학술 작문에서 어법상 틀린 부분을 파악해 고칠 수 있는 능력을 측정하며, 학술적인 자료에서 선정해 각색한 문장으로 구성된다. 각 문장에는 영어를 모국어로 사용하지 않는 비영어권 국가의 사람들이 흔히 저지르는 오류가 포함되어 있으며, 문장에서 밑줄 친 네 부분 중 문법적으로 틀린 부분을 고르면 된다.

일치, 병렬 구조, 단어의 형성, 관사 · 전치사 · 접속사 어법, 명사, 대명사, 형용사, 부사 문제가 출제된다. 필요한 단어가 빠지고 틀린 단어가 삽입된 문장이 출제되거나 형용사 · 부사가 잘못된 위치에 있어서 어순에 오류가 있는 문장이 출제되기도 한다. 하이픈, 어포스트로피나 대문자와 같은 구두점 오류나 철자 등을 묻는 문제는 출제되지 않는다.

Structure and Written Expression 영역의 전략

TOEFL ITP 문법 영역에서는 더 폭넓은 맥락에서 영어 능력을 측정한다. 이 영역에서는 문법 지식을 넘어 직문 실력으로까지 연결되는 능력을 평가한다. 따라서 단순히 문법 규칙만 암기하고 의사소통을 할 때 그 규칙들을 활용하지 못하는 경우보다는, 올바른 영어로 유창하게 글을 쓸 수 있는 능력을 갖춘 경우에 이 영역에서 더 좋은 성적을 거둘 수 있다.

다시 말해서, 문법 규칙에 대한 지식 자체가 의사소통 능력을 일컫는 것이 아니다. 문법 규칙을 외우는 것은 실제로 문법을 활용하지 못한다면 도움이 되지 않는다. 오히려, 문법 규칙을 정확하게 사용할 수 있는 것이 중요하다. 문법을 정확하게 사용하지 못한다면 의미를 제대로 파악할 수 없다.

따라서, TOEFL ITP 문법 영역을 제대로 준비하려면 단순히 문법 규칙을 이해하는 것만으로는 부족하다. 시험 성적과 영어 실력을 향상시키려면 의사소통 상황에서 적극적으로 문장 구조와 규칙을 사용해 연습해야 한다.

특히, 이 영역에서 좋은 점수를 받으려면, 의사소통과 관련이 있는 영어 작문에서 배운 문법을 활용해야 한다. 다양한 읽기, 말하기, 듣기도 도움이 된다. 영어로 의사소통을 하는 데 숙달되면, 연습했던 문법 구조를 좀 더 자연스럽게 사용할 수 있으며 이 영역에서도 좋은 성적을 거둘 수 있다.

STRUCTURE AND WRITTEN EXPRESSION PRACTICE

Practice Set 1   STRUCTURE

해설 p.160

This section is designed to measure your ability to recognize language that is appropriate for standard written English. There are two types of questions in this section, with special directions for each type.

Directions: Questions 1–10 are incomplete sentences. Beneath each sentence you will see four words or phrases, marked (A), (B), (C), and (D). Choose the one word or phrase that best completes the sentence. Then, on your answer sheet, find the number of the question and fill in the space that corresponds to the letter of the answer you have chosen.

Example I

Sample Answer

Geysers have often been compared to volcanoes ------- both emit hot liquids from below Earth's surface.

   (A) despite
   (B) because
   (C) in regard to
   (D) as a result of

The sentence should read: "Geysers have often been compared to volcanoes because both emit hot liquids from below Earth's surface." Therefore, you should choose (B).

Example II

Sample Answer

During the early period of ocean navigation, ------- any need for sophisticated instruments and techniques.

   (A) so that hardly
   (B) when there hardly was
   (C) hardly was
   (D) there was hardly

The sentence should read: "During the early period of ocean navigation, there was hardly any need for sophisticated instruments and techniques." Therefore, you should choose (D).

1. Telephone cables that use optical fibers can be ------- conventional cables, yet they typically carry much more information.

   (A) they are smaller and lighter
   (B) than the smaller and lighter
   (C) smaller and lighter than
   (D) so small and light that

2. In making cheese, -------, is coagulated by enzyme action, by lactic acid, or by both.

   (A) casein is the chief milk protein
   (B) casein, being that the chief milk protein
   (C) the chief milk protein is casein
   (D) casein, the chief milk protein

3. Sensory structures ------- from the heads of some invertebrates are called antennae.

   (A) are growing
   (B) they are growing
   (C) that grow
   (D) grow

4. An étude is a short musical composition written especially ------- a particular technique.

   (A) enable students practicing
   (B) enables students practicing
   (C) enable students to practice
   (D) to enable students to practice

5. ------- the United States consists of many different immigrant groups, many sociologists believe there is a distinct national character.

   (A) In spite of
   (B) Despite
   (C) Even though
   (D) Whether

6. ------- many food preservation methods for inhibiting the growth of bacteria.

   (A) The
   (B) Since
   (C) There are
   (D) Having

7. The safflower plant is grown chiefly for the oil ------- from its seeds.

(A) obtained
(B) is obtaining
(C) which obtains it
(D) obtaining that

8. Newspaper historians feel that Joseph Pulitzer exercised ------- on journalism in the United States during his lifetime.

(A) influence remarkable
(B) remarkable for his influence
(C) influence was remarkable
(D) remarkable influence

9. ------- must have water to lay and fertilize their eggs, while their offspring, tadpoles, need water for development and growth.

(A) Though frogs and toads
(B) Frogs and toads
(C) That frogs and toads
(D) If frogs and toads

10. The philosopher and educator John Dewey rejected -------.

(A) to use authoritarian teaching methods
(B) that authoritarian teaching methods
(C) for authoritarian teaching methods
(D) authoritarian teaching methods

Practice Set 2 WRITTEN EXPRESSION

Directions: In questions 1–10, each sentence has four underlined words or phrases. The four underlined parts of the sentence are marked (A), (B), (C), and (D). Choose the one underlined word or phrase that must be changed for the sentence to be correct. Then, on your answer sheet, find the number of the question and fill in the space that corresponds to the letter of the answer you have chosen.

Example I

Sample Answer
● Ⓑ Ⓒ Ⓓ

Guppies are sometimes <u>call</u> rainbow <u>fish</u> <u>due to</u> the <u>bright</u> colors of the males.
                A   B C   D

The sentence should read: "Guppies are sometimes called rainbow fish due to the bright colors of the males." Therefore, you should choose (A).

Example II

Sample Answer
Ⓐ ● Ⓒ Ⓓ

<u>Serving</u> several <u>term</u> in the United States Congress, Shirley Chisholm became a <u>respected</u>
  A   B   C
United States <u>politician</u>.
                  D

The sentence should read: "Serving several terms in the United States Congress, Shirley Chisholm became a respected United States politician." Therefore, you should choose (B).

1. One of North America's <u>most</u> renowned <u>painters</u>, Grandma Moses was in her seventies when
                              A   B
   <u>her</u> began to paint <u>seriously</u>.
    C   D

2. The novelty, relatively high speed, and <u>advantageously</u> of year-round service <u>made</u> early
                                      A   B
   <u>passenger trains</u> a popular <u>form</u> of transportation.
         C   D

3. Because <u>incomplete</u> records, the <u>number of enlistments</u> in the Confederate army <u>has long</u>
             A   B   C
   <u>been in dispute</u>.
        D

4. Estuaries are <u>highly</u> sensitive and ecologically <u>important</u> habitats, <u>providing</u> breeding and
                 A   B   C
   feeding grounds for <u>much</u> life-forms.
                       D

5. <u>When</u> the temperature drops <u>below</u> 68 degrees Fahrenheit, the body conserves <u>warm</u> by
    A   B   C
   <u>restricting</u> blood flowing to the skin.
       D

6. The Federal Theatre Project, the first federally <u>financed</u> theater project in the United States,
                                              A
   <u>was established</u> <u>to benefit</u> theater personnel <u>while</u> the Depression of the 1930s.
      B   C   D

7. Although best known <u>for great</u> novel *The Grapes of Wrath*, John Steinbeck <u>also</u> published
        A   B
   essays, <u>plays</u>, stories, memoirs, and newspaper <u>articles</u>.
            C   D

8. The political and <u>economic</u> life of the state of Rhode Island <u>was dominated</u> by the owners of
                     A   B
   textile mills <u>well</u> into the <u>twenty</u> century.
                 C   D

9. Lichens <u>grow</u> in a variety of places, <u>ranging</u> from dry <u>area</u> to moist rain forests, to freshwater
           A   B   C
   lakes, and even <u>to</u> bodies of salt water.
                   D

10. Musical instruments are <u>divided into</u> various types, depending <u>on whether</u> the vibration that
                           A   B
    produces <u>their sound</u> is made by striking, strumming, scraping, or <u>is blown</u>.
             C   D

CHAPTER 4

READING COMPREHENSION SECTION

Reading Comprehension Section

Reading Comprehension 영역에서는 영어로 쓰인 짧은 글을 읽고 이해하는 능력을 측정한다. 대학 수준의 교재나 일반 학술서에서 발췌한 지문이 나오고 입문 수준의 다양한 주제가 다뤄진다.

Reading Comprehension 영역의 개요

Reading Comprehension 영역의 시험 시간은 55분이며, 지문이 5개 출제된다. 각 지문의 길이는 300~350단어로, 각 지문마다 보통 9~11개 문제가 출제된다.

강의나 토론에서는 상당 정보가 의사소통을 통해 전달되지만, 대학 교육에서 읽기 역시 중요한 부분이다. 다양한 글을 읽고 지식을 얻으려면 요지와 주요 세부 사항을 이해하고 그 이상의 내용을 파악할 수 있어야 한다. 또한, 읽은 자료를 기반으로 추론을 하거나, 전후 단락을 파악하거나, 맥락으로 잘 모르는 어휘의 의미를 파악하거나, 지문에 언급된 구체적인 생각을 통해 대명사와 추상 명사의 관계를 파악할 수 있어야 한다.

Reading Comprehension 영역의 구성

Reading Comprehension 영역에서는 여섯 가지 유형의 문제가 출제된다. 그 유형은 주제 및 요지 파악 문제, 사실 정보 파악 문제, 단락 구성 및 추론 문제, 지시 대상 찾기 문제, 어휘 문제, 추론 문제이다.

▷ 문제 유형

유형 1. 주제 및 요지 파악

주제 및 요지 파악 유형은 지문 전체의 요지 및 주제를 묻는 문제이다. 지문 전체의 요지나 주제뿐만 아니라 단락의 주제나 요지를 묻는 문제도 출제된다.

질문 유형

- **What does the passage mainly discuss?**
  지문에서는 주로 무엇에 관해 이야기하고 있는가?

- **The passage answers which of the following questions?**
  지문은 다음 중 어느 질문에 답하고 있는가?

- **What is the author's main point in the second paragraph?**
  두 번째 단락에서 글쓴이의 요지는 무엇인가?

유형 2. 사실 정보 파악

사실 정보 파악 유형은 지문에 언급된 중심 정보와 세부 사항을 묻는 문제이다. 일치, 불일치, 지문에 언급되지 않은 사항을 묻는 문제도 출제된다.

질문 유형

- **The author mentions all of the following as a cause of X EXCEPT ...**
  다음 중 글쓴이가 X의 원인으로 언급한 것이 아닌 것은 무엇인가?

- **Where in the passage does the author give an example of X?**
  글쓴이는 지문의 어디에서 X의 예를 제시하는가?

- **According to the passage, what is the least important aspect of X?**
  지문에 따르면, X의 특징 중 가장 중요하지 않은 것은 무엇인가?

- **According to the passage, which of the following is true of X?**
  지문에 따르면, 다음 설명 중 X에 대해 맞는 것은 무엇인가?

유형 3. 단락 구성 및 추론

단락 구성 및 추론 유형은 지문의 구조와 논리를 묻는 문제이다. 저자가 특정 정보를 언급한 이유를 묻는 문제나 전후 단락을 파악하는 추론 문제가 출제된다.

질문 유형

- The paragraph following the passage most likely discusses ...
  이 지문 다음 단락에서 언급될 것 같은 내용은 무엇인가?

- In line *n*, the author mentions X because ...
  n행에서 글쓴이가 X를 언급한 이유는 무엇인가?

- The author mentions X as an example of ...
  글쓴이가 ~의 일례로 X를 언급한 이유는 무엇인가?

유형 4. 지시 대상 찾기

지시 대상 찾기 유형은 대명사와 그 대명사가 가리키는 단어나 구의 관계를 묻는 문제이다. 지문에 언급된 대명사나 추상 명사(예를 들어, this idea나 this characteristic)가 가리키는 것을 묻는 문제도 출제된다.

질문 유형

- The word "these" in line *n* refers to ...
  n행에 언급된 "these"가 가리키는 것은 무엇인가?

- The "characteristic" mentioned by the author in line *n* most probably refers to ...
  글쓴이가 n행에 언급한 "characteristic"이 가리키는 것은 무엇인 것 같은가?

유형 5. 어휘

어휘 유형은 지문에 언급된 특정 단어나 어구의 의미나 유의어를 묻는 문제이다. 지문에서 비유적으로 쓰인 단어나 어구의 동의어를 묻는 문제도 출제되며 상황에 따라 다양한 의미로 쓰이는 다의어의 의미를 묻는 문제도 출제된다.

질문 유형

- The word X in line *n* is closest in meaning to ...
  n행에 언급된 X와 의미상 가장 가까운 것은 무엇인가?

- The word X in line *n* means that ...
  n행에 언급된 X의 의미는 무엇인가?

- The phrase Y in line *n* is closest in meaning to ...
  n행에 언급된 어구 Y와 의미상 가장 가까운 것은 무엇인가?

- In line *n*, the author refers to Y as X to indicate that ...
  n행에서 글쓴이가 X로 Y를 언급한 이유는 무엇인가?

유형 6. 추론

추론 유형은 지문에 명백히 암시된 정보를 묻는 문제이다. 예를 들어, 지문에 결과가 언급되어 있다면 추론 문제는 그 원인을 묻는다. 만약 어떤 것들을 비교하고 있다면, 추론 문제에서는 비교의 근거가 무엇인지를 묻는다. 새로운 현상에 대한 명백한 설명에서 이전 현상에 대한 특성을 추론할 수 있어야 한다.

질문 유형

- It can be inferred from the passage that ...
  지문에서 추론할 수 있는 것은 무엇인가?

- In the first paragraph, the author implies that ...
  첫 번째 단락에서 글쓴이가 암시하는 것은 무엇인가?

- Which of the following can be inferred from the second paragraph about X?
  다음 중 두 번째 단락에서 X에 대해 추론할 수 있는 것은 무엇인가?

- The author suggests ...
  글쓴이가 암시하는 것은 무엇인가?

- The passage supports which of the following conclusions?
  다음 결론들 중 지문에서 지지하는 것은 무엇인가?

Reading Comprehension 영역의 전략

다양한 주제의 학문적인 글을 광범위하게 읽는 것이 읽기 능력을 향상시키는 데 도움이 된다. 예를 들어, 비즈니스 잡지와 과학 교과서, 논픽션 글을 읽는 것이 좋다. 잡지나, 신문, 인터넷에서도 다양한 분야의 학구적인 글을 찾을 수 있다.

▶ 기본 사항 읽기

- 대충 훑어보고 주요 사항 파악하기
  - 각 단어나 문장을 주의 깊게 살펴보는 대신 대충 훑어보면서 요지를 파악하는 연습을 한다.
  - 지문을 훑어본 후에 다시 한 번 정독하면서 요지를 비롯해 주요 사항이나 중요한 사실을 메모한다.
- 지문에서 잘 모르는 단어를 골라 맥락에서 단어의 의미를 추측한 후에 사전에서 그 단어를 찾아 의미를 확인한다.
  - 단어장을 만드는 것도 어휘력 향상에 도움이 된다.
- 대명사(he, him, they, them 등)에 밑줄을 친 후에 지문에서 그 대명사가 가리키는 것을 찾는다.
- 전체 지문이나 특정 단락에 암시된 사실들을 바탕으로 추론하거나 결론을 내리는 연습을 한다.

READING COMPREHENSION PRACTICE

Practice Set READING

해설 p.164

Directions: In the Reading Comprehension section, you will read several passages. Each one is followed by a number of questions about it. For questions 1–21, you are to choose the **one** best answer—(A), (B), (C), or (D)—to each question. Then, on your answer sheet, find the number of the question and fill in the space that corresponds to the letter of the answer you have chosen.

Answer all questions about the information in a passage on the basis of what is **stated** or **implied** in that passage.

Read the following passage:

      The railroad was not the first institution to impose regularity on society or to draw attention to the importance of precise timekeeping. For as long as merchants have set out their wares at daybreak and communal festivities have been celebrated, people have been
Line in rough agreement with their neighbors as to the time of day. The value of this tradition is
(5) today more apparent than ever. Were it not for public acceptance of a single yardstick of time, social life would be unbearably chaotic; the massive daily transfers of goods, services, and information would proceed in fits and starts; the very fabric of modern society would begin to unravel.

Example I

Sample Answer

What is the main idea of the passage?

    (A) In modern society we must make more time for our neighbors.
    (B) The traditions of society are timeless.
    (C) An accepted way of measuring time is essential for the smooth functioning of society.
    (D) Society judges people by the times at which they conduct certain activities.

The main idea of the passage is that societies need to agree about how time is to be measured in order to function smoothly. Therefore, you should choose (C).

Example II

Sample Answer

In line 4, the phrase "this tradition" refers to

    (A) the practice of starting the business day at dawn
    (B) friendly relations between neighbors
    (C) the railroad's reliance on time schedules
    (D) people's agreement on the measurement of time

The phrase "this tradition" refers to the preceding clause, "people have been in rough agreement with their neighbors as to the time of day." Therefore, you should choose (D)

Questions 1–11

As many as a thousand years ago in the Southwest, the Hopi and Zuni Indians of North America were building with adobe—sun-baked brick plastered with mud. Their homes looked remarkably like modern apartment houses. Some were four stories high and contained quarters for perhaps a thousand people, along with storerooms for grain and other goods. These buildings were usually put up against cliffs, both to make construction easier and for defense against enemies. They were really villages in themselves, as later Spanish explorers must have realized, since they called them pueblos, which is Spanish for towns.

The people of the pueblos raised what are called the three sisters—corn, beans, and squash. They made excellent pottery and wove marvelous baskets, some so fine that they could hold water. The Southwest has always been a dry country where water is scarce. The Hopi and Zuni brought water from streams to their fields and gardens through irrigation ditches. Water was so important that it played a major role in their religion.

The way of life of less-settled groups was simpler. Small tribes such as the Shoshone and Ute wandered the dry and mountainous lands between the Rocky Mountains and the Pacific Ocean. They gathered seeds and hunted small animals such as rabbits and snakes. In the Far North the ancestors of today's Inuit hunted seals, walruses, and the great whales. They lived right on the frozen seas in shelters called igloos built of blocks of packed snow. When summer came, they fished for salmon and hunted the lordly caribou.

The Cheyenne, Pawnee, and Sioux tribes, known as the Plains Indians, lived on the grasslands between the Rocky Mountains and the Mississippi River. They hunted bison, commonly called the buffalo. Its meat was the chief food of these tribes, and its hide was used to make their clothing and the covering of their tents and tepees.

1   What does the passage mainly discuss?

   (A) The architecture of early American
       Indian buildings
   (B) The movement of American Indians
       across North America
   (C) Ceremonies and rituals of American
       Indians
   (D) The way of life of American Indian
       tribes in early North America

2. According to the passage, the Hopi and
    Zuni typically built their homes

   (A) in valleys
   (B) next to streams
   (C) on open plains
   (D) against cliffs

3. The word "They" in line 6 refers to

   (A) goods
   (B) buildings
   (C) cliffs
   (D) enemies

4. It can be inferred from the passage that the
    dwellings of the Hopi and Zuni were

   (A) very small
   (B) highly advanced
   (C) difficult to defend
   (D) quickly constructed

5. The author uses the phrase "the three
    sisters" in line 8 to refer to

   (A) Hopi women
   (B) family members
   (C) important crops
   (D) rain ceremonies

6. The word "scarce" in line 10 is closest in
    meaning to

   (A) limited
   (B) hidden
   (C) pure
   (D) necessary

7. Which of the following is true of the
    Shoshone and Ute?

   (A) They were not as settled as the Hopi
       and Zuni.
   (B) They hunted caribou.
   (C) They built their homes with adobe.
   (D) They did not have many religious
       ceremonies.

8. According to the passage, which of the
    following groups lived in the grasslands?

   (A) The Shoshone and Ute
   (B) The Cheyenne and Sioux
   (C) The Hopi and Zuni
   (D) The Pawnee and Inuit

9. Which of the following animals was most important to the Plains Indians?

    (A) The salmon
    (B) The caribou
    (C) The seal
    (D) The bison

10. Which of the following is NOT mentioned by the author as a dwelling place of early North Americans?

    (A) Log cabins
    (B) Adobe houses
    (C) Tepees
    (D) Igloos

11. The author groups North American Indians according to their

    (A) names and geographical regions
    (B) arts and crafts
    (C) rituals and ceremonies
    (D) date of appearance on the continent

PRACTICE SET CONTINUES.
TURN THE PAGE AND READ THE NEXT PASSAGE.

Questions 12–21

If the salinity of ocean waters is analyzed, it is found to vary only slightly from place to place. Nevertheless, some of these small changes are important. There are three basic processes that cause a change in oceanic salinity. One of these is the subtraction of water from the ocean by means of evaporation—conversion of liquid water to water vapor. In this manner, the salinity is increased, since the salts stay behind. If this is carried to the extreme, of course, white crystals of salt would be left behind.

The opposite of evaporation is precipitation, such as rain, by which water is added to the ocean. Here the ocean is being diluted so that the salinity is decreased. This may occur in areas of high rainfall or in coastal regions where rivers flow into the ocean. Thus, salinity may be increased by the subtraction of water by evaporation or decreased by the addition of freshwater by precipitation or runoff.

Normally, in tropical regions where the sun is very strong, the ocean salinity is somewhat higher than it is in other parts of the world where there is not as much evaporation. Similarly, in coastal regions where rivers dilute the sea, salinity is somewhat lower than in other oceanic areas.

A third process by which salinity may be altered is associated with the formation and melting of sea ice. When seawater is frozen, the dissolved materials are left behind. In this manner, seawater directly beneath freshly formed sea ice has a higher salinity than it did before the ice appeared. Of course, when this ice melts, it will tend to decrease the salinity of the surrounding water.

In the Weddell Sea, off Antarctica, the densest water in the oceans is formed as a result of this freezing process, which increases the salinity of cold water. This heavy water sinks and is found in the deeper portions of the oceans of the world.

Line (5) ... (10) ... (15) ... (20)

12. What does the passage mainly discuss?

    (A) The elements of salt
    (B) The bodies of water of the world
    (C) The many forms of ocean life
    (D) The salinity of ocean water

13. The word "this" in line 4 refers to

    (A) ocean
    (B) evaporation
    (C) salinity
    (D) crystals

14. According to the passage, the ocean generally has more salt in

    (A) coastal areas
    (B) tropical areas
    (C) rainy areas
    (D) turbulent areas

15. All of the following are processes that decrease salinity EXCEPT

    (A) evaporation
    (B) precipitation
    (C) runoff
    (D) melting

16. Which of the following statements about the salinity of a body of water can best be inferred from the passage?

    (A) The temperature of the water is the most important factor.
    (B) The speed with which water moves is directly related to the amount of salt.
    (C) Ocean salinity has little effect on sea life.
    (D) Various factors combine to cause variations in the salt content of water.

17. The word "altered" in line 16 is closest in meaning to

    (A) determined
    (B) changed
    (C) accumulated
    (D) needed

18. The word "it" in line 18 refers to

    (A) sea ice
    (B) salinity
    (C) seawater
    (D) manner

19. Why does the author mention the Weddell Sea?

    (A) To show that this body of water has salinity variations
    (B) To compare Antarctic waters with Arctic waters
    (C) To give an example of increased salinity due to freezing
    (D) To point out the location of deep waters

20. Which of the following is NOT a result of the formation of ocean ice?

    (A) The salt remains in the water.
    (B) The surrounding water sinks.
    (C) Water salinity decreases.
    (D) The water becomes denser.

21. What can be inferred about the water near the bottom of oceans?

    (A) It is relatively warm.
    (B) Its salinity is relatively high.
    (C) It does not move.
    (D) It evaporates quickly.

NO TEST MATERIAL ON THIS PAGE.

CHAPTER 5

SAMPLE TEST SECTIONS

CHAPTER 5

Sample Test Sections

이 장에서는 TOEFL ITP 한 세트의 각 영역별 문제를 풀어 본다. 각 영역별로 제한 시간이 있다. 듣기 지시문을 통해 Section 1이 언제 시작되고 언제 끝날지 알 수 있고, Section 2와 3을 풀 때는 시계를 사용해야 한다. 각 영역에 할당된 시간에는 지시문을 읽는 시간도 포함되어 있다는 점에 유의한다. 시험 시간이 끝나기 전에 Section 2와 3의 문제를 다 풀면 남는 시간 동안은 검토를 하도록 한다.

유의사항

- 주의를 기울여 신속히 문제를 푼다. 한 문제에 너무 많은 시간을 할애하지 않도록 한다.
- 어떤 문제는 다른 문제들보다 더 어려울 수도 있지만, 모든 문제를 다 풀도록 한다. 문제에 대한 정답을 모르면 추측해서 문제를 푼 후에 다음 문제로 넘어간다. 비록 추측하여 답한다 해도 모든 문제에 답하는 것이 유리하다.
- 답안지(Answer Sheet)에 정답을 표시해야 한다. 실제 TOEFL ITP 시험 시간에는 메모지를 사용할 수 없으며, 시험 문제지에 낙서를 해서는 안 된다.
- 정답을 한 개만 골라서 원 안의 보기 글씨가 보이지 않을 정도로 완벽하게 칠해야 한다.

Answer Sheet

Section 1	Section 2	Section 3
1 Ⓐ Ⓑ Ⓒ Ⓓ	1 Ⓐ Ⓑ Ⓒ Ⓓ	1 Ⓐ Ⓑ Ⓒ Ⓓ
2 Ⓐ Ⓑ Ⓒ Ⓓ	2 Ⓐ Ⓑ Ⓒ Ⓓ	2 Ⓐ Ⓑ Ⓒ Ⓓ
3 Ⓐ Ⓑ Ⓒ Ⓓ	3 Ⓐ Ⓑ Ⓒ Ⓓ	3 Ⓐ Ⓑ Ⓒ Ⓓ
4 Ⓐ Ⓑ Ⓒ Ⓓ	4 Ⓐ Ⓑ Ⓒ Ⓓ	4 Ⓐ Ⓑ Ⓒ Ⓓ
5 Ⓐ Ⓑ Ⓒ Ⓓ	5 Ⓐ Ⓑ Ⓒ Ⓓ	5 Ⓐ Ⓑ Ⓒ Ⓓ
6 Ⓐ Ⓑ Ⓒ Ⓓ	6 Ⓐ Ⓑ Ⓒ Ⓓ	6 Ⓐ Ⓑ Ⓒ Ⓓ
7 Ⓐ Ⓑ Ⓒ Ⓓ	7 Ⓐ Ⓑ Ⓒ Ⓓ	7 Ⓐ Ⓑ Ⓒ Ⓓ
8 Ⓐ Ⓑ Ⓒ Ⓓ	8 Ⓐ Ⓑ Ⓒ Ⓓ	8 Ⓐ Ⓑ Ⓒ Ⓓ
9 Ⓐ Ⓑ Ⓒ Ⓓ	9 Ⓐ Ⓑ Ⓒ Ⓓ	9 Ⓐ Ⓑ Ⓒ Ⓓ
10 Ⓐ Ⓑ Ⓒ Ⓓ	10 Ⓐ Ⓑ Ⓒ Ⓓ	10 Ⓐ Ⓑ Ⓒ Ⓓ
11 Ⓐ Ⓑ Ⓒ Ⓓ	11 Ⓐ Ⓑ Ⓒ Ⓓ	11 Ⓐ Ⓑ Ⓒ Ⓓ
12 Ⓐ Ⓑ Ⓒ Ⓓ	12 Ⓐ Ⓑ Ⓒ Ⓓ	12 Ⓐ Ⓑ Ⓒ Ⓓ
13 Ⓐ Ⓑ Ⓒ Ⓓ	13 Ⓐ Ⓑ Ⓒ Ⓓ	13 Ⓐ Ⓑ Ⓒ Ⓓ
14 Ⓐ Ⓑ Ⓒ Ⓓ	14 Ⓐ Ⓑ Ⓒ Ⓓ	14 Ⓐ Ⓑ Ⓒ Ⓓ
15 Ⓐ Ⓑ Ⓒ Ⓓ	15 Ⓐ Ⓑ Ⓒ Ⓓ	15 Ⓐ Ⓑ Ⓒ Ⓓ
16 Ⓐ Ⓑ Ⓒ Ⓓ	16 Ⓐ Ⓑ Ⓒ Ⓓ	16 Ⓐ Ⓑ Ⓒ Ⓓ
17 Ⓐ Ⓑ Ⓒ Ⓓ	17 Ⓐ Ⓑ Ⓒ Ⓓ	17 Ⓐ Ⓑ Ⓒ Ⓓ
18 Ⓐ Ⓑ Ⓒ Ⓓ	18 Ⓐ Ⓑ Ⓒ Ⓓ	18 Ⓐ Ⓑ Ⓒ Ⓓ
19 Ⓐ Ⓑ Ⓒ Ⓓ	19 Ⓐ Ⓑ Ⓒ Ⓓ	19 Ⓐ Ⓑ Ⓒ Ⓓ
20 Ⓐ Ⓑ Ⓒ Ⓓ	20 Ⓐ Ⓑ Ⓒ Ⓓ	20 Ⓐ Ⓑ Ⓒ Ⓓ
21 Ⓐ Ⓑ Ⓒ Ⓓ	21 Ⓐ Ⓑ Ⓒ Ⓓ	21 Ⓐ Ⓑ Ⓒ Ⓓ
22 Ⓐ Ⓑ Ⓒ Ⓓ	22 Ⓐ Ⓑ Ⓒ Ⓓ	22 Ⓐ Ⓑ Ⓒ Ⓓ
23 Ⓐ Ⓑ Ⓒ Ⓓ	23 Ⓐ Ⓑ Ⓒ Ⓓ	23 Ⓐ Ⓑ Ⓒ Ⓓ
24 Ⓐ Ⓑ Ⓒ Ⓓ	24 Ⓐ Ⓑ Ⓒ Ⓓ	24 Ⓐ Ⓑ Ⓒ Ⓓ
25 Ⓐ Ⓑ Ⓒ Ⓓ	25 Ⓐ Ⓑ Ⓒ Ⓓ	25 Ⓐ Ⓑ Ⓒ Ⓓ
26 Ⓐ Ⓑ Ⓒ Ⓓ	26 Ⓐ Ⓑ Ⓒ Ⓓ	26 Ⓐ Ⓑ Ⓒ Ⓓ
27 Ⓐ Ⓑ Ⓒ Ⓓ	27 Ⓐ Ⓑ Ⓒ Ⓓ	27 Ⓐ Ⓑ Ⓒ Ⓓ
28 Ⓐ Ⓑ Ⓒ Ⓓ	28 Ⓐ Ⓑ Ⓒ Ⓓ	28 Ⓐ Ⓑ Ⓒ Ⓓ
29 Ⓐ Ⓑ Ⓒ Ⓓ	29 Ⓐ Ⓑ Ⓒ Ⓓ	29 Ⓐ Ⓑ Ⓒ Ⓓ
30 Ⓐ Ⓑ Ⓒ Ⓓ	30 Ⓐ Ⓑ Ⓒ Ⓓ	30 Ⓐ Ⓑ Ⓒ Ⓓ
31 Ⓐ Ⓑ Ⓒ Ⓓ	31 Ⓐ Ⓑ Ⓒ Ⓓ	31 Ⓐ Ⓑ Ⓒ Ⓓ
32 Ⓐ Ⓑ Ⓒ Ⓓ	32 Ⓐ Ⓑ Ⓒ Ⓓ	32 Ⓐ Ⓑ Ⓒ Ⓓ
33 Ⓐ Ⓑ Ⓒ Ⓓ	33 Ⓐ Ⓑ Ⓒ Ⓓ	33 Ⓐ Ⓑ Ⓒ Ⓓ
34 Ⓐ Ⓑ Ⓒ Ⓓ	34 Ⓐ Ⓑ Ⓒ Ⓓ	34 Ⓐ Ⓑ Ⓒ Ⓓ
35 Ⓐ Ⓑ Ⓒ Ⓓ	35 Ⓐ Ⓑ Ⓒ Ⓓ	35 Ⓐ Ⓑ Ⓒ Ⓓ
36 Ⓐ Ⓑ Ⓒ Ⓓ	36 Ⓐ Ⓑ Ⓒ Ⓓ	36 Ⓐ Ⓑ Ⓒ Ⓓ
37 Ⓐ Ⓑ Ⓒ Ⓓ	37 Ⓐ Ⓑ Ⓒ Ⓓ	37 Ⓐ Ⓑ Ⓒ Ⓓ
38 Ⓐ Ⓑ Ⓒ Ⓓ	38 Ⓐ Ⓑ Ⓒ Ⓓ	38 Ⓐ Ⓑ Ⓒ Ⓓ
39 Ⓐ Ⓑ Ⓒ Ⓓ	39 Ⓐ Ⓑ Ⓒ Ⓓ	39 Ⓐ Ⓑ Ⓒ Ⓓ
40 Ⓐ Ⓑ Ⓒ Ⓓ	40 Ⓐ Ⓑ Ⓒ Ⓓ	40 Ⓐ Ⓑ Ⓒ Ⓓ
41 Ⓐ Ⓑ Ⓒ Ⓓ		41 Ⓐ Ⓑ Ⓒ Ⓓ
42 Ⓐ Ⓑ Ⓒ Ⓓ		42 Ⓐ Ⓑ Ⓒ Ⓓ
43 Ⓐ Ⓑ Ⓒ Ⓓ		43 Ⓐ Ⓑ Ⓒ Ⓓ
44 Ⓐ Ⓑ Ⓒ Ⓓ		44 Ⓐ Ⓑ Ⓒ Ⓓ
45 Ⓐ Ⓑ Ⓒ Ⓓ		45 Ⓐ Ⓑ Ⓒ Ⓓ
46 Ⓐ Ⓑ Ⓒ Ⓓ		46 Ⓐ Ⓑ Ⓒ Ⓓ
47 Ⓐ Ⓑ Ⓒ Ⓓ		47 Ⓐ Ⓑ Ⓒ Ⓓ
48 Ⓐ Ⓑ Ⓒ Ⓓ		48 Ⓐ Ⓑ Ⓒ Ⓓ
49 Ⓐ Ⓑ Ⓒ Ⓓ		49 Ⓐ Ⓑ Ⓒ Ⓓ
50 Ⓐ Ⓑ Ⓒ Ⓓ		50 Ⓐ Ⓑ Ⓒ Ⓓ

Section 1

(04) 해설 p.172

Listening Comprehension

In this section of the test, you will have an opportunity to demonstrate your ability to understand conversations and talks in English. There are three parts to this section with special directions for each part. Answer all the questions on the basis of what is stated or implied by the speakers in this test. Do not take notes or write in your test book at any time. Do not turn the pages until you are told to do so.

Part A

Directions: In Part A, you will hear short conversations between two people. After each conversation, you will hear a question about the conversation. The conversations and questions will not be repeated.

After you hear a question, read the four possible answers in your test book and choose the best answer. Then, on your answer sheet, find the number of the question and fill in the space that corresponds to the letter of the answer you have chosen.

Here is an example.

On the recording, you hear:

Sample Answer
● Ⓑ Ⓒ Ⓓ

In your test book, you read:
(A) He does not like the painting either.
(B) He does not know how to paint.
(C) He does not have any paintings.
(D) He does not know what to do.

You learn from the conversation that neither the man nor the woman likes the painting. The best answer to the question "What does the man mean?" is (A), "He does not like the painting either." Therefore, the correct choice is (A).

1. (A) He is majoring in economics.
   (B) He forgot to go to the bookstore.
   (C) He bought the wrong book.
   (D) He is selling his book to the woman.

2. (A) She appreciates the man's help.
   (B) Her presentation was somewhat long.
   (C) She needed more time to prepare.
   (D) She worked hard on her presentation.

3. (A) Search his closet
   (B) Buy a new wallet
   (C) Look in his coat pockets
   (D) Take off his coat

4. (A) He forgot about his appointment with the woman.
   (B) He did not finish his science project on time.
   (C) He cannot help the woman with her science project.
   (D) He will meet the woman at the library in 30 minutes.

5. (A) He has never been to a dormitory party before.
   (B) He does not like his dormitory room.
   (C) He agrees with the woman.
   (D) He finds the party much too noisy.

6. (A) She is happy she does not have so many exams.
   (B) She cannot help the man study.
   (C) She will not do as well on the test as the man.
   (D) The man should not complain.

7. (A) Karen is experienced at making salads.
   (B) It is easy to make a good salad.
   (C) The woman's salads are just as good as Karen's.
   (D) He is not sure why Karen's salads taste so good.

8. (A) Have the store deliver the couch
   (B) Try to get a discount on the couch
   (C) Delay the delivery of the couch
   (D) Rearrange the furniture in her apartment

9. (A) He thought the exhibit had closed.
    (B) He was confused about when the exhibit started.
    (C) He saw the exhibit last weekend.
    (D) He was not interested in meeting the photographer.

10. (A) Trying on clothes
    (B) Buying a mirror
    (C) Packing for a trip
    (D) Looking at travel books

11. (A) Make sure the cables are connected properly
    (B) Get a new printer
    (C) Replace the cables on the printer
    (D) Check the computer for lost files

12. (A) He does not know the way to the golf course.
    (B) He is probably not free in the afternoon.
    (C) He may not be a better golfer than the woman.
    (D) He is glad the woman has her own equipment.

13. (A) Wait for his headache to go away
    (B) Read a book instead
    (C) Take a different kind of medicine
    (D) Find out what the correct dosage is

14. (A) She did not plan to eat supper.
    (B) She is washing up for supper.
    (C) She did not want to come home.
    (D) She was planning to eat at home.

15. (A) The man plays the piano well.
    (B) The man should reconsider taking piano lessons.
    (C) She does not enjoy listening to music.
    (D) She does not have musical ability.

16. (A) He needed to call the bakery again.
    (B) The bakery was not open.
    (C) The bakery was sold out of bread.
    (D) The bakery does not make French bread.

Go on to the next page ➤

17. (A) Go to the interview early
    (B) Do some exercise to relax
    (C) Tell the interviewer about his qualifications
    (D) Wear his new suit to the interview

18. (A) They do not know who painted the pictures.
    (B) They think modern paintings are creative.
    (C) They think children should be taught to paint.
    (D) They do not like the paintings.

19. (A) She will get a ride home with her parents.
    (B) She cannot go home until July.
    (C) She quit her job before summer vacation.
    (D) She is not going home for the summer.

20. (A) Jeff can give her directions to the rehearsal.
    (B) The woman should tell Jeff to come to the rehearsal.
    (C) Jeff might know when the rehearsal will end.
    (D) He does not know whether Jeff will be at the rehearsal.

21. (A) He had to turn it off.
    (B) He could not hear it.
    (C) He enjoyed listening to it while working.
    (D) He was disturbed by it.

22. (A) Putting up posters now is a waste of time.
    (B) Most people have already voted.
    (C) The election results have already been posted.
    (D) Many voters are undecided.

23. (A) She has made a lot of progress.
    (B) She was always good in chemistry.
    (C) She travels a long distance to school.
    (D) She has been studying chemistry for hours.

24. (A) The man is a much better skier than he used to be.
    (B) The man lacks the ability needed to become a good skier.
    (C) The man should not compare his ability to hers.
    (D) The man should have taken skiing lessons as a child.

25. (A) His neighbors no longer grow peaches.
    (B) He keeps forgetting to ask his neighbors for peaches.
    (C) He is not sure what the woman is referring to.
    (D) His neighbors planted a new peach tree after the storm.

26. (A) He knows the manager of Jack's company.
    (B) He wants to help Jack move.
    (C) He is sorry he cannot help Jack manage his business.
    (D) He is doubtful that Jack's plans will succeed.

27. (A) Stay home and watch the news
    (B) Watch the program at a classmate's house
    (C) Tell Professor Jones the news
    (D) Meet Professor Jones at Dave's house

28. (A) Place an ad in the newspaper
    (B) Look in the student paper under apartments for rent
    (C) Check the notices posted on campus
    (D) Look at some apartments located near the student center

29. (A) He hopes the woman will not forget their lunch date.
    (B) There are some tennis courts available right now.
    (C) The tennis courts will be too wet to play on.
    (D) He wants to continue the game tomorrow.

30. (A) The man had already received the phone.
    (B) The phone will be installed soon.
    (C) The phone was already on order.
    (D) The phone had not been ordered.

Go on to the next page

Part B

Directions: In this part of the test, you will hear longer conversations. After each conversation, you will hear several questions. The conversations and questions will not be repeated.

After you hear a question, read the four possible answers in your test book and choose the best answer. Then, on your answer sheet, find the number of the question and fill in the space that corresponds to the letter of the answer you have chosen.

Remember, you are **not** allowed to take notes or write in your test book.

31. (A) A new book
    (B) An exhibit of photographs
    (C) A lecture series on transportation
    (D) Recent developments in urban transportation

32. (A) The editor of the school newspaper
    (B) The professor's student
    (C) The coauthor of the book
    (D) A subway company executive

33. (A) How it was financed
    (B) The engineering of the tunnels
    (C) Its representation in art and literature
    (D) Its effects on city life

34. (A) Show the reporter some photographs
    (B) Read an article in the campus newspaper
    (C) Explain how the subway tunnels were built
    (D) Examine a map of the New York subway system

35. (A) Setting up a computer class
    (B) Meeting a computer software vendor
    (C) Planning a computer fair
    (D) Arranging a trip to a computer company

36. (A) They attended a similar one the day before.
    (B) Too few members are interested in the activity.
    (C) The room is not available that evening.
    (D) The weather may be bad.

37. (A) At a computer software company
    (B) Far from the university
    (C) At the man's house
    (D) On the university campus

38. (A) The man will contact all the members.
    (B) A radio announcement will be made.
    (C) They will talk to the person in charge of publicity.
    (D) They will each call some of the members.

Go on to the next page

Part C

Directions: In this part of the test, you will hear several short talks. After each talk, you will hear some questions. The talks and the questions will not be repeated.

After you hear a question, read the four possible answers in your test book and choose the best answer. Then, on your answer sheet, find the number of the question and fill in the space that corresponds to the letter of the answer you have chosen.

Here is an example.

On the recording, you hear:

Sample Answer

Now listen to a sample question.

In your test book, you read:

(A) To demonstrate the latest use of computer graphics

(B) To discuss the possibility of an economic depression

(C) To explain the workings of the brain

(D) To dramatize a famous mystery story

The best answer to the question "What is the main purpose of the program?" is (C), "To explain the workings of the brain." Therefore, the correct choice is (C).

Now listen to another sample question:

Sample Answer

In your test book, you read:

(A) It is required of all science majors.

(B) It will never be shown again.

(C) It can help viewers improve their memory skills.

(D) It will help with course work.

The best answer to the question "Why does the speaker recommend watching the program?" is (D), "It will help with course work." Therefore, the correct choice is (D).

Remember, you are **not** allowed to take notes or write in your test book.

39. (A) To introduce a recording of a Native American legend
    (B) To encourage young people to become storytellers
    (C) To compare oral and written traditions
    (D) To tell a famous story

40. (A) They were used to teach children the language.
    (B) They carried news from one tribe to another.
    (C) They preserved the society's history.
    (D) They served as chiefs.

41. (A) They are more comprehensive than earlier recordings.
    (B) They provide income for the Crow people.
    (C) Today's children do not enjoy Native American stories.
    (D) Without recordings the stories might be forgotten.

42. (A) Children have better memories than adults do.
    (B) The traditional storytellers have died.
    (C) He is interested in the children's reactions.
    (D) The storytellers are too busy to be interviewed.

43. (A) To prepare students for the next reading assignment
    (B) To provide background information for a class discussion
    (C) To review material from a previous class
    (D) To prepare for a quiz on chapter six

44. (A) Insurance companies
    (B) Sailors
    (C) Manufacturers
    (D) Merchants

45. (A) The distance the merchandise had to be shipped
    (B) The number of insurance companies available at the time
    (C) The amount of danger involved in shipping the goods
    (D) The type of vessel used to transport the goods

46. (A) Only four types of policies still exist today.
    (B) They are cheaper than the ones in the Middle Ages.
    (C) They include features similar to earlier policies.
    (D) The interest rates are based on early methods of calculation.

Go on to the next page

47. (A) How they enjoy their food
    (B) How they communicate with
        each other
    (C) How they depend on the Sun
    (D) How they learn different dances

48. (A) A signal that it is tired
    (B) A message about a food source
    (C) Acceptance of another honeybee
        to its hive
    (D) A warning that danger is near

49. (A) It is not verbal.
    (B) It is not informative.
    (C) It is not effective.
    (D) It is not complicated.

50. (A) Read the chapters on honeybee
        communication
    (B) Discuss the different ways humans
        communicate
    (C) Give examples of other types of
        animal communication
    (D) Write a paper on the various forms
        of communication

THIS IS THE END OF SECTION 1.

NO TEST MATERIAL ON THIS PAGE.

Section 2

해설 p.193

Structure and Written Expression

Time: 25 minutes (including the reading of the directions)

Now set your clock for 25 minutes.

The Structure and Written Expression section is designed to measure your ability to recognize language that is appropriate for standard written English. There are two types of questions in this section, with special directions for each type.

Structure

Directions: Questions 1–15 are incomplete sentences. Beneath each sentence you will see four words or phrases, marked (A), (B), (C), and (D). Choose the one word or phrase that best completes the sentence. Then, on your answer sheet, find the number of the question and fill in the space that corresponds to the letter of the answer you have chosen.

Example I   **Sample Answer**

Ⓐ ● Ⓒ Ⓓ

Geysers have often been compared to volcanoes ------- both emit hot liquids from below Earth's surface.

    (A) despite

    (B) because

    (C) in regard to

    (D) as a result of

The sentence should read: "Geysers have often been compared to volcanoes because both emit hot liquids from below Earth's surface." Therefore, you should choose (B).

Example II

During the early period of ocean navigation, ------- any need for sophisticated instruments and techniques.

    (A) so that hardly

    (B) when there hardly was

    (C) hardly was

    (D) there was hardly

The sentence should read: "During the early period of ocean navigation, there was hardly any need for sophisticated instruments and techniques." Therefore, you should choose (D).

NOW BEGIN WORK ON THE QUESTIONS.

1. Simple photographic lenses cannot ------- sharp, undistorted images over a wide field.

    (A) to form
    (B) are formed
    (C) forming
    (D) form

2. Of all the factors affecting agricultural yields, weather is the one ------- the most.

    (A) it influences farmers
    (B) that influences farmers
    (C) farmers that it influences
    (D) why farmers influence it

3. Beverly Sills, -------, assumed directorship of the New York City Opera in 1979.

    (A) be a star soprano
    (B) was a star soprano
    (C) a star soprano and
    (D) a star soprano

4. ------- of tissues is known as histology.

    (A) Studying scientific
    (B) The scientific study
    (C) To study scientifically
    (D) That is scientific studying

5. With the exception of mercury, ------- at standard temperature and pressure.

    (A) the metallic elements are solid
    (B) which is a solid metallic element
    (C) metallic elements being solid
    (D) since the metallic elements are solid

6. Dehydration is ------- that a land animal faces.

    (A) the often greatest hazard
    (B) the greatest often hazard
    (C) often the greatest hazard
    (D) often the hazard greatest

7. By tracking the eye of a hurricane, forecasters can determine the speed at which -------.

    (A) is a storm moving
    (B) a storm is moving
    (C) is moving a storm
    (D) a moving storm

8. The publication of *Adventures of Huckleberry Finn* helped make Mark Twain one of America's ------- literary figures.

    (A) most famous
    (B) the most famous
    (C) are most famous
    (D) and most famous

9. Technology will play a key role in ------- future lifestyles.

    (A) to shape
    (B) shaping
    (C) shape of
    (D) shaped

10. The computer has dramatically affected ------- many products are designed.

    (A) is the way
    (B) that the way
    (C) which way do
    (D) the way

11. The early railroads were ------- the existing arteries of transportation: roads, turnpikes, and canals and other waterways.

    (A) those short lines connected
    (B) short lines that connected
    (C) connected by short lines
    (D) short connecting lines

12. ------- as a masterpiece, a work of art must transcend the ideals of the period in which it was created.

    (A) Ranks
    (B) The ranking
    (C) To be ranked
    (D) For being ranked

13. Jackie Robinson, ------- to play baseball in the major leagues, joined the Brooklyn Dodgers in 1947.

    (A) the African American who first
    (B) the first African American
    (C) was the first African American
    (D) the first and an African American who

14. During the flood of 1927, the Red Cross, ------- out of emergency headquarters in Mississippi, set up temporary shelters for the homeless.

    (A) operates
    (B) is operating
    (C) has operated
    (D) operating

15. In bacteria and in other organisms, ------- is DNA that provides the genetic information.

    (A) both
    (B) which
    (C) and
    (D) it

SECTION 2 CONTINUES ON THE NEXT PAGE.

Written Expression

Directions: In questions 16–40, each sentence has four underlined words or phrases. The four underlined parts of the sentence are marked (A), (B), (C), and (D). Choose the one underlined word or phrase that must be changed for the sentence to be correct. Then, on your answer sheet, find the number of the question and fill in the space that corresponds to the letter of the answer you have chosen.

Example I   **Sample Answer**
                                                            ● Ⓑ Ⓒ Ⓓ

Guppies are sometimes <u>call</u> rainbow <u>fish</u> <u>due to</u> the <u>bright</u> colors of the males.
                       A   B   C   D

The sentence should read: "Guppies are sometimes called rainbow fish due to the bright colors of the males." Therefore, you should choose (A).

Example II   **Sample Answer**
                                                            Ⓐ ● Ⓒ Ⓓ

<u>Serving</u> several <u>term</u> in the United States Congress, Shirley Chisholm became a <u>respected</u>
   A   B   C
United States <u>politician</u>.
                  D

The sentence should read: "Serving several terms in the United States Congress, Shirley Chisholm became a respected United States politician." Therefore, you should choose (B).

NOW BEGIN WORK ON THE QUESTIONS.

16. Twenty to thirty year after a mature forest is cleared away, a nearly impenetrable thicket
                    A   B   C
    of trees and shrubs develops.
                        D

17. The first national park in world, Yellowstone National Park, was established in 1872.
        A   B   C   D

18. Because it does not have a blood supply, the cornea takes their oxygen directly from the air.
      A   B   C   D

19. Magnificent mountains and coastal scenery is British Columbia's chief tourist attractions.
                    A   B   C   D

20. Scientists at universities are often more involved in theoretical research than in practically
                    A   B   C   D
    research.

21. John Rosamond Johnson he composed numerous songs, including *Lift Every Voice and Sing*,
                          A   B   C
    for which his brother, James Weldon Johnson, wrote the words.
        D

22. Nylon, a synthetic material done from a combination of water, air, and a by-product
                              A   B
    of coal, was first introduced in 1938.
      C   D

23. Ornithology, the study of birds, is one of the major scientific fields in which amateurs play
                                                    A   B   C
    a role in accumulating, researching, and publish data.
                                            D

24. Animation is a technique for creativity the illusion of life in inanimate things.
                    A   B   C   D

25. The nonviolent protest advocated <u>by</u> Dr. Martin Luther King, Jr., <u>proving</u> highly effective in
                              A   B

    an age of <u>expanding</u> television news <u>coverage</u>.
                     C   D

26. <u>On</u> December 7, 1787, Delaware <u>became</u> <u>a</u> first state <u>to ratify</u> the United States Constitution.
    A   B   C   D

27. <u>Nutritionists</u> believe <u>what</u> diet affects <u>how</u> one feels <u>physically</u> and emotionally.
          A   B   C   D

28. Mealii Kalama, creator of <u>over</u> 400 Hawaiian quilts, <u>was granted</u> a National Heritage
                              A   B

    Fellowship in 1985 for <u>herself</u> <u>contributions</u> to folk art.
                           C   D

29. A jetty <u>serves</u> to define and deepen <u>a channel</u>, improve <u>navigate</u>, or protect <u>a harbor</u>.
             A   B   C   D

30. Minoru Yamasaki achieved a reputation as an architect <u>which</u> works <u>departed from</u>
                                                   A   B

    the austerity <u>frequently</u> associated <u>with</u> architecture after the Second World War.
                     C   D

31. Chemical research <u>provides</u> information that is useful <u>when</u> the <u>textile</u> industry in the
                              A   B   C

    <u>development</u> of new fabrics.
        D

32. Because of <u>its</u> vast tracts of <u>virtually</u> uninhabited northern forest, Canada has <u>one</u> of
               A   B   C

    the lowest population <u>density</u> in the world.
                          D

33. Bromyrite crystals <u>have</u> a diamond-like luster and are usually <u>colorless</u>, but they <u>dark</u>
                    A   B   C

    to brown when <u>exposed</u> to light.
                D

34. Stars in our universe vary in temperature, color, bright, size, and mass.
    A   B   C   D

35. Ice is less denser than the liquid from which it is formed.
         A   B   C   D

36. The 1983 Nobel Prize in Medicine was awarded to Barbara McClintock for her
                                     A

    experiments with maize and her discoveries regardless the nature of DNA.
           B   C   D

37. In 1866 to 1883, the bison population in North America was reduced from an estimated
    A   B   C
    13 million to a few hundred.
                   D

38. Most of the damage property attributed to the San Francisco earthquake of 1906 resulted
                A   B   C
    from the fire that followed.
             D

39. James Baldwin's plays and short stories, which are to some degree autobiographical,
                                   A   B
    established them as a leading figure in the United States civil rights movement.
              C   D

40. Thunder can be listened from a maximum distance of about ten miles except under unusual
                A   B   C   D
    atmospheric conditions.

THIS IS THE END OF SECTION 2.

Section 3

해설 p.200

Reading Comprehension

Time: 55 minutes

Now set your clock for 55 minutes. You have 5 minutes to read the directions.

Directions: In the Reading Comprehension section, you will read several passages. Each one is followed by a number of questions about it. For questions 1–50, you are to choose the one best answer—(A), (B), (C), or (D)—to each question. Then, on your answer sheet, find the number of the question and fill in the space that corresponds to the letter of the answer you have chosen.

Answer all questions about the information in a passage on the basis of what is stated or implied in that passage.

Read the following passage:

The railroad was not the first institution to impose regularity on society or to draw attention to the importance of precise timekeeping. For as long as merchants have set out their wares at daybreak and communal festivities have been celebrated, people have been
Line in rough agreement with their neighbors as to the time of day. The value of this tradition is
(5) today more apparent than ever. Were it not for public acceptance of a single yardstick of time, social life would be unbearably chaotic; the massive daily transfers of goods, services, and information would proceed in fits and starts; the very fabric of modern society would begin to unravel.

Example I

Sample Answer

What is the main idea of the passage?

(A) In modern society we must make more time for our neighbors.
(B) The traditions of society are timeless.
(C) An accepted way of measuring time is essential for the smooth functioning of society.
(D) Society judges people by the times at which they conduct certain activities.

The main idea of the passage is that societies need to agree about how time is to be measured in order to function smoothly. Therefore, you should choose (C).

Example II

In line 4, the phrase "this tradition" refers to

    (A) the practice of starting the business day at dawn

    (B) friendly relations between neighbors

    (C) the railroad's reliance on time schedules

    (D) people's agreement on the measurement of time

The phrase "this tradition" refers to the preceding clause, "people have been in rough agreement with their neighbors as to the time of day." Therefore, you should choose (D).

NOW BEGIN WORK ON THE QUESTIONS.

Questions 1–10

In past centuries, Native Americans living in the arid areas of what is now the southwestern United States relied on a variety of strategies to ensure the success of their agriculture. First and foremost, water was the critical factor. The soil was rich because there
Line was little rain to leach out the minerals, but the low precipitation caused its own problems.
(5) Long periods of drought could have made agriculture impossible; on the other hand, a sudden flood could just as easily have destroyed a crop.

Several techniques were developed to solve the water problem. The simplest was to plant crops in the floodplains and wait for the annual floods to water the young crops. A less dangerous technique was to build dikes or dams to control the flooding. These dikes both
(10) protected the plants against excessive flooding and prevented the water from escaping too quickly once it had arrived. The Hopi people designed their fields in a checkerboard pattern, with many small dikes, each enclosing only one or two stalks of maize (corn), while other groups built a series of dams to control the floods. A third technique was to dig irrigation ditches to bring water from the rivers. Water was sometimes carried to the fields in jars,
(15) particularly if the season was dry. Some crops were planted where they could be watered directly by the runoff from cliff walls.

Another strategy Native Americans used to ensure a continuous food supply was to plant their crops in more than one place, hoping that if one crop failed, another would survive. However, since the soil was rich and not easily exhausted, the same patch of ground
(20) could be cultivated year after year, whereas in the woodlands of the eastern United States it was necessary to abandon a plot of ground after a few years of farming. In the Southwest, often two successive crops were planted each year.

It was a common southwestern practice to grow enough food so that some could be dried and stored for emergencies. If emergency supplies ran low, the people turned to the
(25) local wild plants. If these failed, they moved up into the mountains to gather the wild plants that might have survived in the cooler atmosphere.

1. What does the passage mainly discuss?

    (A) Agricultural methods of Native Americans
    (B) Irrigation techniques used by the Hopi
    (C) Soil quality in the American Southwest
    (D) Native American methods of storing emergency food supplies

2. The word "solve" in line 7 is closest in meaning to

    (A) advance toward
    (B) protect from
    (B) keep in
    (D) deal with

3. Planting in the floodplains was not ideal because

    (A) the amount of water could not be controlled
    (B) the crops could be eaten by wild animals
    (C) the floodplains were too remote to be cultivated frequently
    (D) corn grows better at high elevations

4. The word "enclosing" in line 12 is closest in meaning to

    (A) defending
    (B) measuring
    (C) surrounding
    (D) extending

5. The word "they" in line 15 refers to

    (A) fields
    (B) jars
    (C) crops
    (D) walls

6. Why did farmers in the Southwest plant crops in several places at the same time?

    (A) They moved frequently from one place to another.
    (B) They feared that one of the crops might fail.
    (C) The size of each field was quite limited.
    (D) They wanted to avoid overusing the soil.

7. The word "patch" in line 19 is closest in meaning to

    (A) type
    (B) level
    (C) group
    (D) piece

8. Why did farmers in the eastern woodlands periodically abandon their fields?

   (A) Seasonal flooding made agriculture impossible.
   (B) They experienced water shortages.
   (C) They wanted a longer growing season.
   (D) The minerals in the soil were exhausted.

9. What did farmers in the Southwest do when a crop failed?

   (A) They planted in the eastern woodlands.
   (B) They gathered food from wild plants.
   (C) They moved away from the mountains.
   (D) They redesigned their fields for the next season.

10. Farmers in the Southwest would have benefited most from which of the following?

    (A) Steeper cliff walls
    (B) More sunshine
    (C) Regular rain
    (D) Smaller dikes

SECTION 3 CONTINUES.
TURN THE PAGE AND READ THE NEXT PASSAGE.

Questions 11–20

Marianne Moore (1887–1972) once said that her writing could be called poetry only because there was no other name for it. Indeed her poems appear to be extremely compressed essays that happen to be printed in jagged lines on the page. Her subjects were varied:
Line animals, laborers, artists, and the craft of poetry. From her general reading came quotations
(5) that she found striking or insightful. She included these in her poems, scrupulously enclosed in quotation marks, and sometimes identified in footnotes. Of this practice, she wrote, "'Why the many quotation marks?' I am asked … When a thing has been said so well that it could not be said better, why paraphrase it? Hence my writing is, if not a cabinet of fossils, a kind of collection of flies in amber." Close observation and concentration on detail are the
(10) methods of her poetry.

Marianne Moore grew up in Kirkwood, Missouri, near St. Louis. After graduation from Bryn Mawr College in 1909, she taught commercial subjects at the Indian School in Carlisle, Pennsylvania. Later she became a librarian in New York City. During the 1920s she was editor of *The Dial*, an important literary magazine of the period. She lived quietly all
(15) her life, mostly in Brooklyn, New York. She spent a lot of time at the Bronx Zoo, fascinated by animals. Her admiration of the Brooklyn Dodgers baseball team—before the team moved to Los Angeles— was widely known.

Her first book of poems was published in London in 1921 by a group of friends associated with the Imagist movement. From that time on her poetry has been read with
(20) interest by succeeding generations of poets and readers. In 1952 she was awarded the Pulitzer Prize for her *Collected Poems*. She wrote that she did not write poetry "for money or fame. To earn a living is needful, but it can be done in routine ways. One writes because one has a burning desire to objectify what it is indispensable to one's happiness to express."

11. What is the passage mainly about?

   (A) The influence of the Imagists on Marianne Moore
   (B) Essayists and poets of the 1920s
   (C) The use of quotations in poetry
   (D) Marianne Moore's life and work

12. Which of the following can be inferred about Moore's poems?

   (A) They are better known in Europe than the United States.
   (B) They do not use traditional verse forms.
   (C) They were all published in *The Dial*.
   (D) They tend to be abstract.

13. According to the passage, Moore wrote about all of the following EXCEPT

   (A) artists
   (B) animals
   (C) fossils
   (D) workers

14. What does Moore refer to as "flies in amber" (line 9)?

   (A) A common image in her poetry
   (B) Poetry in the twentieth century
   (C) Concentration on detail
   (D) Quotations within her poetry

15. The author mentions all of the following as jobs held by Moore EXCEPT

   (A) commercial artist
   (B) teacher
   (C) magazine editor
   (D) librarian

16. The word "period" in line 14 is closest in meaning to

   (A) movement
   (B) school
   (C) region
   (D) time

17. Where did Moore spend most of her adult life?

   (A) In Kirkwood
   (B) In Brooklyn
   (C) In Los Angeles
   (D) In Carlisle

18. The word "succeeding" in line 20 is closest in meaning to

    (A) inheriting
    (B) prospering
    (C) diverse
    (D) later

19. The word "it" in line 22 refers to

    (A) writing poetry
    (B) becoming famous
    (C) earning a living
    (D) attracting readers

20. It can be inferred from the passage that Moore wrote because she

    (A) wanted to win awards
    (B) was dissatisfied with what others
    (C) felt a need to express herself
    (D) wanted to raise money for the Bronx Zoo

SECTION 3 CONTINUES.
TURN THE PAGE AND READ THE NEXT PASSAGE.

Questions 21–30

Different fish species swim in different ways. Beginning in the 1920s, careful efforts have been made to classify and measure these various means of locomotion. Although the nomenclature and mathematics used to describe fish locomotion have become quite complex, *Line* the basic classification system is still largely the same as it was first outlined.

(5)   The simplest type of swim is "eel-form" (technically, "anguilliform," after the common eel *Anguilla*). As the name suggests, this swimming motion involves undulations, or wavelike motions, of the whole length of the fish's body, the amplitude of the undulation increasing toward the tail. These undulating motions generate a backward thrust of the body against the water, thereby driving it forward. Eel-form swimming is effective but not particularly efficient

(10) because the undulations increase the drag, or resistance in the water. It is employed, therefore, mostly by bottom dwellers that do not move quickly or efficiently. Not only eels but also blennies swim this way, as do flounders, which undulate vertically, top to bottom, rather than horizontally, and certain slow-moving sharks, such as the nurse and wobbegong shark.

Most roaming predators display "jack-form" swimming (technically, "carangiform,"
(15) after the Carangidae family, which includes jacks, scads, and pompanos). Although there is some variation, in general they have certain features in common: a head like the nose of an aircraft, often sloping down on the top, and a tapered posterior that ends in a forked tail. That portion of the body that connects with the forked tail is narrowed. A jack, like other carangiform swimmers, is adapted for acceleration. It thrusts its rather stiff body from side

(20) to side, creating propulsion without much waving of the body, encountering less resistance than eel-form undulations produce. The forked pattern of the tail reduces drag; the narrowed portion of the body connected to the tail minimizes recoil, and thus helps keep the body still. Jack-form fish are efficient swimmers, as they must be to catch their prey.

The least efficient swimmers are those that move trunkfish style (technically,
(25) "ostraciform," after the family Ostraciidae, which includes trunkfishes and cowfishes). Like the jacks, they use their tails for propulsion, but in so inept and clumsy a manner as to make it clear that speed is not their objective. Puffer fish and porcupine fish swim in trunkfish style. Lacking speed, they must depend on body armor or the secretion of toxic substances for protection.

21. The word "suggests" in line 6 is closest in meaning to
    (A) implies
    (B) demands
    (C) describes
    (D) compares

22. The word "it" in line 9 refers to
    (A) tail
    (B) thrust
    (C) body
    (D) water

23. Which of the following does the author mention as the cause of the eel's inefficient swimming style?
    (A) The increased drag produced by the movement of the body
    (B) The eel's habit of usually swimming near the bottom of the water
    (C) The simple structure of the eel's body
    (D) The weakness of the backward thrust of the eel's tail

24. The word "employed" in line 10 is closest in meaning to
    (A) used
    (B) occupied
    (C) developed
    (D) provided

25. It can be inferred from the passage that blennies (line 12) are
    (A) bottom dwellers
    (B) sharks
    (C) predators
    (D) a type of eel

26. The word "minimizes" in line 22 is closest in meaning to
    (A) prevents
    (B) reduces
    (C) determines
    (D) repeats

27. What does the author mention about fish that are "jack-form" swimmers?
    (A) They usually prey on bottom-dwelling fish.
    (B) Their swimming style lets them catch prey effectively.
    (C) They have tails similar to those of eels.
    (D) Their highly flexible skeletal structure allows them to swim efficiently.

28. The word "objective" in line 27 is closest in meaning to
    (A) ability
    (B) preference
    (C) purpose
    (D) method

29. Which of the following fish would most likely emit a poisonous substance?
    (A) A nurse shark
    (B) A jack
    (C) A pompano
    (D) A puffer fish

30. Which of the following statements does the passage support?
    (A) A scientist today would use a system of classification for fish locomotion similar to that used in the 1920s.
    (B) Scientists today still do not understand the mechanics of fish locomotion.
    (C) Mathematical analysis of fish locomotion has remained largely unaltered since the 1920s.
    (D) The classification of fish locomotion has been simplified since it was devised in the 1920s.

SECTION 3 CONTINUES.
TURN THE PAGE AND READ THE NEXT PASSAGE.

Questions 31–40

People appear to be born to compute. The numerical skills of children develop so early and so inexorably that it is easy to imagine an internal clock of mathematical maturity guiding their growth. Not long after learning to walk and talk, they can set the table with
Line impressive accuracy—one plate, one knife, one spoon, one fork, for each of the five chairs.
(5) Soon they are capable of noting that they have placed five knives, spoons, and forks on the table and, a bit later, that this amounts to fifteen pieces of silverware. Having thus mastered addition, they move on to subtraction. It seems almost reasonable to expect that if a child were secluded on a desert island at birth and retrieved seven years later, he or she could enter a second-grade mathematics class without any serious problems of intellectual adjustment.

(10) Of course, the truth is not so simple. In the twentieth century, the work of cognitive psychologists illuminated the subtle forms of daily learning on which intellectual progress depends. Children were observed as they slowly grasped—or, as the case might be, bumped into—concepts that adults take for granted, as they refused, for instance, to concede that quantity is unchanged as water pours from a short stout glass into a tall thin one. Psychologists
(15) have since demonstrated that young children, asked to count the pencils in a pile, readily report the number of blue or red pencils but must be coaxed into finding the total. Such studies have suggested that the rudiments of mathematics are mastered gradually and with effort. They have also suggested that the very concept of abstract numbers—the idea of a oneness, a twoness, a threeness that applies to any class of objects and is a prerequisite
(20) for doing anything more mathematically demanding than setting a table—is itself far from innate.

31. What does the passage mainly discuss?

    (A) Trends in teaching mathematics to children
    (B) The use of mathematics in child psychology
    (C) The development of mathematical ability in children
    (D) The fundamental concepts of mathematics that children must learn

32. It can be inferred from the passage that children normally learn simple counting

    (A) soon after they learn to talk
    (B) by looking at the clock
    (C) when they begin to be mathematically mature
    (D) after they reach second grade in school

33. The word "illuminated" in line 11 is closest in meaning to

    (A) illustrated
    (B) accepted
    (C) clarified
    (D) lighted

34. The author implies that most small children believe that the quantity of water changes when it is transferred to a container of a different

    (A) color
    (B) quality
    (C) weight
    (D) shape

35. According to the passage, when small children were asked to count a pile of red and blue pencils they

    (A) counted the number of pencils of each color
    (B) guessed at the total number of pencils
    (C) counted only the pencils of their favorite color
    (D) subtracted the number of red pencils from the number of blue pencils

36. The word "They" in line 18 refers to

    (A) mathematicians
    (B) children
    (C) pencils
    (D) studies

37. The word "prerequisite" in line 19 is closest in meaning to

    (A) reason
    (B) theory
    (C) requirement
    (D) technique

38. The word "itself" in line 20 refers to

    (A) the total
    (B) the concept of abstract numbers
    (C) any class of objects
    (D) setting a table

39. With which of the following statements would the author be LEAST likely to agree?

    (A) Children naturally and easily learn mathematics.
    (B) Children learn to add before they learn to subtract.
    (C) Most people follow the same pattern of mathematical development.
    (D) Mathematical development is subtle and gradual.

40. Where in the passage does the author give an example of a hypothetical experiment?

    (A) Lines 3–6
    (B) Lines 7–9
    (C) Lines 11–14
    (D) Lines 18–21

SECTION 3 CONTINUES.
TURN THE PAGE AND READ THE NEXT PASSAGE.

Questions 41–50

Botany, the study of plants, occupies a peculiar position in the history of human knowledge. For many thousands of years, it was the one field of awareness about which humans had anything more than the vaguest of insights. It is impossible to know today just what our Stone Age ancestors knew about plants, but from what we can observe of preindustrial societies that still exist, a detailed learning of plants and their properties must be extremely ancient. This is logical. Plants are the basis of the food pyramid for all living things, even for other plants. They have always been enormously important to the welfare of people, not only for food, but also for clothing, weapons, tools, dyes, medicines, shelter, and a great many other purposes. Tribes living today in the jungles of the Amazon recognize literally hundreds of plants and know many properties of each. To them botany, as such, has no name and is probably not even recognized as a special branch of knowledge at all.

Unfortunately, the more industrialized we become the farther away we move from direct contact with plants, and the less distinct our knowledge of botany grows. Yet everyone comes unconsciously on an amazing amount of botanical knowledge, and few people will fail to recognize a rose, an apple, or an orchid. When our Neolithic ancestors, living in the Middle East about 10,000 years ago, discovered that certain grasses could be harvested and their seeds planted for richer yields the next season, the first great step in a new association of plants and humans was taken. Grains were discovered and from them flowed the marvel of agriculture: cultivated crops. From then on, humans would increasingly take their living from the controlled production of a few plants rather than getting a little here and a little there from many varieties that grew wild — and the accumulated knowledge of tens of thousands of years of experience and intimacy with plants in the wild would begin to fade away.

41. Which of the following assumptions about early humans is expressed in the passage?

    (A) They probably had extensive knowledge of plants.
    (B) They divided knowledge into well-defined fields.
    (C) They did not enjoy the study of botany.
    (D) They placed great importance on ownership of property.

42. The word "peculiar" in line 1 is closest in meaning to

    (A) clear
    (B) large
    (C) unusual
    (D) important

43. What does the comment "This is logical" in line 6 mean?

    (A) There is no clear way to determine the extent of our ancestors' knowledge of plants.
    (B) It is not surprising that early humans had a detailed knowledge of plants.
    (C) It is reasonable to assume that our ancestors behaved very much like people in preindustrial societies.
    (D) Human knowledge of plants is well organized and very detailed.

44. The phrase "properties of each" in line 10 refers to each

    (A) tribe
    (B) hundred
    (C) plant
    (D) purpose

45. According to the passage, why has general knowledge of botany declined?

    (A) People no longer value plants as a useful resource.
    (B) Botany is not recognized as a special branch of science.
    (C) Research is unable to keep up with the increasing number of plants.
    (D) Direct contact with a variety of plants has decreased.

46. In line 15, what is the author's purpose in mentioning "a rose, an apple, or an orchid"?

    (A) To make the passage more poetic
    (B) To cite examples of plants that are attractive
    (C) To give botanical examples that most readers will recognize
    (D) To illustrate the diversity of botanical life

47. According to the passage, what was the first great step toward the practice of agriculture?

    (A) The invention of agricultural implements and machinery
    (B) The development of a system of names for plants
    (C) The discovery of grasses that could be harvested and replanted
    (D) The changing diets of early humans

48. The word "controlled" in line 20 is closest in meaning to

    (A) abundant
    (B) managed
    (C) required
    (D) advanced

49. Which of the following can be inferred from the passage about the transition to agriculture?

    (A) It forced humans to study plants more carefully so that they would know how to collect and plant seeds.
    (B) It led to a more narrow understanding of plants as a source of food, but not for other purposes.
    (C) It had a drawback in that humans lost much of their knowledge of wild plants as a result.
    (D) It led to a diet that consisted of a greater variety of plants.

50. Where in the passage does the author describe the benefits people derive from plants?

    (A) Line 1
    (B) Lines 7–9
    (C) Lines 10–11
    (D) Lines 13–15

**THIS IS THE END OF THE READING COMPREHENSION SECTION.
IF YOU FINISH IN LESS THAN 55 MINUTES, CHECK YOUR
WORK IN THIS SECTION ONLY.
DO NOT READ OR WORK ON ANY OTHER SECTION OF THE TEST.**

NO TEST MATERIAL ON THIS PAGE.

Sample Test Sections   **101**

CHAPTER 6

COMPLETE *TOEFL ITP* PRACTICE TEST

Complete *TOEFL ITP* Practice Test

General Directions

This is a test of your ability to understand and use the English language. The test is divided into three sections, and each section or part of a section begins with a set of specific directions. The directions include sample questions. Before you begin to work on a section or part, be sure that you understand what you will need to do.

The supervisor will tell you when to start each section and when to stop and go on to the next section. You should work quickly but carefully. Do not spend too much time on any one question. If you finish a section early, you may review your answers **on that section only**. You may **not** go on to a new section, and you may **not** return to a section that you have already left.

You will find that some of the questions are more difficult than others, but you should try to answer every one. Your score will be based on the number of **correct** answers you give. If you are not sure of the correct answer to a question, make the best guess you can. It is to your advantage to answer every question, even if you have to guess the answer.

Do not mark your answers in the test book. **You must mark all of your answers on the separate answer sheet** that the supervisor will give to you. When you mark your answer to a question on your answer sheet, you must:

- Use a medium-soft (#2 or HB) black lead pencil.
- Check the number of the question, and find that number on your answer sheet. Then, after that number, find the oval with the letter of the answer you have chosen.
- Carefully make a dark mark that completely fills the oval so that you cannot see the letter inside the oval.
- Mark **only one** answer to each question.
- Erase all extra marks completely. If you change your mind about an answer after you have marked it on your answer sheet, erase your old answer completely, and mark your new answer.
- After the supervisor tells you to stop your work, you will not be permitted to make any additional corrections.

The examples below show you the **correct** way and **wrong** ways of marking an answer sheet.

 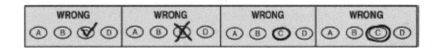

Be sure to fill in the ovals on your answer sheet the **correct** way.

Use the answer sheet on the next page to record your answers for all three sections of the Complete Test.

Answer Sheet

Section 1	Section 2	Section 3
1 Ⓐ Ⓑ Ⓒ Ⓓ	1 Ⓐ Ⓑ Ⓒ Ⓓ	1 Ⓐ Ⓑ Ⓒ Ⓓ
2 Ⓐ Ⓑ Ⓒ Ⓓ	2 Ⓐ Ⓑ Ⓒ Ⓓ	2 Ⓐ Ⓑ Ⓒ Ⓓ
3 Ⓐ Ⓑ Ⓒ Ⓓ	3 Ⓐ Ⓑ Ⓒ Ⓓ	3 Ⓐ Ⓑ Ⓒ Ⓓ
4 Ⓐ Ⓑ Ⓒ Ⓓ	4 Ⓐ Ⓑ Ⓒ Ⓓ	4 Ⓐ Ⓑ Ⓒ Ⓓ
5 Ⓐ Ⓑ Ⓒ Ⓓ	5 Ⓐ Ⓑ Ⓒ Ⓓ	5 Ⓐ Ⓑ Ⓒ Ⓓ
6 Ⓐ Ⓑ Ⓒ Ⓓ	6 Ⓐ Ⓑ Ⓒ Ⓓ	6 Ⓐ Ⓑ Ⓒ Ⓓ
7 Ⓐ Ⓑ Ⓒ Ⓓ	7 Ⓐ Ⓑ Ⓒ Ⓓ	7 Ⓐ Ⓑ Ⓒ Ⓓ
8 Ⓐ Ⓑ Ⓒ Ⓓ	8 Ⓐ Ⓑ Ⓒ Ⓓ	8 Ⓐ Ⓑ Ⓒ Ⓓ
9 Ⓐ Ⓑ Ⓒ Ⓓ	9 Ⓐ Ⓑ Ⓒ Ⓓ	9 Ⓐ Ⓑ Ⓒ Ⓓ
10 Ⓐ Ⓑ Ⓒ Ⓓ	10 Ⓐ Ⓑ Ⓒ Ⓓ	10 Ⓐ Ⓑ Ⓒ Ⓓ
11 Ⓐ Ⓑ Ⓒ Ⓓ	11 Ⓐ Ⓑ Ⓒ Ⓓ	11 Ⓐ Ⓑ Ⓒ Ⓓ
12 Ⓐ Ⓑ Ⓒ Ⓓ	12 Ⓐ Ⓑ Ⓒ Ⓓ	12 Ⓐ Ⓑ Ⓒ Ⓓ
13 Ⓐ Ⓑ Ⓒ Ⓓ	13 Ⓐ Ⓑ Ⓒ Ⓓ	13 Ⓐ Ⓑ Ⓒ Ⓓ
14 Ⓐ Ⓑ Ⓒ Ⓓ	14 Ⓐ Ⓑ Ⓒ Ⓓ	14 Ⓐ Ⓑ Ⓒ Ⓓ
15 Ⓐ Ⓑ Ⓒ Ⓓ	15 Ⓐ Ⓑ Ⓒ Ⓓ	15 Ⓐ Ⓑ Ⓒ Ⓓ
16 Ⓐ Ⓑ Ⓒ Ⓓ	16 Ⓐ Ⓑ Ⓒ Ⓓ	16 Ⓐ Ⓑ Ⓒ Ⓓ
17 Ⓐ Ⓑ Ⓒ Ⓓ	17 Ⓐ Ⓑ Ⓒ Ⓓ	17 Ⓐ Ⓑ Ⓒ Ⓓ
18 Ⓐ Ⓑ Ⓒ Ⓓ	18 Ⓐ Ⓑ Ⓒ Ⓓ	18 Ⓐ Ⓑ Ⓒ Ⓓ
19 Ⓐ Ⓑ Ⓒ Ⓓ	19 Ⓐ Ⓑ Ⓒ Ⓓ	19 Ⓐ Ⓑ Ⓒ Ⓓ
20 Ⓐ Ⓑ Ⓒ Ⓓ	20 Ⓐ Ⓑ Ⓒ Ⓓ	20 Ⓐ Ⓑ Ⓒ Ⓓ
21 Ⓐ Ⓑ Ⓒ Ⓓ	21 Ⓐ Ⓑ Ⓒ Ⓓ	21 Ⓐ Ⓑ Ⓒ Ⓓ
22 Ⓐ Ⓑ Ⓒ Ⓓ	22 Ⓐ Ⓑ Ⓒ Ⓓ	22 Ⓐ Ⓑ Ⓒ Ⓓ
23 Ⓐ Ⓑ Ⓒ Ⓓ	23 Ⓐ Ⓑ Ⓒ Ⓓ	23 Ⓐ Ⓑ Ⓒ Ⓓ
24 Ⓐ Ⓑ Ⓒ Ⓓ	24 Ⓐ Ⓑ Ⓒ Ⓓ	24 Ⓐ Ⓑ Ⓒ Ⓓ
25 Ⓐ Ⓑ Ⓒ Ⓓ	25 Ⓐ Ⓑ Ⓒ Ⓓ	25 Ⓐ Ⓑ Ⓒ Ⓓ
26 Ⓐ Ⓑ Ⓒ Ⓓ	26 Ⓐ Ⓑ Ⓒ Ⓓ	26 Ⓐ Ⓑ Ⓒ Ⓓ
27 Ⓐ Ⓑ Ⓒ Ⓓ	27 Ⓐ Ⓑ Ⓒ Ⓓ	27 Ⓐ Ⓑ Ⓒ Ⓓ
28 Ⓐ Ⓑ Ⓒ Ⓓ	28 Ⓐ Ⓑ Ⓒ Ⓓ	28 Ⓐ Ⓑ Ⓒ Ⓓ
29 Ⓐ Ⓑ Ⓒ Ⓓ	29 Ⓐ Ⓑ Ⓒ Ⓓ	29 Ⓐ Ⓑ Ⓒ Ⓓ
30 Ⓐ Ⓑ Ⓒ Ⓓ	30 Ⓐ Ⓑ Ⓒ Ⓓ	30 Ⓐ Ⓑ Ⓒ Ⓓ
31 Ⓐ Ⓑ Ⓒ Ⓓ	31 Ⓐ Ⓑ Ⓒ Ⓓ	31 Ⓐ Ⓑ Ⓒ Ⓓ
32 Ⓐ Ⓑ Ⓒ Ⓓ	32 Ⓐ Ⓑ Ⓒ Ⓓ	32 Ⓐ Ⓑ Ⓒ Ⓓ
33 Ⓐ Ⓑ Ⓒ Ⓓ	33 Ⓐ Ⓑ Ⓒ Ⓓ	33 Ⓐ Ⓑ Ⓒ Ⓓ
34 Ⓐ Ⓑ Ⓒ Ⓓ	34 Ⓐ Ⓑ Ⓒ Ⓓ	34 Ⓐ Ⓑ Ⓒ Ⓓ
35 Ⓐ Ⓑ Ⓒ Ⓓ	35 Ⓐ Ⓑ Ⓒ Ⓓ	35 Ⓐ Ⓑ Ⓒ Ⓓ
36 Ⓐ Ⓑ Ⓒ Ⓓ	36 Ⓐ Ⓑ Ⓒ Ⓓ	36 Ⓐ Ⓑ Ⓒ Ⓓ
37 Ⓐ Ⓑ Ⓒ Ⓓ	37 Ⓐ Ⓑ Ⓒ Ⓓ	37 Ⓐ Ⓑ Ⓒ Ⓓ
38 Ⓐ Ⓑ Ⓒ Ⓓ	38 Ⓐ Ⓑ Ⓒ Ⓓ	38 Ⓐ Ⓑ Ⓒ Ⓓ
39 Ⓐ Ⓑ Ⓒ Ⓓ	39 Ⓐ Ⓑ Ⓒ Ⓓ	39 Ⓐ Ⓑ Ⓒ Ⓓ
40 Ⓐ Ⓑ Ⓒ Ⓓ	40 Ⓐ Ⓑ Ⓒ Ⓓ	40 Ⓐ Ⓑ Ⓒ Ⓓ
41 Ⓐ Ⓑ Ⓒ Ⓓ		41 Ⓐ Ⓑ Ⓒ Ⓓ
42 Ⓐ Ⓑ Ⓒ Ⓓ		42 Ⓐ Ⓑ Ⓒ Ⓓ
43 Ⓐ Ⓑ Ⓒ Ⓓ		43 Ⓐ Ⓑ Ⓒ Ⓓ
44 Ⓐ Ⓑ Ⓒ Ⓓ		44 Ⓐ Ⓑ Ⓒ Ⓓ
45 Ⓐ Ⓑ Ⓒ Ⓓ		45 Ⓐ Ⓑ Ⓒ Ⓓ
46 Ⓐ Ⓑ Ⓒ Ⓓ		46 Ⓐ Ⓑ Ⓒ Ⓓ
47 Ⓐ Ⓑ Ⓒ Ⓓ		47 Ⓐ Ⓑ Ⓒ Ⓓ
48 Ⓐ Ⓑ Ⓒ Ⓓ		48 Ⓐ Ⓑ Ⓒ Ⓓ
49 Ⓐ Ⓑ Ⓒ Ⓓ		49 Ⓐ Ⓑ Ⓒ Ⓓ
50 Ⓐ Ⓑ Ⓒ Ⓓ		50 Ⓐ Ⓑ Ⓒ Ⓓ

Section 1

05 해설 p.220

Listening Comprehension

In this section of the test, you will have an opportunity to demonstrate your ability to understand conversations and talks in English. There are three parts to this section with special directions for each part. Answer all the questions on the basis of what is stated or implied by the speakers in this test. Do not take notes or write in your test book at any time. Do not turn the pages until you are told to do so.

Part A

Directions: In Part A, you will hear short conversations between two people. After each conversation, you will hear a question about the conversation. The conversations and questions will not be repeated.

After you hear a question, read the four possible answers in your test book and choose the best answer. Then, on your answer sheet, find the number of the question and fill in the space that corresponds to the letter of the answer you have chosen.

Here is an example.

On the recording, you hear:

In your test book, you read:

Sample Answer

    (A) He does not like the painting either.
    (B) He does not know how to paint.
    (C) He does not have any paintings.
    (D) He does not know what to do.

You learn from the conversation that neither the man nor the woman likes the painting. The best answer to the question "What does the man mean?" is (A), "He does not like the painting either." Therefore, the correct choice is (A).

1. (A) Go to the movies with the man
   (B) Take her brother to the movies
   (C) Eat at her brother's home
   (D) Cook dinner with Lois

2. (A) The man should have offered his assistance earlier.
   (B) She does not need the man's help.
   (C) She did not realize the boxes were empty.
   (D) She wants the man to move the boxes.

3. (A) He would like to have the windows open.
   (B) He rarely leaves the windows open.
   (C) He thinks the air is polluted.
   (D) He will help her close the windows.

4. (A) The results might be ready tomorrow.
   (B) The man needs another test tomorrow.
   (C) The results were called in last night.
   (D) The doctor called the lab again.

5. (A) She does not remember much about Portland.
   (B) She has never been to Portland.
   (C) She knows someone else who could help him.
   (D) She would be happy to talk to the man later.

6. (A) Turn down the volume
   (B) Help the man study for a test
   (C) Play a different kind of music
   (D) Speak louder

7. (A) She forgot when the report was due.
   (B) She would like the man to help her with the report.
   (C) She needs more time to finish the report.
   (D) She has not included any data in her report.

8. (A) The cat is causing him problems.
   (B) The cat is quite friendly.
   (C) He does not get along with Debbie.
   (D) He is glad Debbie gave him the cat.

9. (A) Try to get a seat next to the window
   (B) Find another passenger going to Cleveland
   (C) Ask for information about the departure time
   (D) Find out if there are any seats left on the bus

10. (A) She forgot to stop at the store.
    (B) The man should not eat the fish.
    (C) The fish is safe to eat.
    (D) The food should not be reheated.

11. (A) She will not be able to go with the man.
    (B) She does not think Frank is arriving until tomorrow morning.
    (C) She has to pick up Frank at 2:00.
    (D) She does not know when her class will end.

12. (A) He watched the television program with his mother.
    (B) His mother reminded him that his professor was on television.
    (C) Answering the phone caused him to miss the television program.
    (D) His mother missed the television program.

13. (A) The pool will be open all week.
    (B) The weather will cool down soon.
    (C) The woman should go swimming.
    (D) He prefers to stay inside in hot weather.

14. (A) He may not have enough time to cook.
    (B) He may spend more money on food next semester.
    (C) He may gain weight if he does his own cooking.
    (D) He may not enjoy cooking.

15. (A) He is tired.
    (B) He lost the race.
    (C) He has already been to the top of the hill.
    (D) He prefers doing exercise indoors.

16. (A) The doctor only has time on Tuesdays.
    (B) The doctor is busy on Tuesday morning.
    (C) The man must come more than one time.
    (D) The man must arrive on time.

Go on to the next page

17. (A) Eat at the cafeteria more often
    (B) Find out when the cafeteria opens
    (C) Meet her in the cafeteria this evening
    (D) Try to get a job at the cafeteria

18. (A) Cancel their trip
    (B) Make a quick stop for a meal
    (C) Arrive at their destination early
    (D) Have a longer lunch than originally planned

19. (A) She does not want to take the course this semester.
    (B) She thought the class would be easy.
    (C) She is surprised that all the sections are filled.
    (D) There are only thirteen students in the psychology class.

20. (A) He does not like to drink coffee.
    (B) He is not upset by the accident.
    (C) The woman should apologize.
    (D) The woman has spilled coffee on him before.

21. (A) The woman will have to buy a new sweater.
    (B) The sweater looks just like the woman's new one.
    (C) The sweater can be repaired easily.
    (D) The woman should not put sharp objects in her sweater pocket.

22. (A) The jackets sold out quickly.
    (B) The sale ended yesterday.
    (C) He will check with the sales clerk.
    (D) The woman might find a jacket on sale.

23. (A) She likes to drive when she travels.
    (B) She does not want to go to Chicago.
    (C) She does not know how much the train trip will cost.
    (D) It is cheaper to go to Chicago by car.

24. (A) The man paid a lot to join the gym.
    (B) The man has been working too hard.
    (C) The man has improved his physical appearance.
    (D) The man should find a better job.

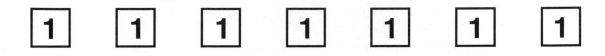

25. (A) She prefers hot weather.
    (B) The man should visit Washington when it is cooler.
    (C) She agrees that going to the beach would have been better.
    (D) Visiting Washington is enjoyable despite the heat.

26. (A) She will help the man clean up the lounge.
    (B) The mother should be more considerate.
    (C) The man should be more understanding.
    (D) The child is not well behaved for his age.

27. (A) He can meet the woman on Wednesday.
    (B) He will not be ready until next week.
    (C) He is available any day except Wednesday.
    (D) He needs to do the history project before Wednesday.

28. (A) Prepare for an important game
    (B) Try out for the field hockey team
    (C) Get tickets to see the championship game
    (D) Receive an award for winning a championship

29. (A) She wants to check the weather before deciding.
    (B) She has a problem with her hearing.
    (C) She would enjoy having dinner another time.
    (D) She wants the man to help her with some work.

30. (A) The back of the drawer has fallen off.
    (B) The man does not have any soap.
    (C) The cabinet is too heavy to move.
    (D) Something is blocking the back of the drawer.

Go on to the next page

Part B

Directions: In this part of the test, you will hear longer conversations. After each conversation, you will hear several questions. The conversations and questions will not be repeated.

After you hear a question, read the four possible answers in your test book and choose the best answer. Then, on your answer sheet, find the number of the question and fill in the space that corresponds to the letter of the answer you have chosen.

Remember, you are **not** allowed to take notes or write in your test book.

31. (A) They lived in caves.
    (B) They traveled in groups.
    (C) They had an advanced language.
    (D) They ate mostly fruit.

32. (A) It was unavailable because dry weather had killed the trees.
    (B) It was used to build shelters in some regions.
    (C) It was used mainly for heating and cooking.
    (D) Ice Age people did not have the tools to work with wood.

33. (A) They wore clothing made of animal skins.
    (B) They used sand as insulation.
    (C) They kept fires burning constantly.
    (D) They faced their homes toward the south.

34. (A) Meet his anthropology teacher
    (B) Lend him her magazine when she is done with it
    (C) Help him with an assignment about the Ice Age
    (D) Help him study for an anthropology test

35. (A) Mating habits of squid and octopus
    (B) The evolution of certain forms of sea life
    (C) The study of marine shells
    (D) Survival skills of sea creatures

36. (A) He did not understand the lecture.
    (B) He wants to borrow her notes next week.
    (C) He needs help preparing for an exam.
    (D) He was sick and unable to attend the lecture.

37. (A) Some sea creatures developed vertebrae.
    (B) The first giant squid was captured.
    (C) Some sea creatures shed their shells.
    (D) Sea life became more intelligent.

38. (A) She has always believed they exist.
    (B) She heard about them in New Zealand.
    (C) Stories about them may be based on giant squid.
    (D) The instructor mentioned them in the lecture.

Go on to the next page

Part C

Directions: In this part of the test, you will hear several short talks. After each talk, you will hear some questions. The talks and the questions will not be repeated.

After you hear a question, read the four possible answers in your test book and choose the best answer. Then, on your answer sheet, find the number of the question and fill in the space that corresponds to the letter of the answer you have chosen.

Here is an example.

On the recording, you hear:

Sample Answer

Now listen to a sample question.

In your test book, you read:

   (A) To demonstrate the latest use of computer graphics
   (B) To discuss the possibility of an economic depression
   (C) To explain the workings of the brain
   (D) To dramatize a famous mystery story

The best answer to the question "What is the main purpose of the program?" is (C), "To explain the workings of the brain." Therefore, the correct choice is (C).

Now listen to another sample question:

Sample Answer

In your test book, you read:

   (A) It is required of all science majors.
   (B) It will never be shown again.
   (C) It can help viewers improve their memory skills.
   (D) It will help with course work.

The best answer to the question "Why does the speaker recommend watching the program?" is (D), "It will help with course work." Therefore, the correct choice is (D).

Remember, you are **not** allowed to take notes or write in your test book.

39. (A) That babies understand language before they can speak
    (B) That babies have simple mathematical skills
    (C) That babies prefer different kinds of toys
    (D) That television has a strong influence on babies

40. (A) Staring at the dolls longer
    (B) Crying loudly
    (C) Blinking their eyes rapidly
    (D) Reaching for the dolls

41. (A) They are born with the ability to count.
    (B) They are exceptionally intelligent.
    (C) They learned to count from playing with dolls.
    (D) They have learned to count from their parents.

42. (A) Language ability might be negatively affected.
    (B) Babies who learn quickly might develop learning problems later.
    (C) Parents might try to teach their children certain skills at too early an age.
    (D) Learning math early might interfere with creativity.

43. (A) To review what students know about volcanic activity
    (B) To demonstrate the use of a new measurement device
    (C) To explain the answer to an examination question
    (D) To provide background for the next reading assignment

44. (A) They occur at regular intervals.
    (B) They can withstand great heat.
    (C) They travel through Earth's interior.
    (D) They can record Earth's internal temperature.

45. (A) When Earth was formed
    (B) The composition of the Earth's interior
    (C) Why lava is hot
    (D) How often a volcano is likely to erupt

46. (A) How deep they are
    (B) Where earthquakes form
    (C) How hot they are
    (D) What purpose they serve

Go on to the next page

47. (A) Photographic techniques common in the early 1900s
    (B) The early life of Alfred Stieglitz
    (C) The influence of weather on Alfred Stieglitz' photography
    (D) Alfred Stieglitz' approach to photography

48. (A) How to analyze photographic techniques
    (B) How to classify photography
    (C) How Alfred Stieglitz contributed to the history of photography
    (D) Whether photography is superior to other art forms

49. (A) They were influenced by his background in engineering.
    (B) They were very expensive to take.
    (C) They were among the first taken under such conditions.
    (D) Most of them were of poor quality.

50. (A) He thought that the copying process took too long.
    (B) He considered each photograph to be an individual work of art.
    (C) He did not have the necessary equipment for reproduction.
    (D) He did not want them to be displayed outside of his home.

THIS IS THE END OF SECTION 1.

STOP WORK ON SECTION 1.

NO TEST MATERIAL ON THIS PAGE.

Section 2

해설 p.240

Structure and Written Expression

Time: 25 minutes

Now set your clock for 25 minutes.

This section is designed to measure your ability to recognize language that is appropriate for standard written English. There are two types of questions in this section, with special directions for each type.

STRUCTURE

Directions: Questions 1–15 are incomplete sentences. Beneath each sentence you will see four words or phrases, marked (A), (B), (C), and (D). Choose the one word or phrase that best completes the sentence. Then, on your answer sheet, find the number of the question and fill in the space that corresponds to the letter of the answer you have chosen.

Example I

Sample Answer

Ⓐ ● Ⓒ Ⓓ

Geysers have often been compared to volcanoes ------- both emit hot liquids from below Earth's surface.

    (A) despite

    (B) because

    (C) in regard to

    (D) as a result of

The sentence should read: "Geysers have often been compared to volcanoes because both emit hot liquids from below Earth's surface." Therefore, you should choose (B).

Example II

During the early period of ocean navigation, ------- any need for sophisticated instruments and techniques.

    (A) so that hardly

    (B) when there hardly was

    (C) hardly was

    (D) there was hardly

The sentence should read: "During the early period of ocean navigation, there was hardly any need for sophisticated instruments and techniques." Therefore, you should choose (D).

NOW BEGIN WORK ON THE QUESTIONS.

1. Tourism is ------- leading source of income for many coastal communities.

   (A) a
   (B) at
   (C) then
   (D) none

2. Although thunder and lightning are produced at the same time, light waves travel faster -------, so we see the lightning before we hear the thunder.

   (A) than sound waves do
   (B) than sound waves are
   (C) do sound waves
   (D) sound waves

3. Beef cattle ------- of all livestock for economic growth in the North American economy.

   (A) the most are important
   (B) are the most important
   (C) the most important are
   (D) that are the most important

4. The discovery of the halftone process in photography in 1881 made it ------- photographs in books and newspapers.

   (A) the possible reproduction
   (B) possible to reproduce
   (C) the possibility of reproducing
   (D) possibly reproduced

5. Flag Day is a legal holiday only in the state of Pennsylvania, -------, according to tradition, Betsy Ross sewed the first American flag.

   (A) which
   (B) where
   (C) that
   (D) has

6. ------- vastness of the Grand Canyon, it is difficult to capture it in a single photograph.

   (A) While the
   (B) The
   (C) For the
   (D) Because of the

7. Speciation, -------, results when an animal population becomes isolated by some factor, usually geographic.

   (A) form biological species
   (B) biological species are formed
   (C) which forming biological species
   (D) the formation of biological species

8. In its pure state antimony has no important uses, but ------- with other substances, it is an extremely useful metal.

   (A) when combined physically or chemically
   (B) combined when physically or chemically
   (C) the physical and chemical combination
   (D) it is combined physically and chemically

9. The dawn redwood appears ------- some 100 million years ago in northern forests around the world.

(A) was flourished
(B) having to flourish
(C) to have flourished
(D) have flourished

10. Beginning in the Middle Ages, composers of Western music used a system of notating their compositions ------- be performed by musicians.

(A) will
(B) that
(C) and when to
(D) so they could

11. Civil rights are the freedoms and rights ------- as a member of a community, state, or nation.

(A) may have a person
(B) may have a person who
(C) a person may have
(D) and a person may have

12. Richard Wright enjoyed success and influence ------- among Black American writers of his era.

(A) were unparalleled
(B) are unparalleled
(C) unparalleled
(D) the unparalleled

13. ------- of large mammals once dominated the North American prairies: the American bison and the pronghorn antelope.

(A) There are two species
(B) With two species
(C) Two species are
(D) Two species

14. Franklin D. Roosevelt was ------- the great force of radio and the opportunity it provided for taking government policies directly to the people.

(A) as the first president he understood fully
(B) the first President that, to fully understand
(C) the first President fully understood
(D) the first President to understand fully

15. During the late fifteenth century, ------- of the native societies of America had professions in the fields of arts and crafts.

(A) only a few
(B) a few but
(C) few, but only
(D) a few only

SECTION 2 CONTINUES ON THE NEXT PAGE.

Written Expression

Directions: In questions 16–40, each sentence has four underlined words or phrases. The four underlined parts of the sentence are marked (A), (B), (C), and (D). Choose the one underlined word or phrase that must be changed for the sentence to be correct. Then, on your answer sheet, find the number of the question and fill in the space that corresponds to the letter of the answer you have chosen.

Example I

Sample Answer

● Ⓑ Ⓒ Ⓓ

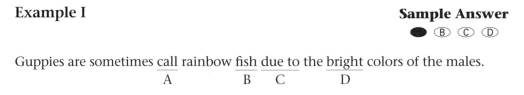

Guppies are sometimes call rainbow fish due to the bright colors of the males.
                   A   B   C   D

The sentence should read: "Guppies are sometimes called rainbow fish due to the bright colors of the males." Therefore, you should choose (A).

Example II

Sample Answer

Ⓐ ● Ⓒ Ⓓ

Serving several term in the United States Congress, Shirley Chisholm became a respected
  A   B   C
United States politician.
              D

The sentence should read: "Serving several terms in the United States Congress, Shirley Chisholm became a respected United States politician." Therefore, you should choose (B).

NOW BEGIN WORK ON THE QUESTIONS.

16. Jane Addams, social worker, author, and <u>spokeswoman</u> for the peace and women's
                                                    A
    suffrage <u>movements, she received</u> the Nobel Peace Prize in 1931 for her <u>humanitarian</u>
                    B   C   D
    achievements.

17. The <u>public ceremonies</u> of the North American Plains Indians are <u>lesser</u> elaborate <u>than</u> those
            A   B   C
    of the Navajo <u>in</u> the Southwest.
                    D

18. In <u>some</u> species of fish, <u>such the</u> three-spined stickleback, the male, not the female, <u>performs</u>
        A   B   C
    the task of <u>caring</u> for the young.
                    D

19. When she <u>retires</u> in September 1989, <u>tennis champion</u> Christine Evert was <u>the most</u> famous
                A   B   C
    <u>woman athlete</u> in the United States.
            D

20. The ancient Romans used vessels <u>equipped</u> with sails <u>and</u> banks of oars <u>to transporting</u>
      A   B   C   D
    their armies.

21. Dinosaurs <u>are</u> traditionally classified as cold-blooded reptiles, <u>but</u> recent evidence based on
              A   B
    eating habits, posture, and skeletal <u>structural</u> suggests some <u>may have been</u> warm-blooded.
                                            C   D

22. Since the Great Depression of the 1930s, government <u>programs</u> such as Social Security have
                                                            A
    <u>been built</u> into the economy <u>to help</u> avert <u>severity</u> business declines.
        B   C   D

23. In the 1970s, <u>consumer</u> activists <u>succeeded in</u> promoting laws that set <u>safety</u> standards for
                    A   B   C
    automobiles, children's clothing, and a <u>widely</u> range of household products.
                                                D

24. Zoos in New Orleans, San Diego, Detroit, and the Bronx <u>have become</u> biological parks <u>where</u>
                                                                A   B
    animals <u>roams freely</u> and people <u>watch from</u> across a moat.
                C   D

25. In primates, as in other <u>mammal</u>, hairs <u>around</u> the eyes and ears and in the nose, <u>prevent</u>
                              A   B   C

    dust, insects, and other matter from <u>entering</u> these organs.
                                               D

26. The Rocky Mountains <u>were</u> explored <u>by</u> fur traders during the early 1800s, in <u>a</u> decades
                            A   B   C

    <u>preceding</u> the United States Civil War.
       D

27. The works of the <u>author</u> Herman Melville are <u>literary</u> creations of a high order, blending <u>fact</u>,
                     A   B   C

    fiction, adventure, and subtle <u>symbolic</u>.
                           D

28. <u>Each chemical</u> element is characterized <u>to</u> the number of protons that <u>an atom</u> of that
          A   B   C

    element contains, called <u>its</u> atomic number.
                            D

29. The <u>body structure</u> that developed in birds <u>over</u> millions of years is <u>well designed</u> for flight,
                A   B   C

    being both <u>lightly</u> in weight and remarkably strong.
                 D

30. From 1905 to 1920, American novelist Edith Wharton <u>was</u> at the height of her writing career,
    <u>A</u>   B

    producing <u>of her</u> three <u>most</u> popular novels.
                   C   D

31. In the early twentieth century, there was considerable <u>interesting</u> among sociologists in the
                                                            A

    fact <u>that</u> in the United States <u>the family</u> was losing its <u>traditional</u> roles.
          B   C   D

32. <u>Although</u> diamond is colorless and transparent <u>when</u> pure, <u>it</u> may appear in various <u>color</u>,
      A   B   C   D

    ranging from pastels to opaque black, if it is contaminated with other material.

33. Comparative anatomy is <u>concerned to</u> the <u>structural</u> differences <u>among</u> animal <u>forms</u>.
                                  A   B   C   D

34. A seismograph records oscillation of the ground <u>caused by</u> seismic waves, vibrations that
                                                 A

    <u>travel</u> from <u>its</u> point of origin <u>through</u> Earth or along its surface.
      B   C   D

35. Electric lamps came into widespread use during the early 1900s and eventually <u>replaced</u>
                                                                                      A
once-popular <u>type</u> of fat, gas, or <u>oil</u> lamps for <u>almost every</u> purpose.
                  B   C   D

36. Located in Canada, the Columbia Icefield <u>covers area</u> of 120 square miles <u>and</u> is 3,300 feet
                                               A   B
<u>thick</u> in some <u>places</u>.
  C   D

37. Composer Richard Rodgers and lyricist Oscar Hammerstein II <u>brought</u> to the musical
                                                                 A
Oklahoma! <u>extensive</u> musical and theatrical backgrounds as well as <u>familiar</u> with the
               B   C
<u>traditional</u> forms of operetta and musical comedy.
  D

38. Although traditional flutes are <u>among</u> the world's oldest musical instruments, <u>but the</u> flute
                                     A   B
<u>used</u> in orchestras today is <u>one of</u> the most technically sophisticated.
  C   D

39. Rice, <u>which it still</u> forms the staple diet of <u>much</u> of the world's population, grows <u>best</u> in <u>hot</u>,
              A   B   C   D
wet lands.

40. Federal funds appropriated <u>for art</u> in the 1930s made possible <u>hundreds of</u> murals and statues
                                 A   B
still <u>admiration</u> in small towns <u>all over</u> the United States.
        C   D

THIS IS THE END OF THE STRUCTURE AND WRITTEN EXPRESSION SECTION.

IF YOU FINISH IN LESS THAN 25 MINUTES, CHECK YOUR WORK IN SECTION 2 ONLY.

DO NOT READ OR WORK ON ANY OTHER SECTION OF THE TEST.

AT THE END OF 25 MINUTES, GO ON TO SECTION 3—READING COMPREHENSION. USE EXACTLY 55 MINUTES TO WORK ON SECTION 3.

Section 3

해설 p.247

Reading Comprehension

Time: 55 minutes

Now set your clock for 55 minutes.

Directions: In this section you will read several passages. Each one is followed by several questions about it. For questions 1–50, choose the one best answer—(A), (B), (C), or (D)—to each question. Then, on your answer sheet, find the number of the question and fill in the space that corresponds to the letter of the answer you have chosen.

Answer all questions following a passage on the basis of what is stated or implied in that passage.

Read the following passage.

The railroad was not the first institution to impose regularity on society or to draw attention to the importance of precise timekeeping. For as long as merchants have set out their wares at daybreak and communal festivities have been celebrated, people have been in rough
Line agreement with their neighbors as to the time of day. The value of this tradition is today more
(5) apparent than ever. Were it not for public acceptance of a single yardstick of time, social life would be unbearably chaotic; the massive daily transfers of goods, services, and information would proceed in fits and starts; the very fabric of modern society would begin to unravel.

Example I

Sample Answer

(A) (B) ● (D)

What is the main idea of the passage?

    (A) In modern society we must make more time for our neighbors.
    (B) The traditions of society are timeless.
    (C) An accepted way of measuring time is essential for the smooth functioning of society.
    (D) Society judges people by the times at which they conduct certain activities.

The main idea of the passage is that societies need to agree about how time is to be measured in order to function smoothly. Therefore, you should choose (C).

Example II

In line 4, the phrase "this tradition" refers to

(A) the practice of starting the business day at dawn
(B) friendly relations between neighbors
(C) the railroad's reliance on time schedules
(D) people's agreement on the measurement of time

The phrase "this tradition" refers to the preceding clause, "people have been in rough agreement with their neighbors as to the time of day." Therefore, you should choose (D).

NOW BEGIN WORK ON THE QUESTIONS.

Questions 1–7

Hotels were among the earliest facilities that bound the United States together. They were both creatures and creators of communities, as well as symptoms of the frenetic quest for community. Even in the first part of the nineteenth century, Americans were already forming
Line the habit of gathering from all corners of the nation for both public and private, business
(5) and pleasure, purposes. Conventions were the new occasions, and hotels were distinctively American facilities making conventions possible. The first national convention of a major party to choose a candidate for president (that of the National Republican Party, which met on December 12, 1831, and nominated Henry Clay for president) was held in Baltimore, at a hotel that was then reputed to be the best in the country. The presence in Baltimore of
(10) Barnum's City Hotel, a six-story building with two hundred apartments, helps explain why many other early national political conventions were held there.

In the longer run, American hotels made other national conventions not only possible but pleasant and convivial. The growing custom of regularly assembling from afar the representatives of all kinds of groups—not only for political conventions, but also for
(15) commercial, professional, learned, and avocational ones—in turn supported the multiplying hotels. By the mid-twentieth century, conventions accounted for over a third of the yearly room occupancy of all hotels in the nation; about 18,000 different conventions were held annually with a total attendance of about ten million persons.

Nineteenth-century American hotelkeepers, who were no longer the genial, deferential
(20) "hosts" of the eighteenth-century European inn, became leading citizens. Holding a large stake in the community, they exercised power to make it prosper. As owners or managers of the local "palace of the public," they were makers and shapers of a principal community attraction. Travelers from abroad were mildly shocked by this high social position.

1. The word "bound" in line 1 is closest in meaning to
   (A) led
   (B) protected
   (C) tied
   (D) strengthened

2. The National Republican Party is mentioned in line 7 as an example of a group
   (A) from Baltimore
   (B) of learned people
   (C) owning a hotel
   (D) holding a convention

3. The word "assembling" in line 13 is closest in meaning to
   (A) announcing
   (B) motivating
   (C) gathering
   (D) contracting

4. The word "ones" in line 15 refers to
   (A) hotels
   (B) conventions
   (C) kinds
   (D) representatives

5. The word "it" in line 21 refers to
   (A) European inn
   (B) host
   (C) community
   (D) public

6. It can be inferred from the passage that early hotelkeepers in the United States were
   (A) active politicians
   (B) European immigrants
   (C) professional builders
   (D) influential citizens

7. Which of the following statements about early American hotels is NOT mentioned in the passage?
   (A) Travelers from abroad did not enjoy staying in them.
   (B) Conventions were held in them.
   (C) People used them for both business and pleasure.
   (D) They were important to the community.

Questions 8–15

With Robert Laurent and William Zorach, direct carving enters into the story of modern sculpture in the United States. Direct carving—in which the sculptors themselves carve stone or wood with mallet and chisel—must be recognized as something more than just a technique. Implicit in it is an aesthetic principle as well: that the medium has certain qualities of beauty and expressiveness with which sculptors must bring their own aesthetic sensibilities into harmony. For example, sometimes the shape or veining in a piece of stone or wood suggests, perhaps even dictates, not only the ultimate form, but even the subject matter.

The technique of direct carving was a break with the nineteenth-century tradition in which the making of a clay model was considered the creative act and the work was then turned over to studio assistants to be cast in plaster or bronze or carved in marble. Neoclassical sculptors seldom held a mallet or chisel in their own hands, readily conceding that the assistants they employed were far better than they were at carving the finished marble.

With the turn-of-the-century Arts and Crafts movement and the discovery of nontraditional sources of inspiration, such as wooden African figures and masks, there arose a new urge for hands-on, personal execution of art and an interaction with the medium. Even as early as the 1880s and 1890s, nonconformist European artists were attempting direct carving. By the second decade of the twentieth century, Americans—Laurent and Zorach most notably—had adopted it as their primary means of working.

Born in France, Robert Laurent (1890–1970) was a prodigy who received his education in the United States. In 1905 he was sent to Paris as an apprentice to an art dealer, and in the years that followed he witnessed the birth of Cubism, discovered primitive art, and learned the techniques of woodcarving from a frame maker.

Back in New York City by 1910, Laurent began carving pieces such as *The Priestess*, which reveals his fascination with African, pre-Columbian, and South Pacific art. Taking a walnut plank, the sculptor carved the expressive, stylized design. It is one of the earliest examples of direct carving in American sculpture. The plank's form dictated the rigidly frontal view and the low relief. Even its irregular shape must have appealed to Laurent as a break with a long-standing tradition that required a sculptor to work within a perfect rectangle or square.

8. The word "medium" in line 4 could be used to refer to

    (A) stone or wood
    (B) mallet and chisel
    (C) technique
    (D) principle

9. What is one of the fundamental principles of direct carving?

    (A) A sculptor must work with talented assistants.
    (B) The subject of a sculpture should be derived from classical stories.
    (C) The material is an important element in a sculpture.
    (D) Designing a sculpture is a more creative activity than carving it.

10. The word "dictates" in line 7 is closest in meaning to

    (A) reads aloud
    (B) determines
    (C) includes
    (D) records

11. How does direct carving differ from the nineteenth-century tradition of sculpture?

    (A) Sculptors are personally involved in the carving of a piece.
    (B) Sculptors find their inspiration in neoclassical sources.
    (C) Sculptors have replaced the mallet and chisel with other tools.
    (D) Sculptors receive more formal training.

12. The word "witnessed" in line 22 is closest in meaning to

    (A) influenced
    (B) studied
    (C) validated
    (D) observed

13. Where did Robert Laurent learn to carve?

    (A) New York
    (B) Africa
    (C) The South Pacific
    (D) Paris

14. The phase "a break with" in line 28 is closest in meaning to

    (A) a destruction of
    (B) a departure from
    (C) a collapse of
    (D) a solution to

15. The piece titled *The Priestess* has all of the following characteristics EXCEPT:

    (A) The design is stylized.
    (B) It is made of marble.
    (C) The carving is not deep.
    (D) It depicts the front of a person.

Questions 16–26

Birds that feed in flocks commonly retire together into roosts. The reasons for roosting communally are not always obvious, but there are some likely benefits. In winter especially, it is important for birds to keep warm at night and conserve precious food reserves. One way

Line
(5) to do this is to find a sheltered roost. Solitary roosters shelter in dense vegetation or enter a cavity—horned larks dig holes in the ground and ptarmigan burrow into snow banks—but the effect of sheltering is magnified by several birds huddling together in the roosts, as wrens, swifts, brown creepers, bluebirds, and anis do. Body contact reduces the surface area exposed to the cold air, so the birds keep each other warm. Two kinglets huddling together were found to reduce their heat losses by a quarter, and three together saved a third of their heat.

(10) The second possible benefit of communal roosts is that they act as information centers. During the day, parties of birds will have spread out to forage over a very large area. When they return in the evening some will have fed well, but others may have found little to eat. Some investigators have observed that when the birds set out again next morning, those birds that did not feed well on the previous day appear to follow those that did. The behavior

(15) of common and lesser kestrels may illustrate different feeding behaviors of similar birds with different roosting habits. The common kestrel hunts vertebrate animals in a small, familiar hunting ground, whereas the very similar lesser kestrel feeds on insects over a large area. The common kestrel roosts and hunts alone, but the lesser kestrel roosts and hunts in flocks, possibly so that one bird can learn from others where to find insect swarms.

(20) Finally, there is safety in numbers at communal roosts since there will always be a few birds awake at any given moment to give the alarm. But this increased protection is partially counteracted by the fact that mass roosts attract predators and are especially vulnerable if they are on the ground. Even those in trees can be attacked by birds of prey. The birds on the edge are at greatest risk since predators find it easier to catch small birds perching at the

(25) margins of the roost.

16. What does the passage mainly discuss?

    (A) How birds find and store food
    (B) How birds maintain body heat in the winter
    (C) Why birds need to establish territory
    (D) Why some species of birds nest together

17. The word "conserve" in line 3 is closest in meaning to

    (A) retain
    (B) watch
    (C) locate
    (D) share

18. Ptarmigan keep warm in the winter by

    (A) huddling together on the ground with other birds
    (B) building nests in trees
    (C) burrowing into dense patches of vegetation
    (D) digging tunnels into the snow

19. The word "magnified" in line 6 is closest in meaning to

    (A) caused
    (B) modified
    (C) intensified
    (D) combined

20. The author mentions kinglets in line 8 as an example of birds that

    (A) protect themselves by nesting in holes
    (B) nest with other species of birds
    (C) nest together for warmth
    (D) usually feed and nest in pairs

21. The word "forage" in line 11 is closest in meaning to

    (A) fly
    (B) assemble
    (C) feed
    (D) rest

22. Which of the following statements about lesser and common kestrels is true?

    (A) The lesser kestrel and the common kestrel have similar diets.
    (B) The lesser kestrel feeds sociably, but the common kestrel does not.
    (C) The common kestrel nests in larger flocks than does the lesser kestrel.
    (D) The common kestrel nests in trees; the lesser kestrel nests on the ground.

23. The word "counteracted' in line 22 is closest in meaning to

    (A) suggested
    (B) negated
    (C) measured
    (D) shielded

24. Which of the following is NOT mentioned in the passage as an advantage derived by birds that huddle together while sleeping?

    (A) Some members of the flock warn others of impending dangers.
    (B) Staying together provides a greater amount of heat for the whole flock.
    (C) Some birds in the flock function as information centers for others who are looking for food.
    (D) Several members of the flock care for the young.

25. Which of the following is a disadvantage of communal roosts that is mentioned in the passage?

    (A) Diseases easily spread among the birds.
    (B) Groups are more attractive to predators than individual birds are.
    (C) Food supplies are quickly depleted.
    (D) Some birds in the group will attack the others.

26. The word "they" in line 23 refers to

    (A) a few birds
    (B) mass roosts
    (C) predators
    (D) trees

SECTION 3 CONTINUES.

TURN THE PAGE AND READ THE NEXT PASSAGE.

Questions 27–38

Perhaps the most striking quality of satiric literature is its freshness, its originality of perspective. Satire rarely offers original ideas. Instead, it presents the familiar in a new form. Satirists do not offer the world new philosophies. What they do is look at familiar conditions
Line from a perspective that makes these conditions seem foolish, harmful, or affected. Satire
(5) jars us out of complacence into a pleasantly shocked realization that many of the values we unquestioningly accept are false. *Don Quixote* makes chivalry seem absurd; *Brave New World* ridicules the pretensions of science; *A Modest Proposal* dramatizes starvation by advocating cannibalism. None of these ideas is original. Chivalry was suspect before Cervantes, humanists objected to the claims of pure science before Aldous Huxley, and people were
(10) aware of famine before Swift. It was not the originality of the idea that made these satires popular. It was the manner of expression, the satiric method, that made them interesting and entertaining. Satires are read because they are aesthetically satisfying works of art, not because they are morally wholesome or ethically instructive. They are stimulating and refreshing because with commonsense briskness they brush away illusions and secondhand opinions.
(15) With spontaneous irreverence, satire rearranges perspectives, scrambles familiar objects into incongruous juxtaposition, and speaks in a personal idiom instead of abstract platitude.

Satire exists because there is need for it. It has lived because readers appreciate a refreshing stimulus, an irreverent reminder that they live in a world of platitudinous thinking, cheap moralizing, and foolish philosophy. Satire serves to prod people into an awareness of
(20) truth, though rarely to any action on behalf of truth. Satire tends to remind people that much of what they see, hear, and read in popular media is sanctimonious, sentimental, and only partially true. Life resembles in only a slight degree the popular image of it. Soldiers rarely hold the ideals that movies attribute to them, nor do ordinary citizens devote their lives to unselfish service of humanity. Intelligent people know these things but tend to forget them
(25) when they do not hear them expressed.

27. What does the passage mainly discuss?

    (A) Difficulties of writing satiric literature
    (B) Popular topics of satire
    (C) New philosophies emerging from satiric literature
    (D) Reasons for the popularity of satire

28. The word "realization" in line 5 is closest in meaning to

    (A) certainty
    (B) awareness
    (C) surprise
    (D) confusion

29. Why does the author mention *Don Quixote*, *Brave New World*, and *A Modest Proposal* in lines 6–7?

    (A) They are famous examples of satiric literature.
    (B) They present commonsense solutions to problems.
    (C) They are appropriate for readers of all ages.
    (D) They are books with similar stories.

30. The word "aesthetically" in line 12 is closest in meaning to

    (A) artistically
    (B) exceptionally
    (C) realistically
    (D) dependably

31. Which of the following can be found in satiric literature?

    (A) Newly emerging philosophies
    (B) Odd combinations of objects and ideas
    (C) Abstract discussion of morals and ethics
    (D) Wholesome characters who are unselfish

32. According to the passage, there is a need for satire because people need to be

    (A) informed about new scientific developments
    (B) exposed to original philosophies when they are formulated
    (C) reminded that popular ideas are often inaccurate
    (D) told how they can be of service to their communities

33. The word "refreshing" in line 18 is closest in meaning to

    (A) popular
    (B) ridiculous
    (C) meaningful
    (D) unusual

34. The word "they" in line 21 refers to

    (A) people
    (B) media
    (C) ideals
    (D) movies

35. The word "devote" in line 23 is closest in meaning to

   (A) distinguish
   (B) feel affection
   (C) prefer
   (D) dedicate

36. As a result of reading satiric literature, readers will be most likely to

   (A) teach themselves to write fiction
   (B) accept conventional points of view
   (C) become better informed about current affairs
   (D) reexamine their opinions and values

37. The various purposes of satire include all of the following EXCEPT

   (A) introducing readers to unfamiliar situations
   (B) brushing away illusions
   (C) reminding readers of the truth
   (D) exposing false values

38. Why does the author mention "service of humanity" in line 24?

   (A) People need to be reminded to take action.
   (B) Readers appreciate knowing about it.
   (C) It is an ideal that is rarely achieved.
   (D) Popular media often distort such stories.

SECTION 3 CONTINUES.
TURN THE PAGE AND READ THE NEXT PASSAGE.

Questions 39–50

Galaxies are the major building blocks of the universe. A galaxy is a giant family of many millions of stars, and it is held together by its own gravitational field. Most of the material in the universe is organized into galaxies of stars, together with gas and dust.

Line
(5) There are three main types of galaxies: spiral, elliptical, and irregular. The Milky Way is a spiral galaxy: a flattish disc of stars with two spiral arms emerging from its central nucleus. About one-quarter of all galaxies have this shape. Spiral galaxies are well supplied with the interstellar gas in which new stars form; as the rotating spiral pattern sweeps around the galaxy, it compresses gas and dust, triggering the formation of bright young stars in its arms. The elliptical galaxies have a symmetrical, elliptical or spheroidal shape with no obvious

(10) structure. Most of their member stars are very old, and since ellipticals are devoid of interstellar gas, no new stars are forming in them. The biggest and brightest galaxies in the universe are ellipticals with masses of about 1013 times that of the Sun; these giants may frequently be sources of strong radio emission, in which case they are called radio galaxies. About two-thirds of all galaxies are elliptical. Irregular galaxies comprise about one-tenth of all galaxies,

(15) and they come in many subclasses.

Measurement in space is quite different from measurement on Earth. Some terrestrial distances can be expressed as intervals of time: the time to fly from one continent to another or the time it takes to drive to work, for example. By comparison, with these familiar yardsticks, the distances to the galaxies are incomprehensibly large, but they too are made

(20) more manageable by using a time calibration, in this case, the distance that light travels in one year. On such a scale, the nearest giant spiral galaxy, the Andromeda galaxy, is two million light years away. The most distant luminous objects seen by telescopes are probably ten thousand million light years away. Their light was already halfway here before the Earth even formed. The light from the nearby Virgo galaxy set out when reptiles still dominated the

(25) animal world.

39. The word "major" in line 1 is closest in meaning to

    (A) intense
    (B) principal
    (C) huge
    (D) unique

40. What does the second paragraph mainly discuss?

    (A) The Milky Way
    (B) Major categories of galaxies
    (C) How elliptical galaxies are formed
    (D) Differences between irregular and spiral galaxies

41. The word "which" in line 7 refers to

    (A) dust
    (B) gas
    (C) pattern
    (D) galaxy

42. According to the passage, new stars are formed in spiral galaxies due to

    (A) an explosion of gas
    (B) the compression of gas and dust
    (C) the combining of old stars
    (D) strong radio emissions

43. The word "symmetrical" in line 9 is closest in meaning to

    (A) proportionally balanced
    (B) commonly seen
    (C) typically large
    (D) steadily growing

44. The word "obvious" in line 9 is closest in meaning to

    (A) discovered
    (B) apparent
    (C) understood
    (D) simplistic

45. According to the passage, which of the following is NOT true of elliptical galaxies?

    (A) They are the largest galaxies.
    (B) They mostly contain old stars.
    (C) They contain a high amount of interstellar gas.
    (D) They have a spherical shape.

46. Which of the following characteristics of radio galaxies is mentioned in the passage?

    (A) They are a type of elliptical galaxy.
    (B) They are usually too small to be seen with a telescope.
    (C) They are closely related to irregular galaxies.
    (D) They are not as bright as spiral galaxies.

47. What percentage of galaxies is irregular?

    (A) 10%
    (B) 25%
    (C) 50%
    (D) 75%

48. The word "they" in line 19 refers to

    (A) intervals
    (B) yardsticks
    (C) distances
    (D) galaxies

49. Why does the author mention the Virgo galaxy and the Andromeda galaxy in the third paragraph?

    (A) To describe the effect that distance has on visibility
    (B) To compare the ages of two relatively young galaxies
    (C) To emphasize the vast distances of the galaxies from Earth
    (D) To explain why certain galaxies cannot be seen by a telescope

50. The word "dominated" in line 24 is closest in meaning to

    (A) threatened
    (B) replaced
    (C) were developing in
    (D) were prevalent in

THIS IS THE END OF THE READING COMPREHENSION SECTION.

IF YOU FINISH IN LESS THAN 55 MINUTES, CHECK YOUR WORK IN THIS SECTION ONLY.

DO NOT READ OR WORK ON ANY OTHER SECTION OF THE TEST.

CHAPTER 7

FREQUENTLY ASKED QUESTIONS

Frequently Asked Questions

*TOEFL® ITP*는 어떤 시험인가요?

TOEFL ITP는 대학교를 비롯해 영어 프로그램, 다른 교육 기관들에게 편리하고 신뢰할 수 있는 영어 평가를 시행할 수 있는 기회를 제공합니다. ITP 시험은 중·고급 수준의 영어 능력을 측정합니다.

시험은 학습과 관련 있는 내용으로 다음 세 가지 영역에서 학생들의 능력을 평가합니다.
- 듣기(Listening Comprehension)
- 문법(Structure and Written Expression)
- 읽기(Reading Comprehension)

해당 기관이 원하는 시험 날짜나 장소를 지정해 TOEFL ITP 시험을 실시할 수 있으며, 성적표에는 각 영역 점수와 총점이 표시됩니다. 기관별 최저 점수 기준은 해당 기관에 직접 문의해서 확인해야 합니다. TOEFL ITP 점수는 2년간 유효하지만, 일반적으로 시험을 실시한 기관에서만 유효하다.

TOEFL® ITP 시험은 어떻게 활용되나요?

TOEFL ITP(기관 토플)는 기관에서 실시하는 영어 평가 시험으로, 다음과 같이 다양하게 활용됩니다.
- 대학이나 대학원 과정에서 필요한 영어 능력을 요구하는 집중 영어 프로그램에서 **반 배정 평가**
- 영어 프로그램에 참여한 학생들의 **영어 능력 향상도 확인**
- 영어 프로그램 수료 시 학생들의 **영어 능력 평가**
- 영어권 국가의 단기 또는 비학위 과정에 **입학하기 위한 자격 요건**으로 활용
- 비영어권 국가에서는 **학사 또는 대학원 과정의 입학 요건**으로 활용
- 복수 학위 과정(Collaborative International Degree)의 **입학 및 반 배정 평가** 도구로 활용
- **장학생 프로그램의 선발** 요건

TOEFL® *ITP* 시험에서는 무엇을 평가하나요?

TOEFL ITP는 3개 영역으로 구성되며, 각 영역별로 다른 능력을 평가합니다.
- 듣기(Listening Comprehension) _ 대학에서 사용되는 구어체 영어에 대한 이해력 평가
- 문법(Structure and Written Expression) _ 문어체 표준 영어의 구조 및 문법 요소에 대한 이해력 평가
- 읽기(Reading Comprehension) _ 학습 요소와 관련된 자료를 읽고 이해하는 능력 평가

TOEFL® *ITP* 시험은 어떻게 구성되어 있나요?

TOEFL ITP는 지필 시험으로, 문제는 4지 선다형이며, 답안지에 정답을 표시하면 됩니다. TOEFL ITP는 듣기(Listening Comprehension)와 문법(Structure and Written Expression), 읽기(Reading Comprehension)의 3개 영역으로 구성됩니다.

영역	문항 수	소요 시간
듣기(Listening Comprehension)	50	35분
문법(Structure and Written Expression)	40	25분
읽기(Reading Comprehension)	50	55분
총점(TOTAL)	140	115분

TOEFL® *ITP* 시험은 어떻게 채점되나요?

현지 지역이나 ETS에서 채점하며, 보통 7일 이내에 성적을 확인할 수 있습니다. 성적은 각 영역별로 채점됩니다. 더 노력해야 할 부진한 부분을 파악할 수 있어, 개개인의 필요에 맞춘 영어 학습이 가능합니다.

정답 및 해설

Listening Comprehension Section

Practice Set 1 **Short Conversations** – 본문 p.22

1. (D)	2. (A)	3. (C)	4. (C)	5. (C)
6. (A)	7. (C)	8. (A)	9. (B)	10. (D)

1. **W** My lease is about to expire and I've decided to get a larger place. Do you know of any two-bedroom apartments for rent?

M Have you checked the off-campus listings at the housing office?

N What does the man imply?

(A) A two-bedroom apartment may be too expensive.

(B) The woman should not move off campus.

(C) The woman should pay the rent by check.

(D) The university has a list of rental properties.

[해석] W 제 임대 계약이 곧 만료되는데, 더 큰 집을 구하려고 해요. 혹시 방 두 개짜리 아파트 나온 거 있나요?

M 기숙사 사무실에서 캠퍼스 인근의 주택 리스트를 확인해 봤어요?

N 남자가 암시하는 것은 무엇인가?

(A) 방 두 개짜리 아파트는 비쌀지도 모른다.

(B) 여자는 캠퍼스 밖으로 이사하면 안 된다.

(C) 여자는 수표로 집세를 지불해야 한다.

(D) 대학에서 임대 주택 리스트를 가지고 있다.

[어휘] lease 임대차 계약   be about to+동사원형 막 ~하려고 하다   expire 만기가 되다   rent 임대(료), 집세   off-campus (대학의) 캠퍼스 밖의   listing 목록, 명단   by check 수표로   property 부동산

[해설] 추론 문제이다. 남자의 말 Have you checked the off-campus listings at the housing office?에서 남자는 여자에게 기숙사 사무실에 문의하라고 제안하고 있으므로 (D)가 정답이다.

2. **M** I've spent the whole morning at the library looking for the information we need — you know, for the assignment that's due Friday?

W I'm stuck, too. Maybe Dr. Boyd will have some suggestions.

N What will the speakers probably do?

(A) Talk to Dr. Boyd about an assignment

(B) Return their books to the library

(C) Meet Dr. Boyd at the library

(D) Make an appointment with their teacher on Friday

[해석] M 나는 아침 내내 필요한 자료를 찾느라 도서관에 있었어. 있잖아, 금요일까지 제출해야 하는 과제 말이야.

W 나도 애를 먹고 있어. 어쩌면 보이드 박사님께서 조언을 해 주실지도 몰라.

N 화자들은 무엇을 할 것 같은가?

(A) 보이드 박사에게 과제에 대해 이야기할 것이다.

(B) 도서관에 책을 반납할 것이다.

(C) 도서관에서 보이드 박사를 만날 것이다.

(D) 금요일에 선생님과 만날 약속을 할 것이다.

[어휘] assignment 숙제, 과제   due (제출) 기일이 된   be stuck 막히다, 궁하다   make an appointment with ~와 만날 약속을 하다

[해설] 다음에 할 일을 예상하는 문제(What ~ probably do?)이다. 화자들은 자료를 찾고 있으며, 여자는 보이드 박사에게 도움을 요청하자(Maybe Dr. Boyd will have some suggestions.)고 제안하고 있으므로 (A)가 정답이다.

3. **M** I think the whole class is going on the field trip next Friday.

W I'm not so sure. Not everyone has paid the transportation fee.

N What does the woman imply?

(A) The transportation for the trip is free.

(B) The class did not enjoy going on the field trip.

(C) Some people may not go on the trip.

(D) Everyone in the class has paid the fee.

[해석] M 우리 반 전체가 다음 주 금요일에 견학을 갈 것 같아.
W 나는 잘 모르겠어. 모든 사람이 교통비를 다 내지는 않았거든.

N 여자가 암시하는 것은 무엇인가?

(A) 견학 교통비는 무료이다.
(B) 그 반에서는 견학 가는 것을 좋아하지 않았다.
(C) 사람들 중 일부가 견학을 가지 않을 수도 있다.
(D) 반 학생 모두가 요금을 지불했다.

[어휘] **field trip** 현장 학습, 견학   **transportation fee** 교통비
free 무료의

[해설] 여자가 암시하는 의미를 묻는 문제이다. 모든 사람이 교통비를 낸 것은 아니다(Not everyone has paid the transportation fee.)라는 여자의 말은 교통비를 내지 않은 사람들은 견학을 가지 않을 수도 있다는 사실을 암시한다. 따라서 (C)가 정답이다.

4. **W** I can't seem to shake this cold.

M Sometimes the only thing that helps is taking it easy.

N What does the man mean?

(A) The woman should avoid getting cold.

(B) It is easy to get sick in cold weather.

(C) The woman should get more rest.

(D) Dressing warmly can prevent illness.

[해석] W 이 감기를 떨쳐 버릴 수가 없어.
M 때로는 편히 쉬는 게 유일한 길이야.

N 남자가 의미하는 것은 무엇인가?

(A) 여자는 감기에 걸리지 않도록 해야 한다.
(B) 추운 날씨에는 아프기 쉽다.
(C) 여자가 더 많이 쉬어야 한다.
(D) 옷을 따뜻하게 입으면 병을 예방할 수 있다.

[어휘] **shake** ~을 떨쳐 버리다, 떼어내다   **take it easy** 편히 쉬다
get cold 감기에 걸리다   **prevent** 예방하다, 막다

[해설] 어휘 문제이다. shake this cold는 '감기를 떨쳐 버리다'라는 의미이며, 남자는 여자에게 편히 쉬라(take it easy)고 제안하고 있다. 따라서 (C)가 정답이다.

5. **W** Congratulations! I understand you got a job. When do you start work?

M You must be thinking of someone else. I'm still waiting to hear.

N What does the man mean?

(A) The woman should get another job.

(B) He will not have to wait much longer.

(C) The woman was mistaken.

(D) He was waiting in the wrong place.

[해석] W 축하해! 일자리를 찾았다면서. 언제부터 일하는 거야?
M 다른 사람으로 착각한 것 같아. 나는 여전히 소식을 기다리고 있거든.

N 남자가 의미하는 것은 무엇인가?

(A) 여자는 다른 일을 찾아야 한다.
(B) 남자는 더 오래 기다릴 필요가 없다.
(C) 여자는 잘못 알았다.
(D) 남자는 잘못된 장소에서 기다리고 있었다.

[어휘] **mistaken** 잘못 생각하고 있는, 오해한

[해설] 요지를 묻는 문제이다. 여자는 남자가 새 일자리를 찾았다고 생각하지만, 남자는 여전히 소식을 기다리고 있다(I'm still waiting to hear.)고 말한다. 따라서 남자의 말은 여자의 말이 틀렸다는 의미이므로 (C)가 정답이다.

6. **M** Have you seen Jim around? We're supposed to play tennis.

W Well, his racket's here on the table.

N What does the woman imply about Jim?

(A) He is probably nearby.

(B) He should pick up his things.

(C) He broke his racket.

(D) He might be playing tennis right now.

[해석] M 이 근처에서 짐 봤니? 나와 함께 테니스 치기로 했거든.
W 글쎄, 그의 라켓은 여기 테이블 위에 있는데.

N 여자는 짐에 대해 무엇을 암시하는가?

(A) 그는 근처에 있을 것이다.
(B) 그는 자기 물건을 가지러 가야 한다.
(C) 그는 자신의 라켓을 부러뜨렸다.
(D) 그는 아마도 지금 테니스를 치고 있을 것이다.

[어휘] **be supposed to+동사원형** ~할 예정이다, ~하기로 되어 있다 **nearby** 바로 가까이에 **pick up** (물건을) 가지러 가다, 찾아가다

[해설] 추론 문제이다. 여자는 짐의 라켓이 테이블 위에 있다(his racket's here on the table)고 했으므로, 짐이 근처에 있다고 추측할 수 있다. 따라서 (A)가 정답이다.

7. **W** I can't remember the due date for our final paper.

M I think it's the twelfth, but the professor said not to wait until the last minute to hand it in.

N What did the professor suggest the students do?

(A) Watch the clock carefully during the final exam

(B) Pick up their papers on the twelfth

(C) Finish their assignment early

(D) Discuss their topics after class

[해석] W 우리 기말 리포트의 제출 기한이 언제인지 잊어버렸어.
M 12일이야. 하지만 교수님께서 마감일까지 기다리지 말고 제출 하라고 하셨어.

N 교수는 학생들에게 어떻게 하라고 제안했는가?

(A) 기말 고사 시험 때 시계를 주의해서 볼 것
(B) 12일에 리포트를 찾아갈 것
(C) 일찍 과제를 끝낼 것
(D) 방과 후에 주제에 대해 논의할 것

[어휘] **due date** 제출 마감일, 지급 기일 **final paper** 기말 리포트, 기말 보고서 **hand in** ~을 제출하다 **last minute** 마지막 순간, 막판

[해설] 제안 사항을 묻는 문제이다. 교수는 보고서 제출 마감일까지 기다리지 말고 그 전에 제출하라(the professor said not to wait until the last minute to hand it in)고 했다. 따라서 (C)가 정답이다.

8. **M** Weren't you trying to get us all together for a picnic this weekend?

W It never really got off the ground.

N What does the woman say about the picnic?

(A) She was not able to organize it.

(B) Its location has been changed.

(C) It has been rescheduled.

(D) She does not know anything about it.

[해석] M 네가 이번 주말에 우리 모두 함께 야유회를 가게 하려고 애쓰 지 않았니?
W 사실 아직 시작도 하지 못했어.

N 여자는 야유회에 대해 뭐라고 말하는가?

(A) 그녀는 야유회를 준비할 수 없었다.
(B) 야유회 장소가 변경되었다.
(C) 야유회 일정이 재조정되었다.
(D) 그녀는 야유회에 대해 전혀 모른다.

[어휘] **get off the ground** (계획을) 실행에 옮기다, (일이) 잘
시작되다 **organize** 계획하다, 준비하다 **location** 위치,
장소 **reschedule** 일정을 다시 잡다

[해설] 어휘 문제이다. to get (something) off the ground는 '(계획
을) 실행에 옮기다, (일이) 잘 시작되다'라는 의미의 관용 표현으로,
여자는 전체 야유회 계획을 시작도 하지 못했다는 것을 알 수 있다.
따라서 (A)가 정답이다.

---

9. **M** I got my grades in the mail and there was
a mistake in my mark for your course.

W I know—there was a problem with the
computer system. It should be straightened
out by next week.

N What does the woman mean?

(A) The man is mistaken.
(B) The error will be corrected.
(C) She did not know about the problem.
(D) Grades were sent late.

[해석] M 성적표를 우편으로 받았는데 교수님 과목에 제 점수가 잘못 기
재되어 있었어요.

W 알아요. 컴퓨터 시스템에 문제가 있었어요. 다음 주까지 수정
될 거예요.

N 여자가 의미하는 것은 무엇인가?

(A) 남자가 틀렸다.
(B) 오류가 수정될 것이다.
(C) 여자는 그 문제에 대해 몰랐다.
(D) 성적표가 늦게 발송되었다.

[어휘] **mark** (성적의) 평점, 점수 **course** 교과 과정, 과목
straighten out ~을 바로잡다, 고치다 **mistaken** 잘못
생각하고 있는, 틀린

[해설] 어휘 문제이다. 여자는 남자의 성적이 컴퓨터 시스템 문제로 잘못
된 것을 알고 있다. 여자의 말 be straightened out은 '바로잡
다, 고치다'라는 의미로, 여자는 남자에게 곧 오류가 수정될 것이라
고 알려주고 있다. 따라서 (B)가 정답이다.

---

10. **W** Can you come to the concert with me this
weekend, or do you have to prepare for
exams?

M I still have a lot to do . . . but maybe a
break would do me good.

N What will the man probably do?

(A) Stay home and prepare for his exams
(B) Attend the concert after his exams are
over
(C) Ask the woman to study with him
(D) Go to the concert with the woman

[해석] W 이번 주말에 나와 함께 음악회에 갈 수 있니, 아니면 시험 공부
를 해야 하니?

M 여전히 할 일이 많아… 하지만 휴식을 취하는 것도 도움이 될
것 같아.

N 남자는 무엇을 할 것인가?

(A) 집에서 시험 공부를 할 것이다.
(B) 시험이 끝난 후에 음악회를 보러 갈 것이다.
(C) 여자에게 함께 공부하자고 요청할 것이다.
(D) 여자와 함께 음악회에 갈 것이다.

[어휘] **break** (짧은) 휴식 **do ~ good** ~에게 도움이 되다
be over 끝나다

[해설] 다음에 할 일을 묻는 문제(What ~ probably do?)이다. 남자
는 휴식을 취하는 것이 좋을 것(maybe a break would do me
good)이라고 했으므로, 여자와 함께 음악회에 갈 것임을 알 수 있
다. 따라서 (D)가 정답이다.

1. (A)	2. (D)	3. (D)	4. (C)

N Listen to a conversation between a college student and his adviser.

W Good morning, Steve. What can I do for you?

M Well, [1]I've decided I want to transfer to a smaller college.

W I know you've had a rough time adjusting, Steve, but I'm sorry to hear you want to leave.

M [1]What I need to do now is find a new college and I was hoping you might have some ideas.

W [2]I might, but first I think I ought to warn you about some of the potential problems with transferring. The main one is how many of your credits will be accepted by your new college.

M You mean they won't all be transferable?

W Not necessarily. [2]It'll depend on what courses you've taken here and how they fit in with the requirements at the other school. So whatever college you choose, be sure to find out about transferring your credits.

M Who would I talk to about something like that?

W First check with the admissions officer, then follow up with the registrar's office. Now ... the other thing I wanted to caution you about is thinking that a transfer will solve all your problems.

M I'm not sure I understand what you mean.

W Well, I know you haven't been happy this semester, but are you sure changing colleges is going to be the answer?

M Uhh ... I like my classes, except for composition. The math department is everything I expected it to be, but ... [3]maybe if my roommate and I had hit it off better ... that's really bothering me more than anything else.

W Really? [4]Did you talk to someone at the residence office? It might be that changing roommates would make all the difference.

M [4]I might just do that!

[해석] **N** 대학생과 지도 교수 간의 대화를 들어 보세요.

W 안녕, 스티브. 무엇을 도와줄까요?

M 음, 더 작은 대학으로 전학하고 싶어요.

W 자네가 적응하느라 힘든 시간을 보냈다는 것은 알지만, 스티브, 전학을 가고 싶다는 말을 들으니 유감이군요.

M 지금 새로 갈 대학을 찾아야 하는데, 교수님께서 조언을 좀 해 주셨으면 합니다.

W 그러지, 하지만 전학 시에 겪을 수 있는 몇 가지 문제점을 먼저 알려줘야 할 것 같군요. 무엇보다 자네가 이수한 학점을 전학 갈 학교에서 얼마나 인정해 주는지가 중요해요.

M 학점을 모두 인정받을 수 없다는 말씀이세요?

W 반드시 모든 학점이 다 인정되는 것은 아니에요. 자네가 여기에서 이수한 과정이 무엇이며, 그 과정이 다른 학교의 필수 과목에 얼마나 적합한지에 따라 달라요. 그러니 자네가 어느 학교를 선택하든지 학점 인정에 대해 반드시 알아봐야 해요.

M 그런 사항은 누구와 상담해야 하나요?

W 먼저 입학 담당자에게 확인한 후에 학적과의 안내에 따라 처리하세요. 자, 또 한 가지 알려주고 싶은 점은 전학이 자신의 모든 문제를 해결해 줄 것인지 생각해 보라는 거예요.

M 무슨 말씀이신지 잘 모르겠어요.

W 어, 자네가 이번 학기에 만족스럽게 지내지 못했다는 것은 알지만, 다른 대학으로 전학 가는 것이 해결책이라고 확신해요?

M 어… 저는 수업이 좋아요, 작문을 제외하고는요. 수학과는 제가 기대했던 그대로예요. 하지만… 어쩌면 저와 룸메이트가 서로 더 잘 맞았더라면… 실은 무엇보다도 그 점이 제가 가장 힘들어요.

W 정말 그래요? 기숙사 사무실 직원과 이야기해 봤어요? 어쩌면 룸메이트를 바꾸는 것이 도움이 될 지도 몰라요.

M 그렇게 해 봐야겠어요!

[어휘] **transfer** 전학하다, 옮기다 cf. transferable 양도할 수 있는, 이동할 수 있는 **adjust** 적응하다 **potential** 잠재적인, 있을 수 있는 **credit** 이수 단위, 학점 **fit in with** ~에 들어맞다 **requirement** 필수조건, 필수 과목 **registrar** (대학의) 학적 담당 직원 **caution** 주의를 주다, 경고하다 **composition** 작문, 작곡 **hit it off** 서로 뜻이 잘 맞다, 사이 좋게 지내다 **bother** 괴롭히다, 고민하게 하다 **make a difference** 변화를 가져 오다, 도움이 되다

---

1. **N** Why does Steve visit the adviser?

(A) To get help in finding a new college

(B) To change his major

(C) To fill out an application for college

(D) To find out how to change dormitories

[해석] N 스티브가 지도 교수를 방문한 이유는 무엇인가?

(A) 새 대학을 찾는 데 도움을 받으려고
(B) 전공을 바꾸려고
(C) 대학 지원서를 작성하려고
(D) 기숙사를 바꾸는 방법에 대해 알아보려고

[어휘] **fill out** ~을 기입하다, 작성하다　**application** 지원(서)　**dormitory** 기숙사

[해설] 요지를 묻는 문제이다. 남자의 첫 번째 말 I've decided I want to transfer to a smaller college.에서 스티브는 다른 대학에 전학 가길 원한다는 것을 알 수 있다. 또, 남자의 두 번째 말 What I need to do now is find a new college and I was hoping you might have some ideas.에서 스티브는 지도 교수에게 도움을 요청하고 있다는 것을 알 수 있다. 따라서 (A)가 정답이다.

2. *N* What is one possible problem the counselor points out to Steve?

(A) A small school does not offer a wide range of courses.
(B) His tuition will not be refunded.
(C) Changing majors involves a lot of paperwork.
(D) He may not be able to transfer all his credits.

[해석] N 지도 교수가 스티브에게 생길 수 있는 한 가지 문제점으로 지적한 것은 무엇인가?

(A) 작은 학교에서는 다양한 과정을 제공하지 않는다.
(B) 수업료를 환불 받지 못할 것이다.
(C) 전공을 바꾸려면 많은 서류 작업을 거쳐야 한다.
(D) 그는 모든 학점을 (새 학교에서) 인정받지 못할 수도 있다.

[어휘] **counselor** 지도 교사, 카운슬러　**tuition** 수업료　**refund** 환불하다, 되돌려주다　**paperwork** 서류 작업, 서류 업무

[해설] 세부 사항을 묻는 문제이다. 지도 교수는 남자에게 생길 수 있는 문제점에 대해 주의를 주면서(I might, but first I think I ought to warn you about some of the potential problems with transferring.), 그가 이수한 학점이 새 학교에서는 인정되지 않을 수도 있다(The main one is how many of your credits will be accepted by your new college. It'll depend on what courses you've taken here and how they fit in with the requirements at the other school. So whatever college you choose, be sure to find out about transferring your credits.)는 우려를 나타낸다. 따라서 (D)가 정답이다.

3. *N* What is Steve's main problem in adjusting to his college?

(A) He does not like his professors.
(B) His classes are too difficult.
(C) He cannot transfer his credits from his previous school.
(D) He does not get along with his roommate.

[해석] N 스티브가 대학에 적응하는 데 가장 주된 문제는 무엇인가?

(A) 그는 자신의 교수들을 좋아하지 않는다.
(B) 그의 수업이 너무 어렵다.
(C) 그는 예전 학교에서 이수한 학점을 인정받을 수 없다.
(D) 그는 자신의 룸메이트와 잘 지내지 못한다.

[어휘] **previous** 이전의, 예전의　**get along with** ~와 잘 지내다

[해설] 세부사항을 묻는 문제이다. 지도교수는 남자가 만족하지 못하는 이유를 정확히 알고 싶어한다. 남자는 자신이 대학에 대해 좋아하는 것이 많지만, 룸메이트와 잘 지내지 못하는 것이 가장 힘들다(maybe if my roommate and I had hit it off better … that's really bothering me more than anything else)고 말한다. 따라서 (D)가 정답이다.

4. *N* Where will Steve probably go to get his problem solved?

(A) The registrar's office
(B) The admissions office
(C) The housing office
(D) The math department

[해석] N 스티브는 자신의 문제를 해결하기 위해 어디에 갈 것인가?

(A) 학적 사무실
(B) 입학처 사무실
(C) 기숙사 사무실
(D) 수학과

[해설] 세부 사항을 묻는 문제로, 화자가 다음에 할 일을 묻고 있다. Did you talk to someone at the residence office?라는 지도 교수의 질문에 스티브는 I might just do that!이라고 대답했으므로, 스티브는 대화 후에 기숙사 사무실에 갈 것임을 알 수 있다. 따라서 (C)가 정답이다.

1. (B)	2. (D)	3. (C)	4. (A)

N Listen to a lecture in an Earth science class.

M [1]Today I'd like to explain the Mohs scale, used in what is called the "scratch test." [2]This scale is based on the simple fact that harder minerals scratch softer ones. For example, a diamond scratches glass, but glass doesn't scratch a diamond; a quartz crystal can scratch a feldspar crystal, but not the other way around.

The scale is named for Friedrich Mohs, the mineralogist who devised it in 1812. His scale spans the range of minerals known at that time, from the softest to the hardest. By performing a scratch test using known minerals and a few common tools, an unidentified mineral sample can be placed between two points on the scale. By referring to the scale, the mineral can then be identified.

I have here a collection of the minerals included on the Mohs scale, as well as the tools necessary to complete this exercise. [3]I'd like you each to take a mineral sample from the basket at the front of the room and classify it according to its place on the Mohs scale. First, however, I should give you a little warning. The hardness of any mineral depends on the strength of the bonds between ions or between atoms—the stronger the bond, the harder the mineral. Because bond strength may differ in various angles of a crystal, [4]the hardness may vary slightly depending on the direction in which the mineral sample is scratched, so be sure to scratch each sample in several different directions.

[해석] *N* 지구 과학 강의를 들어보세요.

M 오늘은 소위 "스크래치 테스트(긋기 시험)"를 하는데 사용되는 모스 경도계에 대해 설명하겠습니다. 모스 경도계는 더 단단한 광석이 더 무른 광석에 흠집을 낸다는 간단한 사실에 기초합니다. 예를 들어, 다이아몬드는 유리에 흠집을 내지만, 유리는 다이아몬드에 흠집을 내지 않습니다. 석영 결정은 장석 결정에 흠집을 낼 수 있지만, 반대로는 흠집이 나지 않습니다.

모스 경도계는 프리드리히 모스의 이름을 따서 명명되었으며, 프리드리히 모스는 1812년에 경도계를 고안했습니다. 경도계는 그 범위가 그 당시에 알려진 광물들의 가장 무른 것에서 가장 단단한 것에 이르기까지 걸쳐 있습니다. 잘 알려진 광물과 흔히 쓰는 도구를 이용하여 스크래치 테스트를 해 보면 확인되지 않은 광물 표본을 모스 경도계의 두 (굳기) 지점 사이에 둘 수 있습니다. 모스 경도계를 참조하여, 광물을 식별할 수 있습니다.

여기 모스 경도계에 포함된 광물들과 스크래치 테스트를 하는 데 필요한 도구들이 있습니다. 여러분 각자 교실 앞의 바구니에서 광물 샘플을 가져가서 모스 경도계의 위치에 따라 광물을 분류해 봅시다. 하지만, 우선 한 가지 주의 사항을 알려드리겠습니다. 광물의 경도는 이온 사이의 결합력이나 원자 사이의 결합력의 강도에 따라 달라집니다. 즉, 그 결합력이 강하면 강할수록 광물은 더 단단해집니다. 결합력의 강도는 광물 결정의 다양한 각도에 따라 달라질 수도 있기 때문에 광물 샘플을 긁는 방향에 따라 경도가 다소 달라질 수도 있으니 각각의 광물 샘플을 다양한 방향으로 긁어보아야 합니다.

[어휘] **Mohs scale** 모스 경도계(광물의 경도 측정 기준) **scratch** 긁기; 긁다 **mineral** 광물, 광석 **quartz** 석영 **crystal** 결정(체) **feldspar** 장석 **the other way around** 반대로, 거꾸로 **mineralogist** 광물학자 **unidentified** 확인되지 않은 **identify** 감정하다, 식별하다 **classify** 분류하다 **hardness** (광물의) 경도 **ion** 이온 **atom** 원자 **direction** 방향, 방위

1. *N* What is the lecture mainly about?

(A) The properties of quartz crystals
(B) A method of identifying minerals
(C) The life of Friedrich Mohs
(D) A famous collection of minerals

[해석] N   주로 무엇에 관한 강의인가?

(A) 석영 결정의 속성
(B) 광물을 식별하는 방법
(C) 프리드리히 모스의 삶
(D) 유명한 광물 모음

[어휘] **property** 고유의 성질, 속성, 특성

[해설] 요지를 묻는 문제이다. 요지는 강연의 서두 부분에 제시되는 경우가 많지만, 때로는 요지를 파악하려면 더 많은 부분을 들어야 하는 경우도 있다. 여기서는 강의의 서두 부분에서 모스 경도계에 관한 강의라는 것을 알 수 있지만, 모스 경도계의 어떤 점을 논의하는지는 강의 중반부까지 들어야 알 수 있다. 광물을 식별하는 방법에 대한 강의이므로, (B)가 정답이다.

---

2. *N*   What aspect of a mineral is the Mohs scale used to identify?

(A) Its estimated value
(B) Its crystalline structure
(C) Its chemical composition
(D) Its relative hardness

[해석] N   모스 경도계는 광물의 어떤 특징을 식별하기 위해 사용되는가?

(A) 산정 가격
(B) 결정형 구조
(C) 화학적 구성
(D) 비교 경도

[어휘] **estimated** 어림의, 예상의   **crystalline** 결정체로 된; 결정(구조)의

[해설] 세부 사항을 묻는 문제이다. 교수는 강의 서두 부분에서 모스 경도계는 광물의 비교 경도를 근거로 한다고 설명하고 있다. 따라서 (D)가 정답이다.

---

3. *N*   What does the teacher ask the class to do?

(A) Collect some minerals as homework
(B) Identify the tools he is using
(C) Apply the information given in the talk
(D) Pass their papers to the front of the room

[해석] N   교수는 학생들에게 어떻게 하라고 요청하는가?

(A) 과제로 광물을 수집해 올 것
(B) 그가 사용하고 있는 도구가 무엇인지 알아낼 것
(C) 강의에서 설명한 정보를 적용할 것
(D) 학생들의 보고서를 교실 앞으로 전달할 것

[해설] 세부 사항을 묻는 문제이다. 교수는 강의 전반부에서 모스 경도계를 설명한 후에 학생들에게 모스 경도계를 사용하여 광물을 분류해 보라(I'd like you each to take a mineral sample from the basket at the front of the room and classify it according to its place on the Mohs scale.)고 했다. 즉, 교수는 학생들에게 강의에서 들은 정보를 적용해 보라고 요청한 것임을 알 수 있으므로, (C)가 정답이다.

---

4. *N*   According to the teacher, when might the hardness of the same mineral seem to vary?

(A) When it is scratched in different directions
(B) When greater pressure is applied
(C) When its surface is scratched too frequently
(D) When the tester uses the wrong tools

[해석] N   교수에 따르면 같은 광물이라도 경도가 달라지는 경우는 언제일 것 같은가?

(A) 다른 방향으로 긁었을 때
(B) 더 큰 압력을 받았을 때
(C) 표면이 너무 자주 긁혔을 때
(D) 실험자가 잘못된 도구를 사용했을 때

[해설] 세부 사항을 묻는 문제이다. 강의 후반부에서 교수는 광물의 경도는 다양한 방향으로 긁었을 때 달라질 수 있다(the hardness may vary slightly depending on the direction in which the mineral sample is scratched)고 했으므로, (A)가 정답이다.

Structure And Written Expression Section

Practice Set 1 Structure — 본문 p.34

1. (C)	2. (D)	3. (C)	4. (D)	5. (C)
6. (C)	7. (A)	8. (D)	9. (B)	10. (D)

1. Telephone cables that use optical fibers can be ------- conventional cables, yet they typically carry much more information.

(A) they are smaller and lighter
(B) than the smaller and lighter
(C) smaller and lighter than
(D) so small and light that

[해석] 광섬유를 사용하는 전화선은 기존의 전화선보다 더 작고 가볍지만 일반적으로 훨씬 더 많은 정보를 전달한다.

[어휘] **optical fiber** 광섬유 **conventional** 전통적인, 기존의 **typically** 대개, 일반적으로

[해설] Telephone cables that use optical fibers와 conventional cables를 비교하고 있다. than 앞에는 형용사 small과 light의 비교급이 와야 하므로, (C)가 정답이다.

2. In making cheese, -------, is coagulated by enzyme action, by lactic acid, or by both.

(A) casein is the chief milk protein
(B) casein, being that the chief milk protein
(C) the chief milk protein is casein
(D) casein, the chief milk protein

[해석] 치즈를 만들 때 주요 우유 단백질인 카세인은 효소 작용이나 젖산 또는 둘 다에 의해 응고된다.

[어휘] **coagulate** 응고시키다, 응결시키다 **enzyme** 효소 **lactic acid** 젖산 **protein** 단백질

[해설] 완전한 문장이 되려면 is의 주어가 필요하므로, 명사구 (D)가 정답이다. casein이 문장의 주어이며, the chief milk protein은 casein을 보충 설명하는 동격어구이다.

3. Sensory structures ------- from the heads of some invertebrates are called antennae.

(A) are growing
(B) they are growing
(C) that grow
(D) grow

[해석] 일부 무척추동물의 머리에서 자라는 감각기관은 더듬이라고 불린다.

[어휘] **sensory** 감각(의); 감각 기관 **invertebrate** 무척추동물 **antenna** (곤충 따위의) 더듬이 *pl.* antennae

[해설] Sensory structures가 문장의 주어이고, are called가 동사인 문장으로, _____ from the heads of some invertebrates는 바로 앞에 온 (Sensory) structures를 수식한다. 따라서 바로 앞의 선행사 structures를 수식하는 관계대명사절이 필요하므로, (C)가 정답이다. 나머지 보기는 명사를 수식할 수 없다.

4. An étude is a short musical composition written especially ------- a particular technique.

(A) enable students practicing
(B) enables students practicing
(C) enable students to practice
(D) to enable students to practice

[해석] 에튀드는 학생들이 특정 테크닉을 연습할 수 있도록 작곡된 짧은 곡이다.

[어휘] **étude** 에튀드, 연습곡 **musical composition** 음악 작품 **technique** 테크닉, 연주법

[해설] 어법상 빈칸에 들어갈 수 있는 알맞은 말은 to부정사구이므로, (D)가 정답이다. 이 문장에서 to는 목적의 의미를 나타내는 in order to와 바꿔 쓸 수 있다.

5. ------- the United States consists of many different immigrant groups, many sociologists believe there is a distinct national character.

(A) In spite of
(B) Despite
(C) Even though
(D) Whether

[해석] 미국은 많은 다양한 이민자 그룹으로 구성되어 있지만, 많은 사회학자들은 독특한 국가별 특성이 있다고 믿는다.

[어휘] **consist of** ~으로 구성되다 **immigrant** 이민, 이주민; 이민자의 **sociologist** 사회학자 **distinct** 독특한, 분명한

[해설] 빈칸 뒤에 주어(the United States)와 동사(consists of)를 갖춘 절이 왔으므로, 전치사(구)인 (A)와 (B)는 오답이 된다. 의미상 '(비록) ~이지만, ~이긴 하지만'이라는 의미를 지닌 접속사 Even though가 들어가야 종속절이 완성된다. 따라서 (C)가 정답이다.

6. ------- many food preservation methods for inhibiting the growth of bacteria.

(A) The
(B) Since
(C) There are
(D) Having

[해석] 박테리아의 성장을 억제하기 위한 다양한 음식 보관 방법들이 있다.

[어휘] **preservation** 보관; 저장 **inhibit** 못하게 막다, 억제하다

[해설] 'there+be동사' 구문을 묻는 문제로, be동사 뒤에 오는 말이 문장의 주어가 된다. 주어 (many food preservation) methods가 복수이므로, 빈칸에는 There are가 들어가야 한다. 따라서 (C)가 정답이다.

7. The safflower plant is grown chiefly for the oil ------- from its seeds.

(A) obtained
(B) is obtaining
(C) which obtains it
(D) obtaining that

[해석] 잇꽃은 주로 씨에서 얻어지는 기름을 위해 재배된다.

[어휘] **safflower** 잇꽃 **chiefly** 주로; 대체로 **seed** 씨, 종자

[해설] The safflower plant가 문장의 주어이고, is grown이 동사인 문장으로, _____ from its seeds는 빈칸 앞의 애를 수식하고 있다. 어법상 수동의 의미를 지닌 과거분사 obtained가 들어가야 하므로, (A)가 정답이다. 참고로, obtained 앞에 that is가 생략되어 있다는 것도 알아둔다.

8. Newspaper historians feel that Joseph Pulitzer exercised ------- on journalism in the United States during his lifetime.

(A) influence remarkable
(B) remarkable for his influence
(C) influence was remarkable
(D) remarkable influence

[해석] 신문 역사학자들은 조셉 퓰리처가 살아 생전에 미국 저널리즘에 막대한 영향력을 끼쳤다고 믿는다.

[어휘] **historian** 역사가 **lifetime** 일생, 생애, 평생

[해설] 빈칸에는 that절의 동사 exercised의 목적어 역할을 할 명사가 들어가야 하므로, (D)가 정답이다. influence는 목적어이고, remarkable은 목적어 influence를 수식하는 형용사이다.

9. ------- must have water to lay and fertilize their eggs, while their offspring, tadpoles, need water for development and growth.

(A) Though frogs and toads
(B) Frogs and toads
(C) That frogs and toads
(D) If frogs and toads

[해석] 개구리와 두꺼비는 알을 낳아 수정하려면 물이 있어야 한다. 반면, 그들의 새끼인 올챙이들은 진화하고 성장하는 데 물이 필요하다.

[어휘] **lay** 알을 낳다 **fertilize** 수정시키다 **offspring** 새끼, 자식 **tadpole** 올챙이 **development** 진화, 발육

[해설] 주절에 들어갈 주어가 필요하다. 따라서 주어 역할을 할 수 있는 명사(구)가 들어가야 하는데, 여기서는 and로 연결된 명사구인 (B) Frogs and toads가 정답이 된다.

10. The philosopher and educator John Dewey rejected -------.

(A) to use authoritarian teaching methods
(B) that authoritarian teaching methods
(C) for authoritarian teaching methods
(D) authoritarian teaching methods

[해석] 철학자이자 교육학자인 존 듀이는 권위주의적인 교수법을 거부했다.

[어휘] **educator** 교육학자, 교육 전문가 **reject** 거부하다, 거절하다 **authoritarian** 권위주의의, 권위주의적인

[해설] The philosopher and educator John Dewey가 주어, rejected가 동사인 문장으로, 빈칸에는 rejected의 목적어가 필요하다. 따라서 목적어 역할을 할 수 있는 명사구 (D) authoritarian teaching methods가 정답이다.

Practice Set 2 Written Expression   – 본문 p.37

1. C	2. A	3. A	4. D	5. C
6. D	7. A	8. D	9. C	10. D

1. One of North America's <u>most</u> renowned <u>painters</u>,
                                    A   B
Grandma Moses was in her seventies when **her**
                                          C
began to paint <u>seriously</u>.
                    D

[해석] 북미의 가장 저명한 화가들 중 한 사람인 그랜마 모제스는 70대에 진지하게 그림을 그리기 시작했다.

[어휘] **renowned** 유명한, 이름 높은, 명성 있는

[해설] 접속사 when 뒤에는 주어와 동사가 나와야 하는데, 여기서는 소유격이나 목적격으로 쓰이는 her가 왔다. began의 주어 역할을 할 수 있는 주격대명사 she가 필요하므로, (C)가 정답이다.

2. The novelty, relatively high speed, and

advantageously of year-round service <u>made</u> early
     A   B
<u>passenger</u> trains a popular <u>form</u> of transportation.
        C   D

[해석] 참신함과 상대적으로 빠른 속도, 연중 운행 가능하다는 이점으로 인해 초기의 여객 열차들은 인기 있는 교통 수단이 되었다.

[어휘] **novelty** 새로움, 신기함, 참신함   **relatively** 상대적으로; 비교적   **year-round** 일 년 내내 계속되는   **transportation** 수송 수단, 교통[수송] 기관

[해설] novelty, speed와 병렬 구조를 이룰 수 있는 명사가 필요하므로, 부사 advantageously가 아니라 명사 advantage가 되어야 한다. 따라서 (A)가 정답이다.

3. <u>**Because incomplete**</u> records, the <u>number of</u>
          A   B
<u>enlistments</u> in the Confederate army <u>has long been</u>
                                                C
<u>in dispute</u>.
    D

[해석] 불완전한 기록 탓에 남부군의 모병 수가 오랫동안 논쟁의 대상이 되어 왔다.

[어휘] **incomplete** 불완전한, 불충분한, 미완성의   **enlistment** 모병, 입대, 복무 기간   **Confederate army** (남북 전쟁 시의) 남부 연합군   **in dispute** 논쟁 중인

[해설] Because 뒤에 incomplete records라는 명사구가 왔으므로, 전치사구인 Because of가 되어야 한다. 따라서 (A)가 정답이다. 참고로, 접속사 because 뒤에는 주어와 동사를 갖춘 절이 와야 한다는 것도 구별해서 알아둔다.

4. Estuaries are <u>highly</u> sensitive and ecologically
                         A
<u>important</u> habitats, <u>providing</u> breeding and feeding
    B   C
grounds for **much** life-forms.
                D

[해석] 강의 하구는 (변화에) 아주 민감하고 생태학적으로 중요한 서식지로, 많은 생명체에게 번식지와 서식지를 제공한다.

[어휘] **estuary** (큰 강의) 하구, 만   **ecologically** 생태학적으로   **habitat** (동·식물의) 서식지   **breeding ground** 번식 장소, 알을 낳는 장소   **feeding ground** 서식지   **life-form** 생명체

[해설] 가산명사의 복수형 명사 life-forms 앞에는 much가 아닌 many가 와야 한다. 따라서 (D)가 정답이다. 참고로, much 뒤에는 셀 수 없는 명사(단수형)가 온다는 것도 알아둔다.

5. <u>When</u> the temperature drops <u>below</u> 68 degrees
          A   B
Fahrenheit, the body conserves **warm** by
                                     C
<u>restricting</u> blood flowing to the skin.
    D

[해석] 기온이 화씨 68도 이하로 떨어지면 신체는 피부에 혈액의 흐름을 제한하여 체온을 유지한다.

[어휘] **temperature** 온도; 기온 **conserve** 보존하다, 유지하다 **restrict** 제한하다, 한정하다

[해설] the body가 주절의 주어, conserves가 동사인 문장이다. conserves 뒤에는 conserves의 목적어 역할을 하는 명사가 와야 하므로, 형용사 warm이 아니라 명사 warmth가 필요하다. 따라서 (C)가 정답이다.

6. The Federal Theatre Project, the first federally

<u>financed</u> theater project in the United States, <u>was</u>
   A   B

<u>established</u> <u>to benefit</u> theater personnel **while** the
              C   **D**

Depression of the 1930s.

[해석] 미국에서 처음으로 정부 차원에서 자금을 댄 연극 사업인 연방 연극 프로젝트는 1930년대 세계 대공황 동안에 연극계 종사자들에게 도움을 주기 위해 설립되었다.

[어휘] **federally** 연방제로, 연방적으로; 연합적으로 **finance** ~에 자금을 대다 **benefit** ~에게 도움이 되다, 혜택을 주다 **personnel** 총인원, 직원 **the Depression** (1929년 미국에서 시작된) 세계 대공황

[해설] 접속사 while 뒤에는 주어와 동사를 갖춘 절이 와야 한다. 그런데 명사구 the Depression of the 1930s가 왔으므로, 종속접속사 while 대신에 전치사 during을 써야 한다. 따라서 (D)가 정답이다.

7. Although best known **for great** novel *The Grapes*
                         A

of Wrath, John Steinbeck <u>also</u> published essays,
                               B

<u>plays</u>, stories, memoirs, and newspaper <u>articles</u>.
 C   D

[해석] 비록 존 스타인벡은 자신의 위대한 소설인 〈분노의 포도〉로 가장 잘 알려져 있지만, 수필과 희곡, 소설, 자서전을 썼으며 신문에 기사도 게재했다.

[어휘] **wrath** 분노, 격노 **play** 희곡, 각본; 극, 연극 **memoir** 자서전, 회고록; 전기 **article** 기사, 논설

[해설] 명사 novel 앞에는 한정사가 필요하다. 문장의 주어 John Steinbeck과 어울리려면 소유격 his가 가장 적합하다. 따라서 형용사 great 앞에 his를 추가해야 하므로, (A)가 정답이다.

8. The political and <u>economic</u> life of the state of
                            A

Rhode Island <u>was dominated</u> by the owners of
                     B

textile mills <u>well</u> into the **twenty** century.
            C   **D**

[해석] 로드 아일랜드 주의 정치적 · 경제적 삶은 20세기에 들어 직물 공장 소유자들에 의해 좌우되었다.

[어휘] **dominate** 지배하다, 통치하다 **textile** 직물, 천 **mill** 공장; 제분소

[해설] '20세기'라고 할 때는 twenty century가 아니라 형용사 역할을 하는 서수 twentieth를 써서 twentieth century라고 한다. 따라서 (D)가 정답이다.

9. Lichens <u>grow</u> in a variety of places, <u>ranging</u> from
          A   B

dry **area** to moist rain forests, to freshwater lakes,
    C

and even <u>to</u> bodies of salt water.
           D

[해석] 이끼는 다양한 장소에서 자라는데, 건조한 지역에서부터 습한 열대 우림, 담수호나 심지어 바다까지 아주 다양하다.

[어휘] **lichen** 이끼, 지의류 **range from A to B** A에서 B까지의 범위에 미치다 **moist** 습한, 축축한 **rain forest** 열대 우림 **freshwater** 민물, 담수

[해설] rain forests, freshwater lakes, bodies of salt water 등과 병렬 구조를 이룰 수 있도록, 단수형 area를 복수형 areas로 바꿔야 한다. 따라서 (C)가 정답이다.

10. Musical instruments are <u>divided into</u> various
                              A

types, depending <u>on whether</u> the vibration
                  B

that produces <u>their sound</u> is made by striking,
                 C

strumming, scraping, or **is blown**.
                    D

[해석] 악기는 소리를 발생시키는 진동을 때려서 내는지, 퉁겨서 내는지, 문질러서 내는지, 불어서 내는지에 따라 다양한 종류로 분류된다.

[어휘] **musical instrument** 악기 **depending on** ~에 따라 **vibration** 진동, 떨림 **strum** (현악기를) 손가락으로 가볍게 쳐서[퉁겨서] 연주하다 **scrape** 문지르다

[해설] striking, strumming, scraping과 병렬 구조를 이뤄야 하므로 is blown을 blowing으로 고쳐야 한다. 따라서 (D)가 정답이다.

Practice Set Reading — 본문 p.46

1. (D)	2. (D)	3. (B)	4. (B)	5. (C)
6. (A)	7. (A)	8. (B)	9. (D)	10. (A)
11. (A)	12. (D)	13. (B)	14. (B)	15. (A)
16. (D)	17. (B)	18. (C)	19. (C)	20. (C)
21. (B)				

Questions 1–11

[1]As many as a thousand years ago in the Southwest, [10, 11]the Hopi and Zuni Indians of North America were building with adobe—sun-baked brick plastered with mud. [4]Their homes looked remarkably like modern apartment houses. Some were four stories high and contained quarters for perhaps a thousand people, along with storerooms for grain and other goods. [2]These buildings were usually put up against cliffs, both to make construction easier and for defense against enemies. [3]They were really villages in themselves, as later Spanish explorers must have realized, since they called them pueblos, which is Spanish for towns.

The people of the pueblos raised what are called [5]the three sisters—corn, beans, and squash. They made excellent pottery and wove marvelous baskets, some so fine that they could hold water. The Southwest has always been a dry country where water is [6]scarce. The Hopi and Zuni brought water from streams to their fields and gardens through irrigation ditches. Water was so important that it played a major role in their religion.

The way of life of [7]less-settled groups was simpler. Small tribes such as [11]the Shoshone and Ute wandered the dry and mountainous lands between the Rocky Mountains and the Pacific Ocean. They gathered seeds and hunted small animals such as rabbits and snakes. In the Far North the ancestors of today's Inuit hunted seals, walruses, and the great whales. [10]They lived right on the frozen seas in shelters called igloos built of blocks of packed snow. When summer came, they fished for salmon and hunted the lordly caribou.

[8, 11]The Cheyenne, Pawnee, and Sioux tribes, known as the Plains Indians, lived on the grasslands between the Rocky Mountains and the Mississippi River. [9]They hunted bison, commonly called the buffalo. Its meat was the chief food of these tribes, and [10]its hide was used to make their clothing and the covering of their tents and tepees.

[해석] 무려 1천 년 전 남서부 지역에서 북미의 호피족 인디언과 주니족 인디언들은 진흙으로 회반죽하여 햇볕에 말린 벽돌인 흙벽돌로 집을 지었다. 인디언들의 집은 오늘날의 아파트와 아주 유사해 보였다. 어떤 집들은 4층 건물이었으며, 천 명의 사람들을 수용할 수 있는 숙소가 있었고, 곡식이나 다른 물건들을 보관할 수 있는 창고도 딸려 있었다. 이 건물들은 보통 더 쉽게 짓고 적들을 방어하기 위해 절벽에 세워졌다. 그 건물들 자체는 실제로 마을이었는데, 이후의 스페인 탐험가들은 그 사실을 알았던 것 같다. 스페인 탐험가들은 그 건물들을 pueblos라고 불렀는데, pueblos는 스페인어로 마을들을 의미하기 때문이다.

그 마을 사람들은 소위 세 자매라고 불리는 옥수수와 콩, 호박을 재배했다. 그들은 훌륭한 도자기를 만들었고 멋진 바구니를 짰는데, 어떤 바구니들은 아주 고와서 물을 담을 수도 있었다. 남서부 지역은 물이 부족한 건조한 땅이었다. 호피족 인디언과 주니족 인디언들은 관개수로를 통해 강에서 물을 끌어와 들판과 정원에 물을 댔다. 물은 아주 중요해서 종교에도 주요한 역할을 했다.

완전히 정착하지 않은 사람들의 삶의 방식은 더 단순했다. 쇼쇼니족과 유트족 같은 소규모 부족들은 로키 산맥과 태평양 사이의 건조한 산악 지대에서 방랑 생활을 했다. 그들은 열매를 모았으며 토끼와 뱀 같은 작은 동물들을 사냥했다. 극북 지역에서는 오늘날 이뉴잇족의 선조들이 바다표범과 바다코끼리, 큰 고래들을 사냥했다. 그들은 얼어붙은 바다 위에서 눈 벽돌로 지어진 이글루라고 불리는 집에서 살았다. 여름이 오면 그들은 연어를 낚시하고 장대한 순록을 사냥했다.

평원 인디언으로 알려진 샤이엔족과 포니족, 수족들은 로키 산맥과 미시시피 강 사이의 초원 지대에서 살았다. 그들은 흔히 버팔로라고 불리는 들소를 사냥했다. 들소 고기는 이 종족의 주식이었으며, 그 가죽은 옷을 만들고 천막과 천막집의 덮개를 만드는 데 사용되었다.

1. What does the passage mainly discuss?

(A) The architecture of early American Indian
buildings

(B) The movement of American Indians across
North America

(C) Ceremonies and rituals of American Indians

**(D) The way of life of American Indian tribes in
early North America**

[해석] 주로 무엇에 관해 이야기하고 있는가?
(A) 초기 아메리카 인디언 건물의 건축술
(B) 북미 전역에 걸친 아메리카 인디언의 이동
(C) 아메리카 인디언의 의식과 종교 의식
(D) 초기 북미의 아메리카 인디언 부족의 생활 방식

[어휘] architecture 건축; 건축술   ritual 종교 의식, 의례

[해설] 요지를 묻는 문제이다. 건축술(architecture), 이동
(movement), 의식(ceremonies and rituals) 등의 내용
이 지문에 언급되기는 했으나, 지문 전체의 요지를 가장 잘 요
약한 것은 (D)이다.

2. According to the passage, the Hopi and Zuni
typically built their homes

(A) in valleys

(B) next to streams

(C) on open plains

(D) against cliffs

[해석] 지문에 따르면, 호피족과 주니족 인디언들은 주로 어디에 집
을 지었는가?
(A) 계곡에
(B) 강 옆에
(C) 대평원에
(D) 절벽에

[어휘] valley 골짜기, 계곡

[해설] 사실적인 정보 파악 문제이다. 첫 단락의 5행 These
buildings were usually put up against cliffs에서 단서
를 찾을 수 있다. 따라서 (D)가 정답이다.

3. The word "They" in line 6 refers to

(A) goods

(B) buildings

(C) cliffs

(D) enemies

[해석] 6행에 언급된 "They"가 가리키는 것은 무엇인가?
(A) 물건들
(B) 건물들
(C) 절벽들
(D) 적들

[어휘] refer to ~를 가리키다

[해설] 지시 대상을 찾는 문제이다. 보기로 제시된 명사들이 모두 복
수 명사이기는 하지만, 논리적으로 대명사 "They"는 바로 앞
문장(These buildings were usually put up against
cliffs, both to make construction easier and for
defense against enemies.)에 언급된 These buildings
를 가리킨다. 따라서 (B)가 정답이다.

4. It can be inferred from the passage that the
dwellings of the Hopi and Zuni were

(A) very small

(B) highly advanced

(C) difficult to defend

(D) quickly constructed

6. The word "scarce" in line 10 is closest in meaning to

(A) limited

(B) hidden

(C) pure

(D) necessary

[해석] 10행에 언급된 "scarce"와 의미상 가장 가까운 것은?
  (A) **부족한**
  (B) 숨겨진
  (C) 순수한
  (D) 필요한

[해설] 어휘 문제이다. 10행의 dry country나 11행의 brought water from streams to their fields and gardens through irrigation ditches에서 scarce의 의미에 대한 단서를 찾을 수 있는데, 여기서 scarce는 '부족한, 불충분한'의 의미이므로 (A)가 정답이다.

[해석] 이 지문에서 호피족과 주니족 인디언들의 주거지에 대해 추론할 수 있는 것은 무엇인가?
(A) 아주 작았다
(B) 고도로 발전되었다
(C) 방어하기 어려웠다
(D) 급히 지어졌다

[어휘] dwelling 주거(지), 주택   advanced 진보한, 선진의

[해설] 추론 문제이다. 건물이 오늘날의 아파트와 아주 유사했다 (Their homes looked remarkably like modern apartment houses)는 내용이나 일부는 4층 높이였다 (Some were four stories high)는 내용으로 미루어 주거지가 고도로 발전되어 있었다는 것을 유추할 수 있다. 따라서 (B)가 정답이다.

5. The author uses the phrase "the three sisters" in line 8 to refer to

(A) Hopi women

(B) family members

(C) important crops

(D) rain ceremonies

[해석] 글쓴이가 8행에서 인용한 "the three sisters"가 가리키는 것은 무엇인가?
  (A) 호피족 여자들
  (B) 가족 구성원들
  (C) 중요한 작물들
  (D) 기우제

[어휘] rain ceremony 기우제

[해설] 지칭 대상을 찾는 문제이다. the three sisters 뒤에 주요 작물인 옥수수와 콩, 호박(corn, beans, and squash)이 언급되어 있다. 따라서 corn, beans, and squash를 important crops라고 바꿔서 표현한 (C)가 정답이다.

7. Which of the following is true of the Shoshone and Ute?

(A) They were not as settled as the Hopi and Zuni.

(B) They hunted caribou.

(C) They built their homes with adobe.

(D) They did not have many religious ceremonies.

[해석] 다음 중 쇼쇼니족과 유트족에 대한 설명으로 맞는 것은 무엇인가?
  (A) 그들은 호피족이나 주니족과 달리 정착하지 않았다.
  (B) 그들은 순록을 사냥했다.
  (C) 그들은 흙벽돌로 집을 지었다.
  (D) 그들은 종교 의식이 많지 않았다.

[해설] 사실적인 정보 파악 문제이다. 첫 문단에서 호피족과 주니족 인디언들은 마을을 이루어 주택에서 살았다고 나오고 세 번째 단락에서 쇼쇼니족과 유트족은 완전히 정착하지 않았다 (less-settled groups)고 나온다. 따라서 (A)가 정답이다.

8. According to the passage, which of the following groups lived in the grasslands?

(A) The Shoshone and Ute

(B) The Cheyenne and Sioux

(C) The Hopi and Zuni

(D) The Pawnee and Inuit

[해석] 지문에 따르면, 다음 중 어느 그룹이 초원에서 살았는가?
　　(A) 쇼쇼니족과 유트족
　　(B) 샤이엔족과 수족
　　(C) 호피족과 주니족
　　(D) 포니족과 이뉴잇족

[해설] 사실적인 정보 파악 문제이다. 네 번째 단락 첫 문장 The Cheyenne, Pawnee, and Sioux tribes, known as the Plains Indians, lived on the grasslands between the Rocky Mountains and the Mississippi River.에서 문제 해결의 단서를 찾을 수 있는데, 샤이엔족과 포니족, 수족들이 로키 산맥과 미시시피강 사이의 초원 지대에서 살았다고 나온다. 따라서 (B)가 정답이다.

9. Which of the following animals was most important to the Plains Indians?

(A) The salmon

(B) The caribou

(C) The seal

(D) The bison

[해석] 다음 동물들 중 평원 인디언들에게 가장 중요했던 동물은 무엇인가?
　　(A) 연어
　　(B) 순록
　　(C) 바다표범
　　(D) 들소

[해설] 사실적인 정보 파악 문제이다. 네 번째 단락의 They hunted bison, commonly called the buffalo. Its meat was the chief food of these tribes, and its hide was used to make their clothing and the covering of their tents and tepees.에서 들소 고기가 주식이었으며 그 가죽이 의복 및 덮개로 쓰였다고 나온다. 따라서 (D)가 정답이다. 참고로, 지문의 chief는 most important를 의미한다는 것도 알아둔다.

10. Which of the following is NOT mentioned by the author as a dwelling place of early North Americans?

(A) Log cabins

(B) Adobe houses

(C) Tepees

(D) Igloos

[해석] 다음 중 글쓴이가 초기 북아메리카 원주민들의 주거지로 언급하지 않은 것은 무엇인가?
　　(A) 통나무집
　　(B) 흙벽돌집
　　(C) 천막집
　　(D) 이글루

[해설] 사실적인 정보 파악 문제이다. "NOT" 질문으로, 지문에 언급되지 않은 것을 묻고 있으므로, 지문에 언급되지 않은 (A) Log cabins가 정답이 된다. (B)는 첫 단락(the Hopi and Zuni Indians of North America were building with adobe)에, (C)는 네 번째 단락(its hide was used to make their clothing and the covering of their tents and tepees)에, (D)는 세 번째 단락(They lived right on the frozen seas in shelters called igloos built of blocks of packed snow.)에 언급되어 있다.

11. The author groups North American Indians according to their

(A) names and geographical regions

(B) arts and crafts

(C) rituals and ceremonies

(D) date of appearance on the continent

[해석] 글쓴이가 북아메리카 인디언을 분류한 기준은 무엇인가?
　　(A) 이름 및 지역
　　(B) 예술과 공예
　　(C) 종교 의식과 의식
　　(D) 대륙에 출현한 날짜

[어휘] **craft** 수공업, 공예　**ritual** 종교 의식　**ceremony** 의식, 의전　**continent** 대륙

[해설] 문단 구성 및 추론 문제이다. 필자는 종족의 이름과 지역으로 인디언들을 지칭하고 있으므로 (A)가 정답이 된다.

[12]If the salinity of ocean waters is analyzed, it is found to vary only slightly from place to place. Nevertheless, some of these small changes are important. [16]There are three basic processes that cause a change in oceanic salinity. One of these is the subtraction of water from the ocean [15]by means of evaporation—conversion of liquid water to water vapor. In [13]this manner, the salinity is increased, since the salts stay behind. If this is carried to the extreme, of course, white crystals of salt would be left behind.

The opposite of evaporation is precipitation, such as rain, by which water is added to the ocean. Here the ocean is being diluted so that the salinity is decreased. This may occur in areas of high rainfall or in coastal regions where rivers flow into the ocean. Thus, salinity may be increased by the subtraction of water by evaporation or decreased by the addition of freshwater by precipitation or runoff.

[14]Normally, in tropical regions where the sun is very strong, the ocean salinity is somewhat higher than it is in other parts of the world where there is not as much evaporation. Similarly, in coastal regions where rivers dilute the sea, salinity is somewhat lower than in other oceanic areas.

A third process by which salinity may be [17]altered is associated with the formation and melting of sea ice. When seawater is frozen, the dissolved materials are left behind. In this manner, [20]seawater directly beneath freshly formed sea ice has a higher salinity than [18]it did before the ice appeared. Of course, when this ice melts, it will tend to decrease the salinity of the surrounding water.

[19]In the Weddell Sea, off Antarctica, the densest water in the oceans is formed as a result of this freezing process, which increases the salinity of cold water. [21]This heavy water sinks and is found in the deeper portions of the oceans of the world.

[해석] 해수의 염도를 분석해 보면 장소에 따라 아주 미미한 차이가 있다는 것을 알 수 있다. 그럼에도 불구하고 이 미미한 차이는 중요하다. 해수의 염도에 변화를 야기하는 세 가지 기본적인 과정이 있다. 그 중 하나는 증발 작용을 통해 바다에서 물이 감소하는 것이다. 즉, 액체인 물이 수증기로 변하는 것이다. 이런 방식으로 소금이 뒤에 남기 때문에 염도가 증가한다. 물론 이런 과정이 막다른 데까지 이르면 흰색 소금 결정이 남게 된다.

증발 작용의 반대가 비와 같은 강우인데, 이를 통해 바다에 물이 증가한다. 이때는 바다가 희석되어 염도가 감소한다. 이런 현상은 비가 많이 내리는 지역이나 강물이 바다에 유입되는 연안 지역에서 일어난다. 이런 식으로, 증발 작용으로 물이 감소하면 염도가 증가하고, 강수나 지표에 흐르는 빗물로 담수가 증가하면 염도는 감소한다.

보통 햇빛이 아주 강한 열대 지역에서는 증발 작용이 그리 많지 않은 전 세계의 다른 지역에서보다 해수의 염도가 다소 높다. 마찬가지로 강이 해수의 농도를 묽게 하는 연안 지역에서는 다른 해양 지역보다 염도가 다소 더 낮다.

염도가 달라지게 되는 세 번째 과정은 해빙이 형성되거나 녹는 것과 관련 있다. 해수가 얼 때, 용해된 물질은 얼지 않고 그대로 남아 있다. 이런 방식으로 새로 형성된 해빙 바로 밑의 해수는 얼음이 얼기 전보다 염도가 더 높다. 물론, 이 얼음이 녹으면 그 주변 물의 염도가 낮아질 것이다.

남극 연안의 웨델 해에서 가장 농도가 짙은 물은 이런 동결 과정의 결과로 형성되는데, 이 과정에서 찬 물의 염도가 증가된다. 이 무거운 물은 가라앉아 전 세계 바다의 가장 깊은 곳에서 발견된다.

[어휘] salinity 염분, 염도 analyze 분석하다, 분해하다 process 과정, 절차; 변화 subtraction 빼기, 감하기, 공제 by means of ~에 의하여, ~으로 evaporation 증발 (작용) conversion 전환, 변환 water vapor 수증기 crystal 결정(체) precipitation 강수(량), 강우 dilute 묽게 하다, 희석하다 runoff (땅 속으로 스며들지 않고 흐르는) 빗물 tropical 열대의 alter 바꾸다, 고치다 be associated with ~와 관련되다 formation 형성, 구성; 층 sea ice 해빙 dissolved 용해된 decrease 감소하다, 줄이다 dense (액체·증기 따위가) 짙은, (물질이) 고밀도의 portion 부분, 일부

12. What does the passage mainly discuss?

(A) The elements of salt

(B) The bodies of water of the world

(C) The many forms of ocean life

(D) The salinity of ocean water

[해석] 주로 무엇에 관한 글인가?
(A) 소금의 구성 성분
(B) 전 세계의 바다
(C) 해양 생물의 다양한 형태
(D) 해수의 염도

[어휘] element 구성 성분

[해설] 요지를 묻는 문제이다. 이 글은 해수의 염도가 높아지거나 낮아지는 과정을 설명하고 있으므로, (D)가 정답이다.

13. The word "this" in line 4 refers to

(A) ocean

(B) evaporation

(C) salinity

(D) crystals

[해석] 4행에 언급된 "this"가 가리키는 것은 무엇인가?
(A) 바다
(B) 증발
(C) 염도
(D) 결정

[해설] 지시 대상을 찾는 문제이다. 바로 앞의 문장에서 증발 과정에 대해 언급하고 있으므로, "this"는 증발을 가리킨다. 따라서 (B)가 정답이다.

14. According to the passage, the ocean generally has more salt in

(A) coastal areas

(B) tropical areas

(C) rainy areas

(D) turbulent areas

[해석] 이 지문에 따르면, 일반적으로 어느 지역의 바다에 더 많은 소금이 함유되어 있는가?
(A) 연안 지역
(B) 열대 지역
(C) 우림 지역
(D) 난기류 지역

[어휘] turbulent (풍파 · 날씨 따위가) 소용돌이치는; 난기류의

[해설] 사실적인 정보 파악 문제이다. 세 번째 단락의 Normally, in tropical regions where the sun is very strong, the ocean salinity is somewhat higher than it is in other parts of the world where there is not as much evaporation.에서 보통 해수의 염도는 열대 지역에서 더 높다고 하므로, (B)가 정답이다.

15. All of the following are processes that decrease salinity EXCEPT

(A) evaporation

(B) precipitation

(C) runoff

(D) melting

[해석] 다음 중 염도를 낮추는 과정이 아닌 것은 무엇인가?
(A) 증발
(B) 강우
(C) 빗물
(D) 해빙

[해설] 사실적인 정보 파악 문제이다. "EXCEPT" 문제이므로, 글의 내용과 일치하지 않는 것을 고르면 된다. 첫 단락의 ~ by means of evaporation — conversion of liquid water to water vapor. In this manner, the salinity is increased, since the salts stay behind.에서 증발은 염도를 낮추는 것이 아니라 높인다고 하므로, (A)가 정답이다.

16. Which of the following statements about the salinity of a body of water can best be inferred from the passage?

(A) The temperature of the water is the most important factor.

(B) The speed with which water moves is directly related to the amount of salt.

(C) Ocean salinity has little effect on sea life.

(D) Various factors combine to cause variations in the salt content of water.

[해석] 다음의 바다 염도에 대한 설명 중 이 지문에서 추론할 수 있는 것은 무엇인가?
(A) 물의 온도가 가장 중요한 요인이다.
(B) 물의 이동 속도는 소금의 양과 직접적인 관계가 있다.
(C) 해수의 염도는 해양 생물에 거의 영향을 미치지 않는다.
(D) 다양한 요인들이 결합하여 해수의 소금 함량에 차이가 생긴다.

[어휘] **salt content** 소금 함량

[해설] 추론 문제이다. 이 지문은 해수의 염도에 영향을 미치는 다양한 요인에 대해 설명하고 있으므로 (D)가 정답이다. 나머지 보기는 지문에 언급되어 있지 않다.

17. The word "altered" in line 16 is closest in meaning to

(A) determined

(B) changed

(C) accumulated

(D) needed

[해석] 16행의 "altered"와 의미상 가장 가까운 것은 무엇인가?
(A) 결정된
(B) 달라진
(C) 축적된
(D) 필요한

[해설] 어휘 문제이다. 이 지문에서는 염도의 증가와 감소에 대해 논의하고 있다는 점에서 altered가 '달라진'의 의미로 쓰였다는 단서를 찾을 수 있다. 따라서 (B)가 정답이다.

18. The word "it" in line 18 refers to

(A) sea ice

(B) salinity

(C) seawater

(D) manner

[해석] 18행의 "it"이 가리키는 것은 무엇인가?
(A) 해빙
(B) 염도
(C) 해수
(D) 방식

[해설] 지시 대상을 찾는 문제이다. 네 번째 단락의 "seawater directly beneath freshly formed sea ice has a higher salinity than it did before the ice appeared."에서 it은 앞에 언급된 seawater를 가리킨다는 것을 알 수 있다. 따라서 (C)가 정답이다.

19. Why does the author mention the Weddell Sea?

(A) To show that this body of water has salinity variations

(B) To compare Antarctic waters with Arctic waters

(C) To give an example of increased salinity due to freezing

(D) To point out the location of deep waters

[해석] 글쓴이가 웨델 해를 언급한 이유는 무엇인가?
(A) 이 해수의 염도가 다르다는 것을 보여주려고
(B) 남극 해수와 북극 해수를 비교하려고
(C) 결빙으로 염도가 증가하는 일례를 보여주려고
(D) 심해의 위치를 가리켜주려고

[어휘] **Arctic** 북극(의)

[해설] 문단 구성 및 추론 문제이다. 네 번째 단락에서 해빙의 형성 과정에 대해 설명하고 있으며, 이어지는 단락, 즉 웨델 해를 언급한 단락에서 해빙 형성으로 염도가 증가하는 구체적인 사례를 제시하고 있다. 따라서 (C)가 정답이다.

20. Which of the following is NOT a result of the formation of ocean ice?

(A) The salt remains in the water.

(B) The surrounding water sinks.

(C) Water salinity decreases.

(D) The water becomes denser.

[해석] 다음 중 해빙 형성의 결과가 아닌 것은 무엇인가?

　(A) 소금이 물 속에 남아 있다.

　(B) 주변의 물이 가라앉는다.

　(C) 해수의 염도가 낮아진다.

　(D) 해수의 농도가 높아진다.

[해설] 사실 정보 파악 문제로, 글의 내용과 일치하지 않는 정보를 묻고 있다. 네 번째 단락의 seawater directly beneath freshly formed sea ice has a higher salinity than it did before the ice appeared에서 해빙 바로 밑에 있는 해수의 염도가 더 높다고 했으므로, (C)는 글의 내용과 일치하지 않는다.

21. What can be inferred about the water near the bottom of oceans?

(A) It is relatively warm.

(B) Its salinity is relatively high.

(C) It does not move.

(D) It evaporates quickly.

[해석] 해저 가까이에 있는 해수에 대해 추론할 수 있는 것은 무엇인가?

　(A) 비교적 따뜻하다.

　(B) 비교적 염도가 높다.

　(C) 움직이지 않는다.

　(D) 빨리 증발한다.

[어휘] **relatively** 상대적으로; 비교적

[해설] 추론 문제이다. 마지막 단락에서 염도가 높은 해수에 대해 설명하고 있다. 특히 마지막 문장 This heavy water sinks and is found in the deeper portions of the oceans of the world.에서 (B)가 정답임을 알 수 있다.

Sample Test Sections

Section 1 **Listening Comprehension** — 본문 p.61

Part A

1. (C)	2. (D)	3. (C)	4. (A)	5. (C)
6. (A)	7. (A)	8. (A)	9. (B)	10. (A)
11. (A)	12. (C)	13. (D)	14. (D)	15. (D)
16. (B)	17. (C)	18. (D)	19. (D)	20. (C)
21. (D)	22. (A)	23. (A)	24. (C)	25. (A)
26. (D)	27. (B)	28. (C)	29. (C)	30. (D)

Part B

31. (A)	32. (C)	33. (D)	34. (A)	35. (C)
36. (D)	37. (D)	38. (D)		

Part C

39. (A)	40. (C)	41. (D)	42. (B)	43. (B)
44. (D)	45. (C)	46. (C)	47. (B)	48. (B)
49. (A)	50. (C)			

Part A

1. **W** No, no. I asked you to get me the economics test book, not the textbook.

M Oh, no wonder the cashier looked at me that way.

N What can be inferred about the man?

(A) He is majoring in economics.
(B) He forgot to go to the bookstore.
(C) He bought the wrong book.
(D) He is selling his book to the woman.

[해석] W 이런, 아니야. 내가 사다 달라고 부탁했던 것은 경제학 문제집이었어, 교과서가 아니라.
M 아, 그래서 점원이 나를 그렇게 봤구나.

N 남자에 대해 추론할 수 있는 것은 무엇인가?

(A) 그는 경제학을 전공한다.
(B) 그는 서점에 가는 것을 잊었다.
(C) 그는 책을 잘못 샀다.
(D) 그는 여자에게 자신의 책을 팔고 있다.

[어휘] **economics** 경제학 **textbook** 교과서 **no wonder** ~은 당연하다, ~은 놀라운 일이 아니다 **cashier** 계산대 (점원) **major in** ~을 전공하다

[해설] 여자의 말에 주의를 기울여 들어야 한다. 여자는 남자에게 경제학 문제집을 사다 달라고 요청했으며, "not"에서 남자가 여자의 말을 잘못 이해했다는 것을 알 수 있으므로 (C)가 정답이다.

2. **M** You did an excellent job on that presentation.

W Thanks. I put a lot of time into it.

N What does the woman mean?

(A) She appreciates the man's help.
(B) Her presentation was somewhat long.
(C) She needed more time to prepare.
(D) She worked hard on her presentation.

[해석] M 발표를 아주 잘하셨어요.
W 고마워요. 발표 준비에 많은 시간을 들였거든요.

N 여자가 의미하는 것은 무엇인가?

(A) 그녀는 남자의 도움에 감사한다.
(B) 그녀의 발표가 다소 길었다.
(C) 그녀는 준비할 시간이 더 필요했다.
(D) 그녀는 열심히 발표 준비를 했다.

[어휘] **put a lot of time into** ~에 많은 시간을 들이다 **appreciate** 감사하다 **presentation** 프레젠테이션, 발표

[해설] put a lot of time into는 '오랫동안 뭔가를 열심히 준비하다'라는 의미이다. 따라서 여자는 열심히 발표 준비를 했다는 것을 알 수 있으므로 (D)가 정답이다.

3.
M I can't find my wallet! And it has more than a hundred dollars in it!

W Calm down a minute. Have you checked the coat you had on this morning?

N What does the woman suggest the man do?

(A) Search his closet

(B) Buy a new wallet

(C) Look in his coat pockets

(D) Take off his coat

[해석] M 지갑을 찾을 수가 없어! 그 안에 100달러 넘게 들어 있는데!
W 잠시 진정해 봐. 오늘 아침에 입었던 코트 살펴봤어?

N 여자는 남자에게 어떻게 하라고 권하는가?

(A) 옷장을 찾아볼 것
(B) 새 지갑을 살 것
(C) 코트 주머니를 살펴볼 것
(D) 코트를 벗을 것

[어휘] **calm down** 진정하다

[해설] 여자는 남자에게 코트를 살펴봤는지(Have you checked the coat)를 묻고 있으므로, 여자가 남자에게 권하는 것은 코트 주머니를 살펴보라는 것이다. 따라서 (C)가 정답이다.

4.
W I waited for you at the library for more than 30 minutes yesterday. Weren't we supposed to meet at noon?

M Oh that's right! I'm sorry, I've been so wrapped up in my science project it just slipped my mind.

N What does the man mean?

(A) He forgot about his appointment with the woman.

(B) He did not finish his science project on time.

(C) He cannot help the woman with her science project.

(D) He will meet the woman at the library in 30 minutes.

[해석] W 어제 도서관에서 30분 넘게 널 기다렸어. 우리 정오에 만나기로 하지 않았니?
M 아, 맞아! 미안해. 내가 과학 숙제에 너무 몰두해서 약속을 깜빡 잊어버렸어.

N 남자가 의미하는 것은 무엇인가?

(A) 그는 여자와의 약속을 잊어버렸다.
(B) 그는 과학 숙제를 제때 끝내지 못했다.
(C) 그는 여자의 과학 숙제를 도와 줄 수 없다.
(D) 그는 30분 후에 도서관에서 여자를 만날 것이다.

[어휘] **be supposed to+동사원형** ~하기로 되어 있다, ~할 예정이다   **wrap up in** ~에 몰두하다   **slip one's mind** 깜빡 잊어버리다   **appointment** 약속

[해설] slip one's mind는 '~를 잊다'라는 의미로, 남자는 도서관에서 여자와 만나기로 한 약속을 잊어버렸다. 따라서 (A)가 정답이다. 설령 slip one's mind의 의미를 모르더라도, 어제 30분 넘게 기다렸다는 여자의 말(I waited for you at the library for more than 30 minutes yesterday.)에서도 남자가 여자와 만나기로 한 약속을 잊어버렸다는 것을 알 수 있다.

5.
W This is the most boring dormitory party I've ever been to.

M It certainly could use some livening up.

N What does the man imply?

(A) He has never been to a dormitory party before.

(B) He does not like his dormitory room.

(C) He agrees with the woman.

(D) He finds the party much too noisy.

[해석] W 이번 기숙사 파티는 내가 가 본 파티 중 가장 지루했어.
M 분명 좀 더 활기를 불어 넣을 수도 있었는데.

N 남자가 암시하는 것은 무엇인가?

(A) 그는 이전에 기숙사 파티에 가 본적이 없다.
(B) 그는 자신의 기숙사 방을 좋아하지 않는다.
(C) 그는 여자의 의견에 동의한다.
(D) 그는 파티가 너무 시끄럽다고 생각한다.

[어휘] **dormitory** 기숙사   **liven up** 활기를 불어 넣다, 생기를 불어 넣다   **noisy** 시끄러운, 떠들썩한

[해설] liven up은 '생기를 불어 넣다'라는 의미이다. 파티에 생기를 불어 넣을 수도 있었다(It certainly could use some livening up.)는 남자의 말에서, 남자는 파티가 지루했다(This is the most boring dormitory party I've ever been to.)는 여자의 의견에 동의한다는 것을 알 수 있다. 따라서 (C)가 정답이다.

6. **M** I've got three exams tomorrow! I can't possibly study for all of them!

W I'm just glad I'm not in your shoes!

N What does the woman mean?

(A) She is happy she does not have so many exams.

(B) She cannot help the man study.

(C) She will not do as well on the test as the man.

(D) The man should not complain.

[해석] **M** 내일 시험이 세 과목이나 있어! 아마 전부 다 공부할 수는 없을 거야!

W 내가 너와 같은 처지가 아니라니 정말 다행이구나!

N 여자가 의미하는 것은 무엇인가?

(A) 여자는 시험이 그렇게 많지 않아서 기쁘다.

(B) 여자는 남자가 공부하는 것을 도와줄 수 없다.

(C) 여자는 남자만큼 시험을 잘 보지 못할 것이다.

(D) 남자는 불평을 해서는 안 된다.

[어휘] **possibly** 어쩌면, 아마 **in one's shoes** ~의 입장이 되어; ~을 대신하여 **do well** 잘하다, 성공하다 **complain** 불평[푸념]하다, 불만을 말하다

[해설] in one's shoes는 '~의 입장이 되어'라는 의미이다. 여자는 남자와 달리 시험이 그렇게 많지 않다는 사실에 기뻐하고 있다. 따라서 (A)가 정답이다.

7. **W** My roommate Karen makes the best salads. I don't understand why mine never taste as good as hers.

M It's not such a mystery—she's a vegetarian and has simply perfected the art.

N What does the man mean?

(A) Karen is experienced at making salads.

(B) It is easy to make a good salad.

(C) The woman's salads are just as good as Karen's.

(D) He is not sure why Karen's salads taste so good.

[해석] **W** 내 룸메이트 카렌은 최고로 맛있는 샐러드를 만들어. 왜 내가 만든 샐러드는 그녀가 만든 샐러드만큼 맛있지 않은지 잘 모르겠어.

M 그렇게 신비스러울 것도 없어. 그녀는 채식주의자이니 (그렇게 맛있는 샐러드를 만드는) 솜씨가 있는 거야.

N 남자가 의미하는 것은 무엇인가?

(A) 카렌은 샐러드 만드는 것에 능숙하다.

(B) 맛있는 샐러드를 만들기는 쉽다.

(C) 여자가 만든 샐러드는 카렌이 만든 샐러드만큼 맛있다.

(D) 그는 카렌이 만든 샐러드가 그렇게 맛있는 이유를 잘 모른다.

[어휘] **mystery** 신비, 불가사의 **vegetarian** 채식주의자 **art** 요령, 기교, 재량 **be experienced at** ~에 능숙하다

[해설] perfect the art는 '~을 하는 것에 전문가가 되다'라는 의미이다. 남자는 카렌이 채식가인 탓에 많은 샐러드를 만들어 봤기 때문에 샐러드를 잘 만든다고 했다. 따라서 (A)가 정답이다.

8. **W** Do you think you could help me get a new couch into my apartment this weekend?

M Didn't you make arrangements to have it delivered? That'd be easier and it's free.

N What does the man suggest the woman do?

(A) Have the store deliver the couch

(B) Try to get a discount on the couch

(C) Delay the delivery of the couch

(D) Rearrange the furniture in her apartment

[해석] **W** 이번 주말에 내 아파트에 새 소파를 들여놓을 건데 나 좀 도와줄 수 있어?

M 배달해 달라고 하지 않았어? 그 편이 더 쉬울 거야. 그리고 무료이기도 하고.

N 남자는 여자에게 어떻게 하라고 제안하는가?

(A) 가게에 소파를 배달해 달라고 할 것

(B) 소파 가격을 할인 받을 것

(C) 소파 배달을 연기할 것

(D) 그녀 아파트의 가구를 재배치할 것

[어휘] **couch** 소파(= sofa)　**make arrangements** 협의하다
deliver 배달하다 *cf.* delivery 배달　**free** 무료의, 공짜의
get a discount 할인 받다　**rearrange** 재배치하다

[해설] 남자의 말 Didn't you make arrangements to have it delivered? That'd be easier and it's free.에서 남자는 배달해서 받는 편이 더 쉽고, 배달비도 무료라고 했다. 따라서 남자는 여자에게 소파를 배달 받으라고 한 것이므로, (A)가 정답이다.

---

9. *W*　The opening of the new photo exhibit was great. I thought you said you were coming, too—to meet the artist.

M　[*surprised*] Oh, no. That was last weekend?

N　What can be inferred about the man?

(A) He thought the exhibit had closed.
(B) He was confused about when the exhibit started.
(C) He saw the exhibit last weekend.
(D) He was not interested in meeting the photographer.

[해석] *W* 새 사진 전시회 개막식은 훌륭했어. 네가 올 거라고 말했던 것 같은데. 작가를 만나려고 말이야.
M [놀라며] 오 이런. 그게 지난 주말이었어?

N 남자에 대해 추론할 수 있는 것은 무엇인가?

(A) 그는 전시회가 끝났다고 생각했다.
(B) 그는 전시회 시작일을 혼동했다.
(C) 그는 지난 주말에 전시회를 봤다.
(D) 그는 사진작가를 만나는 것에 관심이 없었다.

[어휘] **exhibit** 전시회　**confuse** 혼동하다

[해설] 여자의 말에 대한 남자의 반응(Oh, no. That was last weekend?)으로 미루어, 남자는 전시회가 언제 열리는지 잊고 있었다는 것을 알 수 있다. 따라서 (B)가 정답이다.

---

10. *W*　[*with disapproval*] Are you going to buy that? I'm not sure I like it on you.

M　Well, it is comfortable—perfect for our trip. Maybe I'd better find a mirror so I can see how it looks.

N　What is the man doing?

(A) Trying on clothes
(B) Buying a mirror
(C) Packing for a trip
(D) Looking at travel books

[해석] *W* [반대하며] 너 그거 살 거야? 그건 너한테 어울리지 않는 것 같아.
M 글쎄, 편해서 우리 여행에 딱이야. 어쩌면 이 옷이 어떤지 거울에 비춰 보는 게 낫겠군.

N 남자는 무엇을 하고 있는가?

(A) 옷을 입어보고 있다
(B) 거울을 사고 있다
(C) 여행 짐을 싸고 있다
(D) 여행책자를 보고 있다

[어휘] **disapproval** 반대, 동의하지 않음　**try on** ~을 입어보다
pack 짐을 싸다

[해설] 여자의 어조로 보아 남자가 사려는 것에 반대한다는 것을 알 수 있다. 또, 여자의 말 Are you going to buy that? I'm not sure I like it on you.에서 남자가 옷을 입어보고 있다는 것을 알 수 있다. 남자의 말 Maybe I'd better find a mirror so I can see how it looks.에서도 남자가 옷을 입어 보고 있다는 것을 알 수 있다. 따라서 (A)가 정답이다.

---

11. *M*　[*grunt of disgust*] Ugh, I can't figure out why I can't get my computer to print.

W　Did you check the cables? Sometimes they just get loose.

N　What does the woman suggest the man do?

(A) Make sure the cables are connected properly
(B) Get a new printer
(C) Replace the cables on the printer
(D) Check the computer for lost files

[해석]　M　[넌더리 치며] 어휴, 왜 내 컴퓨터에서 인쇄가 안 되는지 알 수가 없어.
　　　W　전선 확인해 봤어? 가끔 전선이 느슨해져.

　　　N　여자는 남자에게 어떻게 하라고 제안하는가?

　　　(A) 전선이 제대로 연결되었는지 확인할 것
　　　(B) 새 프린터를 살 것
　　　(C) 프린터에 전선을 교체할 것
　　　(D) 컴퓨터에서 잃어버린 파일을 확인할 것

[어휘]　**grunt** 투덜대는 불평[불만]　**disgust** 싫증, 혐오감, 질색
　　　figure out 알아내다　**cable** 케이블, 전선　**loose** 풀린,
　　　헐렁헐렁한　**properly** 제대로, 적절히　**replace** 교체하다,
　　　갈다

[해설]　여자의 질문 Did you check the cables?에서 여자는 남자에게 전선을 확인해 보라고 했다. 따라서 (A)가 정답이다.

12.　W　I'm going out to the golf course this afternoon. Would you like to come along? I could use a few pointers on my game.
　　　M　I'd be glad to, but I'm not sure what I could show you.

　　　N　What does the man mean?

　　　(A) He does not know the way to the golf course.
　　　(B) He is probably not free in the afternoon.
　　　(C) He may not be a better golfer than the woman.
　　　(D) He is glad the woman has her own equipment.

[해석]　W　오늘 오후에 골프장에 갈 거예요. 당신도 함께 갈래요? 제가 경기하면서 당신 조언을 좀 적용해 볼 수 있을 거예요.
　　　M　나도 가고 싶어요. 그런데 내가 당신에게 무엇을 보여 줄 수 있을지는 모르겠군요.

　　　N　남자가 의미하는 것은 무엇인가?

　　　(A) 그는 골프장 가는 길을 모른다.
　　　(B) 그는 아마도 오후에 한가하지 않을 것이다.
　　　(C) 그는 아마도 여자보다 골프를 더 잘 치지 못할 것이다.
　　　(D) 그는 여자가 자신의 장비를 가지고 있어 기쁘다.

[어휘]　**golf course** 골프장, 골프 코스　**come along** 같이 가다　**pointer** 조언, 힌트　**free** 한가한, 선약이 없는; 무료의　**equipment** 장비, 기술

[해설]　이 대화에서 pointers는 '힌트, 조언'이라는 의미로 쓰였다. 여자는 남자에게 골프에 대한 조언을 요청하고 있으며, 남자의 말 I'm not sure what I could show you.에서 남자는 여자를 도와줄 만큼 충분히 골프를 잘 치지 못한다는 것을 알 수 있다. 따라서 (C)가 정답이다.

13.　M　I think I'll take three of these tablets. My head is killing me!
　　　W　You'd better read the label carefully first.

　　　N　What does the woman imply the man should do?

　　　(A) Wait for his headache to go away
　　　(B) Read a book instead
　　　(C) Take a different kind of medicine
　　　(D) Find out what the correct dosage is

[해석]　M　이 알약을 세 개 먹어야 할 것 같아. 머리가 아파 죽겠어!
　　　W　먼저 라벨을 꼼꼼히 읽어 보는 게 좋아.

　　　N　여자는 남자에게 어떻게 해야 한다고 암시하는가?

　　　(A) 그의 두통이 나을 때까지 기다릴 것
　　　(B) 대신 책을 읽을 것
　　　(C) 다른 종류의 약을 먹을 것
　　　(D) 정확한 복용량을 확인할 것

[어휘]　**tablet** 정제 알약　**kill** ~에게 지독한 고통을 주다　**label** 라벨, 상표　**go away** (고통이) 가시다, 낫다　**dosage** 투약량, 복용량

[해설]　(D)에서 dosage는 한 사람이 1회에 복용해야 할 약의 복용량을 뜻한다. 여자의 말 You'd better read the label carefully first.는 너무 많은 약을 복용하지 않도록 약병에서 라벨을 확인하라는 의미이다. 따라서, 여자는 남자에게 정확한 복용량을 확인하라고 주의를 주고 있으므로 (D)가 정답이다.

14. **M** I thought you weren't planning to come home for supper.

  W Oh, but I was.

  N What does the woman mean?

  (A) She did not plan to eat supper.
  (B) She is washing up for supper.
  (C) She did not want to come home.
  (D) She was planning to eat at home.

[해석] **M** 난 네가 집에 와서 저녁 식사할 거라고는 생각하지 못했어.
  W 오, 하지만 그럴 작정이었는데.

  N 여자가 의미하는 것은 무엇인가?

  (A) 그녀는 저녁 식사를 할 계획이 없었다.
  (B) 그녀는 저녁 식사를 하려고 손을 씻고 있다.
  (C) 그녀는 집에 오기를 원치 않았다.
  (D) 그녀는 집에서 식사를 할 계획이었다.

[어휘] **wash up** (얼굴이나 손을) 씻다, 세수하다; 설거지를 하다

[해설] 여자의 말 but에서 여자는 남자의 말(you weren't planning to come home for supper)에 반박하고 있음을 알 수 있다. 따라서 여자는 집에서 식사를 할 계획이었음을 알 수 있으므로 (D)가 정답이다.

---

15. **M** I'm really looking forward to taking up piano this semester.

  W I hope you do better than I did when I took lessons. I just don't have an ear for music.

  N What does the woman mean?

  (A) The man plays the piano well.
  (B) The man should reconsider taking piano lessons.
  (C) She does not enjoy listening to music.
  (D) She does not have musical ability.

[해석] **M** 나는 이번 학기에 피아노 배우는 것을 손꼽아 기다리고 있어.
  W 너는 내가 레슨을 받았을 때보다 더 잘하길 바라. 나는 음악에는 별 소질이 없는 것 같아.

  N 여자가 의미하는 것은 무엇인가?

  (A) 남자는 피아노를 잘 친다.
  (B) 남자는 피아노 레슨 받는 것을 다시 생각해 봐야 한다.
  (C) 여자는 음악을 듣는 것을 좋아하지 않는다.
  (D) 여자는 음악적인 재능이 없다.

[어휘] **look forward to -ing** ~하기를 고대하다 **take up** ~를 배우다 **semester** 학기 **have an ear for** ~을 알다, ~에 대한 일가견이 있다 **reconsider** 재고하다, 고쳐 생각하다

[해설] don't have an ear for music은 '음악에 대한 재능이 없다'는 의미로, 여자는 음악에 대한 재능이 없어서 레슨을 받을 때 잘하지 못했다고 말하고 있다. 또, 여자의 말 I hope you do better than I did when I took lessons.에서도 여자는 음악적인 재능이 없음을 알 수 있으므로 (D)가 정답이다.

---

16. **W** Did you pick up some French bread at the bakery?

  M A sign on the window said "Closed. Please call again."

  N What does the man mean?

  (A) He needed to call the bakery again.
  (B) The bakery was not open.
  (C) The bakery was sold out of bread.
  (D) The bakery does not make French bread.

[해석] **W** 빵집에서 바게트 빵은 사왔어?
  M 창문에 "휴무 중. 다음에 다시 오세요"라는 표지판이 있었어.

  N 남자가 의미하는 것은 무엇인가?

  (A) 그는 빵집에 다시 전화해야 했다.
  (B) 빵집이 문을 열지 않았다.
  (C) 빵집의 빵이 다 팔렸다.
  (D) 빵집에서 바게트 빵을 만들지 않는다.

[어휘] **pick up** 사다, 집어 올리다 **French bread** 긴 바게트 빵 **sign** 표지판 **call** 방문하다(= visit) **be sold out of** ~이 품절이다, 매진이다

[해설] 남자의 말 "Closed. Please call again."에서 closed는 '휴업한, 폐점의(= not open for business)'라는 의미이며, call은 '다시 오다(= come back)'의 의미로 쓰였다. 따라서 빵집이 문을 열지 않았다는 의미이므로 (B)가 정답이다.

17. **M** I'm nervous about the job interview I have this afternoon.

W Relax. Just let them know about your background. It's perfect for the job.

N What does the woman suggest the man do?

(A) Go to the interview early

(B) Do some exercise to relax

(C) Tell the interviewer about his qualifications

(D) Wear his new suit to the interview

18. **M** I really don't see the value of these modern paintings. They look like the kind of pictures my four-year-old nephew paints.

W And I'll bet he uses brighter colors, too!

N What can be inferred about the speakers?

(A) They do not know who painted the pictures.

(B) They think modern paintings are creative.

(C) They think children should be taught to paint.

(D) They do not like the paintings.

[해석] **M** 오늘 오후에 있을 취직 면접 때문에 긴장 돼.

W 진정해. 네 학력에 대해 알려주기만 하면 돼. 그 일에는 딱 안성맞춤이잖아.

N 여자가 남자에게 제안하는 것은 무엇인가?

(A) 면접에 일찍 갈 것

(B) 진정하기 위해 운동을 좀 할 것

(C) 그의 자격 요건에 대해 면접관에게 말할 것

(D) 면접에 새 옷을 입고 갈 것

[어휘] **nervous** 긴장되는, 불안한, 초조한 **job interview** 취직 면접 **relax** 편안하게 하다, 느긋하게 하다 **background** 성장 환경, 출신 배경; 경력, 학력 **interviewer** 면접관 cf. interviewee 면접을 받는 사람 **qualifications** 자격 요건, 자질, 능력

[해설] 여자의 말 Just let them know about your background.에서 background는 '직업을 충족시킬 경력이나 학력'을 의미한다. 여자는 남자에게 충분한 자격 요건을 갖추고 있으니(It's perfect for the job.) 면접관에게 자신의 자격 요건을 말하기만 하면 된다고 했다. 따라서 (C)가 정답이다.

[해석] **M** 나는 정말 이런 현대 미술의 가치를 잘 모르겠어. 4살짜리 내 조카가 그린 그림 같아 보여.

W 그리고 네 조카는 분명 더 밝은 색깔을 쓸 거야!

N 화자들에 대해 추론할 수 있는 것은 무엇인가?

(A) 그들은 누가 그림을 그렸는지 모른다.

(B) 그들은 현대 미술이 창의적이라고 생각한다.

(C) 그들은 아이들이 그림 그리는 것을 배워야 한다고 생각한다.

(D) 그들은 그 그림들을 좋아하지 않는다.

[어휘] **nephew** 조카 **I'll bet** 단언하다, 틀림없다(= I'm sure) **creative** 독창적인, 창조적인

[해설] 남자의 말 They look like the kind of pictures my four-year-old nephew paints.에서 남자는 현대 미술이 4살짜리 조카가 그린 그림처럼 보인다고 했으므로, 현대 미술을 높이 사지 않는다는 것을 알 수 있다. 또, 여자의 말 And에서 여자 역시 남자의 말에 동의하고 있으며, 이어지는 말 I'll bet he uses brighter colors, too!에서 여자는 현대 미술의 색조도 좋아하지 않는다는 것을 알 수 있다. 따라서, 두 사람 다 그림을 좋아하지 않으므로 (D)가 정답이다.

19. **M** Are you flying or taking the train home for the summer?

W Neither. Since I've got this job at the university library, my parents are just going to come visit sometime in July.

N What does the woman mean?

(A) She will get a ride home with her parents.

(B) She cannot go home until July.

(C) She quit her job before summer vacation.

(D) She is not going home for the summer.

[해석] M 여름 방학 때 집에 비행기 타고 갈 거야, 아니면 기차 타고 갈 거야?

W 둘 다 아니야. 대학교 도서관에서 일자리를 얻어서, 우리 부모님께서 7월 중에 오실 거야.

N 여자가 의미하는 것은 무엇인가?

(A) 그녀는 부모님과 함께 차를 타고 집에 갈 것이다.

(B) 그녀는 7월까지는 집에 갈 수 없다.

(C) 그녀는 여름 방학 전에 일을 그만뒀다.

(D) 그녀는 여름에 집에 가지 않을 것이다.

[어휘] **get a ride** 차를 얻어 타다 **quit** 그만두다

[해설] 여자의 말 Since I've got this job at the university library, my parents are just going to come visit sometime in July.에서 여자는 여름에 대학 도서관에서 일해야 해서 부모님이 자신을 방문하실 거라고 했다. 따라서 여자가 집에 가지 않을 것임을 알 수 있으므로, (D)가 정답이다.

20. **W** Do you have any idea when tonight's rehearsal will be over?

M Beats me. You could try asking Jeff.

N What does the man mean?

(A) Jeff can give her directions to the rehearsal.

(B) The woman should tell Jeff to come to the rehearsal.

(C) Jeff might know when the rehearsal will end.

(D) He does not know whether Jeff will be at the rehearsal.

[해석] W 혹시 오늘밤 예행 연습이 언제 끝나는지 알아?

M 나도 몰라. 제프에게 물어 봐.

N 남자가 의미하는 것은 무엇인가?

(A) 제프는 여자에게 예행 연습 장소에 가는 길을 알려줄 수 있다.

(B) 여자는 제프에게 예행 연습에 오라고 말해야 한다.

(C) 제프는 예행 연습이 언제 끝날지 알 수도 있다.

(D) 남자는 제프가 예행 연습에 올지 어떨지 모른다.

[어휘] **rehearsal** 예행 연습 **be over** 끝나다 **(It) Beats me.** 모르겠어, 두 손 들었어. **directions** 길 안내

[해설] 남자의 말 Beats me.는 '잘 모른다'라는 의미로, 남자는 자신도 예행 연습이 언제 끝나는지 모르니 제프에게 물어보라(You could try asking Jeff.)고 했다. 따라서 (C)가 정답이다.

21. **W** The music we were playing last night didn't disturb you, did it?

M [*sarcastically*] I was trying to get some work done.

N What does the man imply about the music?

(A) He had to turn it off.

(B) He could not hear it.

(C) He enjoyed listening to it while working.

(D) He was disturbed by it.

[해석] W 어젯밤 저희가 연주한 음악이 폐가 되지는 않았나요, 그랬나요?

M [비꼬듯이] 일을 좀 하려고 했었어요.

N 남자가 음악에 대해 암시하는 것은 무엇인가?

(A) 그는 음악을 꺼야 했다.

(B) 그는 음악을 들을 수 없었다.

(C) 그는 일하면서 음악 듣는 것을 즐겼다.

(D) 그는 음악 소리 때문에 방해를 받았다.

[어휘] **disturb** 방해하다, 폐를 끼치다 **sarcastically** 빈정대듯이, 비꼬듯이 **turn off** ~을 끄다(↔ **turn on** ~을 켜다)

[해설] 비꼬는 듯한 어조나, 남자의 말 I was trying to get some work done.에서 남자는 음악 연주로 인해 방해 받았다는 것을 알 수 있다. 따라서 (D)가 정답이다.

22. **W** The election's tomorrow. Do you want to help me put up some more campaign posters?

M I don't see why we should bother. The people who are going to vote have already made up their minds.

N What does the man imply?

(A) Putting up posters now is a waste of time.

(B) Most people have already voted.

(C) The election results have already been posted.

(D) Many voters are undecided.

[해석] **W** 선거가 내일이야. 내가 선거 운동 포스터 붙이는 것 좀 도와줄래?

M 나는 우리가 왜 애를 써야 하는지 이해가 안 돼. 투표를 할 사람들은 이미 마음의 결정을 했을 텐데.

N 남자가 암시하는 것은 무엇인가?

(A) 지금 포스터를 붙이는 것은 시간 낭비이다.

(B) 대부분의 사람들이 이미 투표를 했다.

(C) 선거 결과가 이미 게재되었다.

(D) 많은 투표자들이 결정을 하지 못했다.

[어휘] **election** 선거, 투표 **campaign** 선거 운동, 유세 **bother** 신경 쓰다, ~하려고 애쓰다 **make up one's mind** 마음의 결정을 하다, 결심하다 **a waste of time** 시간 낭비 **post** 게시하다, 붙이다 **undecided** 미결정의, 미정의

[해설] 남자는 I don't see why we should bother. The people who are going to vote have already made up their minds.에서 투표자들의 마음을 바꾸기에는 너무 늦었으니 포스터를 더 붙이는 것은 아무런 소용이 없다고 했다. 따라서 (A)가 정답이다.

23. **W** Jessie's doing well in chemistry now, isn't she?

M Yes, she's really come a long way.

N What does the man say about Jessie?

(A) She has made a lot of progress.

(B) She was always good in chemistry.

(C) She travels a long distance to school.

(D) She has been studying chemistry for hours.

[해석] **W** 제시는 이제 화학을 잘해요, 그렇지 않아요?

M 맞아요, 그녀는 정말 상당히 좋아졌어요.

N 남자는 제시에 대해 뭐라고 말하는가?

(A) 그녀는 많이 향상되었다.

(B) 그녀는 늘 화학을 잘했다.

(C) 그녀는 학교까지 먼 거리를 이동한다.

(D) 그녀는 몇 시간째 화학을 공부하고 있다.

[어휘] **come a long way** 상당히 좋아지다, 크게 발전하다 **make progress** 발전을 하다, 진전을 보이다

[해설] come a long way는 '많은 발전을 하다, 진전을 보이다'라는 의미로, 남자는 제시의 화학 실력이 많이 향상되었다고 하였다. 따라서 (A)가 정답이다.

24. **M** I give up! I'll never learn how to ski as well as you!

W Don't be discouraged. Remember, I practically grew up on skis.

N What does the woman imply?

(A) The man is a much better skier than he used to be.

(B) The man lacks the ability needed to become a good skier.

(C) The man should not compare his ability to hers.

(D) The man should have taken skiing lessons as a child.

[해석] M 나는 포기할래! 나는 절대 너처럼 잘 탈 정도로 스키를 배울 수 없을 것 같아!

W 낙담하지 마. 생각해 봐, 사실 나는 자라면서 내내 스키를 탔잖아.

N 여자가 암시하는 것은 무엇인가?

(A) 남자는 예전보다 스키를 훨씬 더 잘 탄다.
(B) 남자는 스키를 잘 타기 위해 필요한 재능이 부족하다.
(C) 남자는 자신의 능력을 여자의 능력과 비교해서는 안 된다.
(D) 남자는 어렸을 때 스키 강습을 받았어야 했다.

[어휘] give up 포기하다　discouraged 낙담한, 의욕을 잃어버린　practically 사실상(은), 실제로는　grow up 자라다, 성장하다　compare A to B A를 B와 비교하다　should have p.p. ~했어야 했는데 (하지 않았다)

[해설] 여자는 막 스키를 배우고 있는 남자를 격려하고 있는데, 여자의 말 Remember, I practically grew up on skis.에서 여자는 어린 시절부터 스키를 타 왔다고 말하고 있다. 이는 스키를 막 배우기 시작한 남자에게 자신과 비교하지 말라고 우회적으로 말하는 것이므로 (C)가 정답이다.

---

25. W Your neighbors used to grow the most wonderful peaches!

M You have a good memory. The tree went down in a storm a few years ago, and I'd completely forgotten about it.

N What does the man imply?

(A) His neighbors no longer grow peaches.
(B) He keeps forgetting to ask his neighbors for peaches.
(C) He is not sure what the woman is referring to.
(D) His neighbors planted a new peach tree after the storm.

[해석] W 당신 이웃사람들이 아주 훌륭한 복숭아 나무를 키웠었죠!

M 당신은 기억력이 좋군요. 그 나무는 몇 년 전에 폭우로 쓰러졌는데, 나는 완전히 잊어버리고 있었어요.

N 남자가 암시하는 것은 무엇인가?

(A) 그의 이웃 사람들은 더 이상 복숭아 나무를 기르지 않는다.
(B) 그는 이웃 사람들에게 복숭아를 달라고 말하는 것을 계속 잊어버린다.
(C) 그는 여자가 무슨 말을 하고 있는지 잘 모른다.
(D) 그의 이웃들은 폭풍 후에 새 복숭아 나무를 심었다.

[어휘] go down 쓰러지다　refer to ~을 언급하다

[해설] 여자의 말 Your neighbors used to grow the most wonderful peaches!의 used to grow에서 남자의 이웃 사람들이 더 이상 복숭아 나무를 기르지 않는다는 것을 알 수 있다. 또, 남자의 말 The tree went down in a storm a few years ago에서도 이웃 사람들이 더 이상 복숭아 나무를 기르지 않는다는 것을 알 수 있다. 따라서 (A)가 정답이다.

---

26. W Jack's plan to move across the country and start his own business is really brave, but I hope he knows what he's doing.

M Oh, I know. I can't help but wonder how he's ever going to manage it.

N What does the man mean?

(A) He knows the manager of Jack's company.
(B) He wants to help Jack move.
(C) He is sorry he cannot help Jack manage his business.
(D) He is doubtful that Jack's plans will succeed.

[해석] W 나라 반대편으로 이사 가서 새로운 사업을 시작하려는 잭의 계획은 정말 용감하지만, 나는 그가 자신이 무슨 일을 하고 있는 건지 알았으면 좋겠어요.

M 오, 나도 알아요. 그가 어떻게 그 일을 감당할지 의문을 가지지 않을 수 없어요.

N 남자가 의미하는 것은 무엇인가?

(A) 그는 잭이 다니는 회사의 관리자를 알고 있다.
(B) 그는 잭의 이사를 돕기를 원한다.
(C) 그는 잭의 사업 운영을 도울 수 없어 유감이다.
(D) 그는 잭의 계획이 성공할지 의심스럽다.

[어휘] can't help but+동사원형 ~하지 않을 수 없다　doubtful 의심스러운, 미심쩍은

[해설] 남자의 말 I can't help but wonder how he's ever going to manage it.에서 남자는 잭에게 새 사업을 성공할 능력이 있는지 의심스러워하고 있다는 것을 알 수 있으므로 (D)가 정답이다.

27.
M I hear that Professor Jones is going to be on the news tonight. Could I come over and watch it?

W Well, a bunch of us from class are going to go over to Dave's to watch it. Want to join us?

N What will the speakers probably do this evening?

(A) Stay home and watch the news

(B) Watch the program at a classmate's house

(C) Tell Professor Jones the news

(D) Meet Professor Jones at Dave's house

[해석] M 존스 교수님이 오늘밤 뉴스에 나오신대. 내가 (네 집에) 가서 볼 수 있을까?

W 글쎄, 우리 반 친구들 몇 명이 데이브의 집에 가서 볼 거야. 너도 함께 갈래?

N 화자들은 오늘 저녁에 무엇을 할 것 같은가?

(A) 집에 머물러 뉴스를 볼 것이다

(B) 같은 반 친구의 집에서 프로그램을 볼 것이다

(C) 존스 교수에게 뉴스를 말할 것이다

(D) 데이브의 집에서 존스 교수를 만날 것이다

[해설] 남자는 여자의 집에 가서 뉴스를 보고 싶어 하지만(Could I come over and watch it?), 여자는 데이브의 집에 가서 뉴스를 볼 거(Well, a bunch of us from class are going to go over to Dave's to watch it.)라고 했다. 따라서 (B)가 정답이다.

28.
W I've been combing the classifieds for an apartment.

M I think there're some good rentals on the bulletin board outside the student center.

N What does the man suggest the woman do?

(A) Place an ad in the newspaper

(B) Look in the student paper under apartments for rent

(C) Check the notices posted on campus

(D) Look at some apartments located near the student center

[해석] W 아파트를 찾기 위해 광고를 샅샅이 뒤지고 있어.

M 학생회관 밖의 게시판에 좋은 셋집들이 나와 있을 거야.

N 남자는 여자에게 어떻게 하라고 제안하는가?

(A) 신문에 광고를 낼 것

(B) 학생 신문에서 아파트 임대 섹션을 살펴볼 것

(C) 캠퍼스에 게재된 공고문을 확인해 볼 것

(D) 학생회관 근처의 아파트를 찾아볼 것

[어휘] **comb** 샅샅이 찾다[뒤지다] **classified** 광고 **rental** 임대 물건, 셋집; 임대료 **bulletin board** 게시판, 알림판 **place an ad** 광고를 내다 **notice** 공고(문), 공지 **post** 게시하다, 붙이다

[해설] 여자의 말 I've been combing the classifieds for an apartment.에서 comb은 '~을 샅샅이 찾다'라는 의미로, 여자는 아파트를 찾고 있음을 알 수 있으며, 남자는 학생회관의 게시판에 게재된 공고문을 보라(I think there're some good rentals on the bulletin board outside the student center.)고 제안하고 있다. 따라서 (C)가 정답이다.

29.
W Look at it pour! So much for our tennis game.

M Yeah, and since it's supposed to keep up all night, we ought to forget about tomorrow's lunch game too.

N What does the man imply?

(A) He hopes the woman will not forget their lunch date.

(B) There are some tennis courts available right now.

(C) The tennis courts will be too wet to play on.

(D) He wants to continue the game tomorrow.

[해석] W 비가 억수같이 내리는 것 좀 봐! 우리가 테니스 게임을 하기에는 너무 많이 내리고 있어.

M 그래, 밤새 내내 비가 온다고 하니 내일 점심 경기 역시 잊어버려야 할 것 같아.

N 남자가 암시하는 것은 무엇인가?

(A) 그는 여자가 점심 약속을 잊지 않기를 바란다.

(B) 지금 당장 사용할 수 있는 테니스 코트가 몇 곳 있다.

(C) 테니스 코트가 너무 젖어서 경기를 할 수 없을 것이다.

(D) 그는 내일 경기를 계속 하기를 원한다.

[어휘] **pour** 퍼붓다 **be supposed to+동사원형** ~할 예정이다,
~하기로 되어 있다 **keep up** (특정한 날씨가) 계속되다
available 이용할 수 있는, 사용할 수 있는

[해설] 비가 억수같이 내리고(Look at it pour!) 있으며, 밤새 비가 계
속 내릴 것이므로 내일 경기는 잊어버려야 할 것 같다는 남자의 말
(since it's supposed to keep up all night, we ought to
forget about tomorrow's lunch game)로 미루어 테니스 코
트가 너무 젖어서 경기를 할 수 없을 것임을 알 수 있다. 따라서
(C)가 정답이다.

---

30. *M* The phone will be installed tomorrow.
    W Oh, so you did order it.

    N What had the woman assumed?

    (A) The man had already received the phone.
    (B) The phone will be installed soon.
    (C) The phone was already on order.
    (D) The phone had not been ordered.

[해석] *M* 내일 전화기가 설치될 거예요.
    W 오, 당신이 주문을 했었군요.

    N 여자가 짐작했던 것은 무엇인가?

    (A) 남자는 이미 전화를 받았다.
    (B) 전화가 곧 설치될 것이다.
    (C) 전화기를 이미 주문해 놓은 상태였다.
    (D) 전화기를 주문하지 않았었다.

[어휘] **install** 설치하다 **order** 주문하다; 주문 **on order**
(물건이) 주문 중인, 발주가 끝난

[해설] 여자의 어조와, 여자가 Oh, so you ordered it.이 아니라 Oh,
so you did order it.이라고 말한 것으로 미루어 여자는 남자가
이미 전화기를 주문했다는 것을 몰랐다는 것을 알 수 있다. 따라서
(D)가 정답이다.

Part B
Questions 31–34

N Listen to part of an interview between a student
newspaper reporter and a professor.

W ³¹Professor Smith, let me make sure my
information is accurate. The title of your book
is *Moving People: The New York Subway and
Urban Development*. It's 312 pages long, and it
will be published next month.

M That's right. ³²You should be sure to make clear
that I'm not the sole author. My coauthor is
Kathleen Douglas.

W Yes. I have that. So why write about the
subways?

M ³³I'm a cultural historian, and I'm interested in
the impact of technology on people's lives. The
subways increased everyone's mobility. How
cheap, efficient transportation changed life in
New York—that's really the focus.

W Have the subways been around a long time?

M Some unsuccessful attempts were made as
far back as the 1870s, but the history of the
subways really begins with the founding of the
IRT, the Interborough Rapid Transit Company,
in 1900. Today we call it the IRT.

W So the IRT built the first subway in 1900?

M They started work in 1900, but it took four
years to dig the tunnel and lay the track for the
first line.

W And it was a success?

M Oh, yes. People knew it would transform their
lives—a hundred thousand rode the train the
first day. I've got some great pictures of that
day.

W Are they in the book?

M Yes. ³⁴Those and quite a few others. Actually,
Kathleen collected the photographs. I was
going over this set when you arrived.

CHAPTER 5

[해석] N 학생 신문 기자와 교수의 인터뷰 중 일부를 들어 보세요.

W 스미스 교수님, 제 정보가 정확한지 확인해 볼게요. 교수님께서 쓰신 책의 제목은 〈이동하는 사람들: 뉴욕의 지하철과 도시 개발〉입니다. 312페이지 분량이고, 다음 달에 발간됩니다.

M 맞아요. 제가 단독 저자가 아니라는 점을 분명히 해주셔야 해요. 공동 집필자는 캐슬린 더글러스예요.

W 예, 알겠습니다. 그런데 왜 지하철에 관해 쓰셨나요?

M 나는 문화 역사가이고, 기술이 사람들의 삶에 미치는 영향에 관심이 있어요. 지하철은 모든 사람들의 이동성을 증진시켰어요. 저렴하고 효율적인 교통수단이 뉴욕의 삶을 얼마나 바꿨는가, 바로 그것이 주안점이에요.

W 지하철은 생긴 지 오래 되었나요?

M 1870년대로 거슬러 올라가면 몇몇 성공하지 못한 시도들도 있었지만, 지하철의 역사는 사실 1900년에 인터보로우 철도 회사인 IRT의 설립과 함께 시작됩니다. 오늘날 우리는 그때 생긴 지하철 노선을 IRT라고 부르죠.

W 그럼 IRT에서 1900년에 첫 번째 지하철을 건설했나요?

M 1900년에 건설하기 시작했지만, 터널을 파고 1호선 철도를 까는데 4년이 걸렸어요.

W 그래서 성공했나요?

M 오, 그럼요. 사람들은 지하철이 자신들의 삶을 바꿔 놓을 것을 알았어요. 첫날 10만 명이 지하철에 탑승했어요. 그날의 영광스러운 사진들을 좀 갖고 있어요.

W 책에 그 사진들이 수록되어 있나요?

M 네. 그 사진들과 몇몇 다른 사진들이 수록되어 있어요. 실은, 캐슬린이 그 사진들을 수집했어요. 당신이 도착했을 때 이것을 정리하고 있었어요.

[어휘] **accurate** 정확한, 흠이 없는　**urban** 도시의, 도시에 사는　**sole** 한 사람뿐인, 유일한　**coauthor** 공저자, 공동 집필자　**impact** 효과, 영향　**mobility** 이동성, 기동성　**efficient** 능률적인, 효율적인　**as far back as** ~으로 멀리 거슬러 올라가서　**founding** 창립　**lay the track** 철도를 깔다　**transform** 바꾸다, 변형시키다

---

31. *N*　What is the main topic of the interview?

(A) **A new book**

(B) An exhibit of photographs

(C) A lecture series on transportation

(D) Recent developments in urban transportation

[해석] N 인터뷰의 주제는 무엇인가?

(A) **새 책**

(B) 사진 전시회

(C) 교통기관에 관한 일련의 강의

(D) 최근의 도시 교통기관 개발

[어휘] **exhibit** 전시(회)

[해설] 화자들은 곧 발간될 책에 관해 이야기하고 있으므로 (A)가 정답이다. 특히, 여자의 첫 번째 말 Professor Smith, let me make sure my information is accurate. The title of your book is *Moving People: The New York Subway and Urban Development*. It's 312 pages long, and it will be published next month.에서 결정적인 단서를 찾을 수 있다.

---

32. *N*　Who is Kathleen Douglas?

(A) The editor of the school newspaper

(B) The professor's student

(C) **The coauthor of the book**

(D) A subway company executive

[해석] N 캐슬린 더글러스는 누구인가?

(A) 학교 신문 편집자

(B) 교수의 학생

(C) **책의 공동 집필자**

(D) 지하철 회사 임원

[어휘] **editor** 편집자　**executive** 중역, 임원

[해설] 남자의 첫 번째 말 You should be sure to make clear that I'm not the sole author. My coauthor is Kathleen Douglas.에서 캐슬린 더글러스가 공동 집필자라고 밝히고 있다. 따라서 (C)가 정답이다.

---

33. *N*　What aspect of the New York subway especially interests the professor?

(A) How it was financed

(B) The engineering of the tunnels

(C) Its representation in art and literature

(D) **Its effects on city life**

N 교수는 뉴욕 지하철의 어떤 면에 특히 관심이 있는가?

(A) 재원 마련 방법
(B) 터널의 공학 기술
(C) 예술과 문학에서의 표현
(D) 도시 생활에 미치는 영향

[어휘] **aspect** 측면, 양상 **finance** 자금을 마련하다
representation 표현 **literature** 문학

[해설] 남자의 두 번째 말 I'm a cultural historian, and I'm interested in the impact of technology on people's lives.에서 교수는 기술이 사람들의 삶에 미치는 영향에 관심이 있다고 했다. 따라서 the impact of technology on people's lives를 Its effects on city life라고 바꿔서 표현한 (D)가 정답이다.

---

34. *N* What will the professor probably do next?

(A) Show the reporter some photographs
(B) Read an article in the campus newspaper
(C) Explain how the subway tunnels were built
(D) Examine a map of the New York subway system

[해석] *N* 교수는 다음에 무엇을 할 것 같은가?

(A) 기자에게 사진을 몇 장 보여줄 것이다
(B) 학교 신문의 기사를 읽을 것이다
(C) 지하철 터널이 어떻게 건설되었는지 설명할 것이다
(D) 뉴욕 지하철 시스템의 지도를 살펴볼 것이다

[어휘] **article** 기사 **examine** 조사하다, 검토하다

[해설] 인터뷰 후반부에서 두 사람은 책에 수록될 사진에 대해 언급하고 있으며, 특히 인터뷰의 마지막 말 Those and quite a few others. Actually, Kathleen collected the photographs. I was going over this set when you arrived.에서 교수는 기자에게 사진을 보여줄 것임을 알 수 있다. 따라서 (A)가 정답이다.

Questions 35–38

N Listen to a conversation between two students who are members of the computer club.

M Sorry to say this, Pam, but [35]I think we're going to have to cancel tonight's planning meeting.

W You're kidding, Tom. [35]With the computer fair only two weeks away? Is the weather that bad?

M Well, I just listened to the noon forecast on the radio, and [36]the snow's supposed to start between 2:00 and 3:00 and continue throughout the afternoon and evening. Some other campus clubs have already announced they're not meeting.

W Gee ... I'd hate to cancel, though ... There's so much to do to get ready.

M [37]I know what you mean, but if the weather's bad, we probably wouldn't get much of a turnout anyway. Remember how many computer club members live far from campus.

W Maybe you're right. And Kathy told me yesterday that the publicity's all taken care of ...

M And I've made the arrangements for the rooms we'll be using, so that's all set, too.

W Sounds as if we're further ahead than I thought. Maybe we could just postpone the meeting till tomorrow night.

M I think we'd better wait a couple of days until the roads clear. How about the day after tomorrow? I could get on the phone and let everyone know.

W [38]I'll split the list with you. That way we'll each have only ten calls to make.

M Great. And when I talk to Sara, I'll find out how the response from the computer vendors has been.

W Last I heard, there were about twenty software companies coming.

M [35]I guess everything's coming along all right then. Let's just hope we have good weather the day of the fair.

CHAPTER 5

[해석] N 컴퓨터 클럽 회원인 두 학생 간의 대화를 들어 보세요.

M 팸, 이런 말을 해서 미안하지만, 오늘밤에 예정된 기획 모임을 취소해야 할 것 같아.

W 톰, 농담하지 마. 컴퓨터 박람회가 2주밖에 안 남았는데 그러려고? 날씨가 그 정도로 안 좋아?

M 음, 라디오에서 정오의 일기예보를 들었는데, 2~3시 사이에 눈이 오기 시작해서 오후 내내 내리고 저녁 동안에도 계속 내린대. 다른 캠퍼스 클럽들은 벌써 모임을 취소한다고 발표했대.

W 이런… 그래도 나는 취소하기 싫은데… 준비하려면 할 게 얼마나 많은데.

M 나도 무슨 말인지는 알지만, 날씨가 나쁘면, 아마 참석하는 사람들도 많지 않을 거야. 얼마나 많은 컴퓨터 클럽 회원들이 학교 캠퍼스에서 먼 곳에 사는지 생각해 봐.

W 네 말이 맞을 수도 있겠다. 그리고 어제 캐시가 내게 홍보도 다 마쳤다고 말했어…

M 그리고 나는 우리가 쓸 방들을 준비해 뒀으니, 모든 준비가 다 끝났어.

W 내가 생각했던 것보다 많이 준비가 된 것 같네. 아마도 내일 밤까지 모임을 연기해도 될 것 같아.

M 도로가 치워질 때까지 2~3일 기다리는 편이 좋겠어. 모레는 어때? 내가 전화를 걸어서 모든 사람들에게 알릴게.

W 나와 명단을 나누자. 그러면 각자 10통씩 전화하면 돼.

M 좋아. 그리고 사라와 통화하면서 컴퓨터 판매자들의 반응이 어땠는지 알아볼게.

W 내가 마지막으로 들은 이야기로는 대략 20곳의 소프트웨어 회사에서 올 거래.

M 그럼 모든 게 순조롭게 진행되고 있네. 그저 박람회 날에 날씨가 좋기만 바라자.

[어휘] cancel 취소하다 fair 전시회, 박람회 forecast 일기예보 throughout ~동안 내내, ~의 전역에 걸쳐 turnout 출석자, 참가자 수 publicity 일반에게 알려져 있음, 공표, 광고 take care of ~를 돌보다, 처리하다 make the arrangements 준비하다 all set 다 준비된 postpone 연기하다, 미루다 the day after tomorrow 모레 split the list 쪼개다, 나누다 response 응답, 대답 vendor 판매자, 판매 회사 come along 일이 순조롭게 진행되다

---

35. *N* What are the speakers working on?

(A) Setting up a computer class

(B) Meeting a computer software vendor

(C) Planning a computer fair

(D) Arranging a trip to a computer company

[해석] N 화자들은 무엇을 하고 있는가?

(A) 컴퓨터 수업을 개설하고 있다

(B) 컴퓨터 소프트웨어 판매자를 만나고 있다

(C) 컴퓨터 박람회를 계획하고 있다

(D) 컴퓨터 회사 방문을 준비하고 있다

[어휘] set up 개설하다

[해설] 주제를 묻는 문제이다. 컴퓨터 클럽 회원인 두 학생은 다가올 컴퓨터 박람회에 대한 계획을 논의하고 있다. 남자의 첫 번째 말 I think we're going to have to cancel tonight's planning meeting.에서 planning meeting이 언급되었고, 여자의 말 With the computer fair only two weeks away? 에서 컴퓨터 박람회가 2주 후에 있을 거라는 사실을 알 수 있다. 또한, 이어지는 내용에서 다가올 행사에 대한 구체적인 사항들(the publicity, the arrangements for the rooms, about twenty software companies coming)이 나온다. 남자의 마지막 말 I guess everything's coming along all right then. Let's just hope we have good weather the day of the fair.에서 앞으로 있을 행사가 박람회임을 알 수 있으므로, (C)가 정답이다.

---

36. *N* Why do the speakers decide to cancel the meeting?

(A) They attended a similar one the day before.

(B) Too few members are interested in the activity.

(C) The room is not available that evening.

(D) The weather may be bad.

[해석] N 화자들이 모임을 취소하기로 결정한 이유는 무엇인가?

(A) 바로 전날 비슷한 모임에 참석했다.

(B) 그 활동에 관심이 있는 회원들이 너무 적다.

(C) 그날 저녁에 사용할 수 있는 방이 없다.

(D) 날씨가 나쁠 것 같다.

[해설] 대화의 서두 부분에서 나쁜 날씨(the snow's supposed to start between 2:00 and 3:00 and continue throughout the afternoon and evening)와 모임 취소(I think we're going to have to cancel tonight's planning meeting.)에 대해 이야기하고 있다. 따라서 (D)가 정답이다.

37. *N* Where is the planning meeting scheduled to take place?

(A) At a computer software company
(B) Far from the university
(C) At the man's house
(D) On the university campus

[해석] *N* 기획 모임은 어디에서 열릴 예정인가?

(A) 컴퓨터 소프트웨어 회사에서
(B) 대학에서 멀리 떨어진 곳에서
(C) 남자의 집에서
(D) 대학 캠퍼스에서

[어휘] **take place** 열리다, 일어나다

[해설] 추론 문제이다. 남자의 말 I know what you mean, but if the weather's bad, we probably wouldn't get much of a turnout anyway. Remember how many computer club members live far from campus.에서 많은 클럽 회원들이 캠퍼스에서 먼 곳에 산다고 했으므로 그 모임은 캠퍼스에서 열릴 것임을 추론할 수 있다. 따라서 (D)가 정답이다.

38. *N* How are the speakers going to let club members know about the change in plans?

(A) The man will contact all the members.
(B) A radio announcement will be made.
(C) They will talk to the person in charge of publicity.
(D) They will each call some of the members.

[해석] *N* 화자들은 클럽 회원들에게 계획 변경을 어떻게 알릴 것인가?

(A) 남자가 모든 회원들에게 연락할 것이다.
(B) 라디오에서 발표할 것이다.
(C) 그들은 홍보 담당자에게 말할 것이다.
(D) 그들 각자 회원들에게 전화할 것이다.

[어휘] **contact** 연락하다 **in charge of** ~을 맡아서, 담당해서

[해설] 대화 후반부 여자의 말 I'll split the list with you. That way we'll each have only ten calls to make.에서 두 사람이 각자 회원들에게 전화를 걸어 변경된 모임 일정을 알릴 것임을 알 수 있다. 따라서 (D)가 정답이다.

Part C
Questions 39–42

N Listen to a talk by an anthropologist.

M [39]To continue our series of recordings from the museum's archives, this afternoon you will have the opportunity to hear a preeminent Native American storyteller, Joseph Medicine Crow. This museum is fortunate to have some of the recordings of legends and other stories he has collected from his native Crow culture, which is one of the Plains Indian groups.

[40]To understand the significance of these recordings, it is important to remember that the history and traditions of Native Americans were not written down. Instead they were passed down from one generation to the next by tribal storytellers. Often these storytellers were specially trained. They were chosen for the role when young and charged with remembering and sharing their people's oral history—a tradition that no longer exists.

[41]Joseph Medicine Crow recorded and saved the stories of his grandfather, one of the Crow people's last war chiefs. He also collected the memoirs of other tribal elders. [42]Today, the traditional tribal storytellers Joseph Crow knew as a young man are all gone, so he must now gather information from their children and grandchildren.

Now we'll hear a tape of this great storyteller as he recounts a legend of the Crow people. The slides you will see accompanying this story are pictures of artifacts of various Plains Indian cultures.

인류학자의 강연을 들어보세요.

M 박물관 아카이브의 녹음 테이프를 계속 살펴보기 위해, 오늘 오후에는 뛰어난 아메리카 원주민 이야기꾼인 조셉 메디슨 크로에 대해 들어보는 시간을 갖겠습니다. 다행히 이 박물관에는 그가 자신의 부족인 크로족 문화에서 수집한 전설과 다른 이야기들을 녹음한 기록물들이 있습니다. 크로족은 대평원 인디언 집단의 한 부족입니다.

이 기록물들의 중요성을 이해하기 위해, 아메리카 원주민들의 역사와 전통은 기록으로 남아있지 않다는 점을 기억하는 것이 중요합니다. 그 대신 그 역사와 전통들은 부족의 이야기꾼들에 의해 한 세대에서 다음 세대로 전해졌습니다. 종종 이 이야기꾼들은 특별한 훈련을 받기도 했습니다. 이들은 어릴 때 그 역할을 하도록 선발되어서 자기 부족의 구전 역사, 즉 더 이상 존재하지 않는 전통을 기억하고 공유하는 일을 담당했습니다.

조셉 메디슨 크로는 크로족의 마지막 전쟁 추장이었던 자신의 할아버지 이야기를 기록하여 남겼습니다. 그는 또한 다른 부족 원로들의 회고록도 수집했습니다. 오늘날, 조셉 크로가 젊었을 때 알던 전통적인 부족 이야기꾼들은 모두 사라져서, 그는 그들의 자녀나 손자들에게 정보를 수집해야만 합니다.

이제 우리는 이 위대한 이야기꾼의 (녹음) 테이프로 그가 이야기하는 크로족의 전설을 듣도록 하겠습니다. 이 이야기와 함께 여러분이 보게 될 슬라이드는 다양한 대평원 인디언 문화의 공예품 사진들입니다.

[어휘] anthropologist 인류학자   archive 아카이브, 기록 보관소   preeminent 탁월한   storyteller 이야기 작가, 소설가   legend 전설 (문학)   Plains Indian 대평원 인디언   significance 중요성, 중대성   tradition 전통, 관습   pass down (후세에) 전하다   generation 세대   tribal 부족의   be charged with ~ 책임을 맡고 있다   oral 구두의, 구술의   no longer 더 이상 ~아니다   memoir 회고록   elder 연장자, 조상   recount 이야기하다, 열거하다, 묘사하다   accompany 동반하다, 수반하다   artifact 공예품

---

39. N What is the speaker's main purpose?

(A) To introduce a recording of a Native American legend

(B) To encourage young people to become storytellers

(C) To compare oral and written traditions

(D) To tell a famous story

[해석] N 화자의 주요 목적은 무엇인가?

(A) 아메리카 원주민의 전설에 관한 녹음을 소개하려고

(B) 젊은이들에게 이야기꾼이 되도록 격려하려고

(C) 구전되는 전통과 기록으로 남겨진 전통을 비교하려고

(D) 유명한 이야기를 말하려고

[해설] 서두 부분 To continue our series of recordings from the museum's archives, this afternoon you will have the opportunity to hear a preeminent Native American storyteller, Joseph Medicine Crow.에서 화자는 박물관 아카이브의 녹음 기록물을 계속 살펴볼 것이라고 했으며, 아메리카 원주민 이야기꾼인 조셉 메디슨 크로에 대해 들어보는 시간을 갖겠다고 했다. 따라서 (A)가 정답이다.

---

40. N Why were storytellers important to Plains Indian cultures?

(A) They were used to teach children the language.

(B) They carried news from one tribe to another.

(C) They preserved the society's history.

(D) They served as chiefs.

[해석] N 평원 인디언 문화에서 이야기꾼들이 중요한 이유는 무엇인가?

(A) 그들은 아이들에게 언어를 가르쳤다.

(B) 그들은 한 부족에서 다른 부족으로 소식을 전했다.

(C) 그들은 그 사회의 역사를 보존했다.

(D) 그들은 추장으로 일했다.

[어휘] preserve 보존하다

[해설] 두 번째 단락의 To understand the significance of these recordings, it is important to remember that the history and traditions of Native Americans were not written down. Instead they were passed down from one generation to the next by tribal storytellers.에서 아메리카 원주민의 역사와 전통은 기록으로 남아 있지 않으며 부족의 이야기꾼들에 의해 한 세대에서 다음 세대로 전해졌다고 했다. 따라서 이야기꾼들은 그 사회의 역사를 보존하기 때문에 중요하다는 것을 알 수 있으므로 (C)가 정답이다.

---

41. N According to the talk, why are Joseph Medicine Crow's recordings especially important now?

(A) They are more comprehensive than earlier recordings.
(B) They provide income for the Crow people.
(C) Today's children do not enjoy Native American stories.
(D) Without recordings the stories might be forgotten.

[해석] *N* 담화에 따르면, 조셉 메디슨 크로의 녹음 기록이 오늘날 특히 중요한 이유는 무엇인가?

(A) 초기의 기록보다 더 광범위해서
(B) 크로족 사람들에게 소득을 제공해서
(C) 오늘날 아이들은 아메리카 원주민들의 이야기를 좋아하지 않아서
(D) 녹음 기록이 없다면 이야기가 잊혀질 수 있어서

[어휘] **comprehensive** 종합적인, 광범위한   **income** 수입, 소득

[해설] 세 번째 단락에서 조셉 메디슨 크로는 할아버지와 다른 부족의 원로들로부터 이야기를 수집했지만, 현재는 젊은 시절 알던 전통적인 부족 이야기꾼들이 모두 사라진 상황이라고 했다. 따라서, 조셉 메디슨 크로의 녹음 기록물이 전통적이 이야기들을 사라지지 않고 보존하는 방법이라는 것을 알 수 있으므로 (D)가 정답이다.

42. *N* Why does Joseph Medicine Crow collect material from storytellers' children?

(A) Children have better memories than adults do.
(B) The traditional storytellers have died.
(C) He is interested in the children's reactions.
(D) The storytellers are too busy to be interviewed.

[해석] *N* 조셉 메디슨 크로가 이야기꾼들의 자녀들에게 자료를 수집한 이유는 무엇인가?

(A) 아이들이 어른들보다 기억력이 더 좋아서
(B) 전통적인 이야기꾼들이 죽어서
(C) 아이들의 반응에 관심이 있어서
(D) 이야기꾼들이 너무 바빠서 인터뷰를 할 수 없어서

[어휘] **material** 자료, 소재   **reaction** 반응, 대응

[해설] 화자는 전통적인 부족 이야기꾼들이 사라진 상황이어서, 이야기꾼들의 자녀들에게서만 구전 역사를 들을 수 있다고 했다. 따라서 (B)가 정답이다.

Questions 43–46

N Listen to a professor in a business class.

W I hope you've all finished reading the assigned chapter on insurance—so that you're prepared for our discussion today. [43]But, before we start, I'd like to mention a few things your text doesn't go into.

It's interesting to note that insurance has existed in some form for a very long time. [44]The earliest insurance policies were what were called bottomry contracts. They provided shipping protection for merchants as far back as 3000 B.C.E.

In general, the contracts were often no more than verbal agreements. They granted loans to merchants with the understanding that if a particular shipment of goods was lost at sea, the loan didn't have to be repaid. [45]Interest on the loans varied according to how risky it was to transport the goods. During periods of heavy piracy at sea, for example, the amount of interest and the cost of the policy went up considerably.

So, you can see how insurance helped encourage international trade. Even the most cautious merchants became willing to risk shipping their goods over long distances—not to mention in hazardous weather conditions—when they had this kind of protection available.

[46]Generally speaking, the basic form of an insurance policy has been pretty much the same since the Middle Ages. There are four points that were salient then and remain paramount in all policies today. These were outlined in chapter six and will serve as the basis for the rest of today's discussion. Can anyone tell me what one of those points might be?

W 나는 여러분들이 과제로 내 준 보험에 관한 장을 모두 다 읽었기를 바랍니다. 그러면 여러분들은 오늘 논의할 준비가 된 것입니다. 하지만 시작하기 전에 여러분의 교과서에 언급되지 않은 몇 가지 내용을 언급하고자 합니다.

보험이 아주 오랫동안 어떤 형태로 존재해 왔다는 점은 주목할만한 흥미로운 사실입니다. 최초의 보험 증권은 이른바 선박 저당 계약이었습니다. 그 계약들은 기원전 3,000년으로 거슬러 올라가 상인들에게 선적 보호책을 제공했습니다.

일반적으로, 계약은 종종 구두 계약에 지나지 않았습니다. 만약 바다에서 특정 선적 물품을 분실하면, 그 대출을 상환하지 않아도 된다는 조건 하에 상인들에게 대출을 해주었습니다. 대출 이자는 물품 수송이 얼마나 위험한지에 따라 달랐습니다. 예를 들어, 해적의 약탈 행위가 기승을 부리는 기간 동안에는 이자의 액수와 보험료가 상당히 올라갔습니다.

따라서, 보험이 어떻게 국제 무역을 장려하는 데 도움이 되었는지 알 수 있을 것입니다. 가장 신중한 상인들조차도 이런 보호책이 있어서 험악한 날씨는 물론 위험을 무릅 쓰고 기꺼이 장거리 물품을 수송했습니다.

일반적으로 말해서, 보험 제도의 기본 형태는 중세 이후로 (오늘날과) 아주 같아졌습니다. 그 당시에 두드러진 점들이 4가지 있었는데 오늘날에도 모든 보험제도에서 가장 중요한 요소로 남아 있습니다. 이 요소들은 6장에 개략적으로 나와 있으며 이는 오늘 하게 될 토론의 기반이 될 것입니다. 그런 요소 중 하나가 무엇인지 말해 볼 사람 있습니까?

[어휘] **assign** 할당하다, 배정하다 **insurance** 보험 **go into** ~에 언급하다, ~을 연구하다 **insurance policy** 보험 증권, 보험 증서 **bottomry** 선박 저당 계약(선박을 담보로 항해 비용을 빌어 쓰는 계약) **contract** 계약(서) **merchant** 상인 **B.C.E.** 기원전(= Before the Common[Current, Christian] Era) **in general** 일반적으로, 대체로 **no more than** 단지 ~에 지나지 않다, ~일 뿐(= only) **verbal agreement** 구두 계약 **grant** 허가하다, 주다 **loan** 대출, 대여 **interest** 이자 **transport** 수송하다, 운반하다 **piracy** 해적 행위 **considerably** 꽤, 상당히 **international trade** 국제 무역 **cautious** 조심성 있는, 주의 깊은, 신중한 **not to mention** ~은 말할 것도 없고, ~은 물론 **hazardous** 위험한 **available** 이용할 수 있는 **generally speaking** 일반적으로 (말하면), 대부분은 **salient** 현저한, 두드러진 **paramount** 가장 중요한, 최고의 **outline** ~의 개요를 말하다, 약술하다 **basis** 기반, 기초

---

43. *N* What is the purpose of the professor's talk?

(A) To prepare students for the next reading assignment

(B) To provide background information for a class discussion

(C) To review material from a previous class

(D) To prepare for a quiz on chapter six

[해석] N 교수의 강의 목적은 무엇인가?

(A) 학생들에게 다음 읽기 과제를 준비시키려고
(B) 수업 시간에 토론할 주제에 대한 배경 지식을 알려 주려고
(C) 이전 수업에서 학습한 자료를 복습하려고
(D) 6장에 대한 퀴즈 시험을 준비하려고

[어휘] **assignment** 과제 **background information** 배경 지식 **review** 복습하다

[해설] 첫 단락의 But, before we start, I'd like to mention a few things your text doesn't go into.에서 교수는 토론을 시작하기 전에 교과서에 나오지 않는 몇 가지 부가 정보를 언급하겠다고 했다. 따라서 (B)가 정답이다.

---

44. *N* Who were the first insurance contracts designed to protect?

(A) Insurance companies

(B) Sailors

(C) Manufacturers

(D) Merchants

[해석] N 최초의 보험 계약은 누구를 보호하기 위한 것이었는가?

(A) 보험 회사
(B) 선원
(C) 생산자
(D) 상인

[어휘] **manufacturer** 제조업자, 생산자

[해설] 두 번째 단락의 The earliest insurance policies were what were called bottomry contracts. They provided shipping protection for merchants as far back as 3000 B.C.E.에서 최초의 계약은 선박 저당 계약이었는데, 이는 상인들을 보호하기 위한 것이라고 했으므로 (D)가 정답이다.

45. **N** What does the professor say determined the cost of early insurance policies?

(A) The distance the merchandise had to be shipped

(B) The number of insurance companies available at the time

(C) The amount of danger involved in shipping the goods

(D) The type of vessel used to transport the goods

[해석] *N* 교수는 초기의 보험료를 결정지었던 것은 무엇이라고 말하는가?

(A) 물품 수송 거리
(B) 그 당시 이용 가능했던 보험회사 수
(C) 물품 수송에 관련된 위험 정도
(D) 물품 수송에 사용된 배의 종류

[어휘] **available** 이용할 수 있는, 유용한　**vessel** 선박, 배

[해설] 세 번째 단락 Interest on the loans varied according to how risky it was to transport the goods. During periods of heavy piracy at sea, for example, the amount of interest and the cost of the policy went up considerably.에서 초기 보험은 대출이었으며, 대출 이자는 물품 수송의 위험도에 따라 달랐다고 했다. 그 일례로 해적의 약탈 행위가 기승을 부리는 기간 동안에는 이자의 액수와 보험료가 상당히 올라갔다고 했다. 따라서 (C)가 정답이다.

46. **N** What does the professor say about current insurance policies?

(A) Only four types of policies still exist today.

(B) They are cheaper than the ones in the Middle Ages.

(C) They include features similar to earlier policies.

(D) The interest rates are based on early methods of calculation.

[해석] *N* 교수는 현재의 보험 제도에 관해 뭐라고 말하는가?

(A) 오늘날은 네 가지 종류의 보험 제도만 존재한다.
(B) 중세의 보험 제도보다 더 저렴하다.
(C) 초기 제도와 유사한 점들이 있다.
(D) 이율이 초기 계산법에 근거한다.

[어휘] **current** 현재의, 지금의　**feature** 특징, 기능　**be based on** ~에 근거하다　**calculation** 계산

[해설] 다섯 번째 단락 Generally speaking, the basic form of an insurance policy has been pretty much the same since the Middle Ages. There are four points that were salient then and remain paramount in all policies today.에서 보험 제도의 기본 형태는 중세 이후로 (오늘날과) 아주 같아졌으며, 4가지 두드러진 점들이 있었는데 오늘날에도 모든 보험 제도에서 가장 중요한 요소로 남아 있다고 했다. 따라서 (C)가 정답이다.

Questions 47–50

N Listen to part of a talk about honeybees.

W Communication—what is communication? Some of you will say it is language. But is communication just limited to human language? [47]You might be surprised to learn that scientists have discovered that honeybees have a form of communication that is as complicated and as effective as human language. Honeybees communicate by dancing. [48]For example, when a honeybee finds food it returns to its hive and performs a dance. This dance communicates a message about the food. Basically, there are three types of dances: the round dance, the sickle dance, and the tail-wagging dance. In all three dances, the number of turns in the bee's dance tells the other bees how far the food is from the hive. The angle of the bee's dance in relation to the Sun tells the direction of food from the hive.

[49]So you see, honeybees communicate using one form of nonverbal communication. [50]Can anyone suggest another form of nonverbal communication used by animals?

[해석] N 꿀벌에 관한 담화의 일부를 들어 보세요.

W 의사소통 — 의사소통이란 무엇인가? 여러분 중 일부는 의사소통은 언어라고 말할 것입니다. 하지만 의사소통이 단지 인간의 언어에만 한정될까요? 아마도 여러분은 과학자들이 꿀벌들도 인간의 언어만큼 복잡하고 효과적인 의사소통의 형태를 갖고 있다는 사실을 발견했다는 것을 알게 된다면 놀랄 것입니다. 꿀벌들은 춤을 춰서 의사소통을 합니다. 예를 들어, 꿀벌 한 마리가 먹이를 발견하면 그 꿀벌은 벌집으로 돌아가 춤을 춥니다. 이 춤은 먹이를 발견했다는 메시지를 전달합니다. 기본적으로, 세 가지 종류의 춤이 있습니다. 원 모양 춤과 낫 모양 춤, 꼬리를 흔드는 춤이 있습니다. 모든 세 가지 춤에서, 꿀벌이 추는 춤의 회전 수로 그 먹이가 벌집에서 얼마나 멀리 떨어져 있는지를 다른 꿀벌들에게 알립니다. 태양과 관련된 꿀벌의 춤의 각도로 벌집으로부터 먹이가 있는 방향을 알립니다.

이제 꿀벌들은 비언어적인 의사소통 형태를 이용해 의사소통을 하고 있다는 점을 알 수 있습니다. 동물들이 사용하는 또 다른 비언어적인 의사소통 형태에 대해 이야기해 볼 사람 있나요?

[어휘] **honeybee** 꿀벌 **communication** 통신, 의사소통 **complicated** 복잡한 **effective** 효력이 있는, 효과적인 **communicate** 의사소통하다 **hive** 벌집 **basically** 기본적으로 **sickle** 낫 (모양) **tail-wagging** 꼬리 흔드는 **angle** 각, 각도 **direction** 방향 **nonverbal** 말을 쓰지 않는

47. *N* What aspect of honeybees does the speaker discuss?

(A) How they enjoy their food

(B) How they communicate with each other

(C) How they depend on the Sun

(D) How they learn different dances

[해석] N 화자는 꿀벌의 어떤 측면에 관해 이야기하고 있는가?

(A) 먹이를 먹는 방법

(B) 서로 의사소통하는 방법

(C) 태양에 의존하는 방법

(D) 다른 춤을 배우는 방법

[어휘] **aspect** 측면, 양상

[해설] 서두 부분의 Communication — what is communication? 에서 화자는 의사소통에 관해 논의할 것임을 알 수 있으며, 네 번째 문장 You might be surprised to learn that scientists have discovered that honeybees have a form of communication that is as complicated and as effective as human language. 이하에서 꿀벌들이 서로 의사소통하는 방법에 대해 이야기했다. 따라서 (B)가 정답이다.

48. *N* According to the speaker, what does the honeybee communicate through its dances?

(A) A signal that it is tired

(B) A message about a food source

(C) Acceptance of another honeybee to its hive

(D) A warning that danger is near

[해석] N 화자에 따르면, 꿀벌들은 춤을 통해 무엇을 의사소통하는가?

(A) 피곤하다는 신호

(B) 먹이가 있는 곳에 대한 메시지

(C) 벌집에 다른 벌이 들어오는 것에 대한 허용

(D) 위험이 가까이에 있다는 경고

[어휘] **acceptance** 수락, 허용

[해설] 중반부의 For example, when a honeybee finds food it returns to its hive and performs a dance.에서 꿀벌들은 춤을 통해 먹이 위치에 관한 정보를 전달한다고 했다. 따라서 (B)가 정답이다.

49. *N* What does the speaker say about the honeybee's system of communication?

(A) It is not verbal.

(B) It is not informative.

(C) It is not effective.

(D) It is not complicated.

[해석] N 화자는 꿀벌의 의사소통 체계에 관해 뭐라고 말하는가?

(A) 비언어적이다.

(B) 유익하지 않다.

(C) 효과적이지 않다.

(D) 복잡하지 않다.

[어휘] **verbal** 언어적인 **informative** 유익한, 지식을 주는

[해설] 담화를 요약한 후반부 단락의 첫 문장 So you see, honeybees communicate using one form of nonverbal communication.에서 꿀벌들은 비언어적인 의사소통을 한다고 했다. 따라서 (A)가 정답이다.

50. *N* What does the speaker ask the listeners to do at the end of the talk?

(A) Read the chapters on honeybee communication

(B) Discuss the different ways humans communicate

(C) Give examples of other types of animal communication

(D) Write a paper on the various forms of communication

[해석] *N* 화자는 담화의 마지막 부분에서 청자들에게 어떻게 하라고 요청하는가?

(A) 꿀벌의 의사소통에 관한 장을 읽을 것
(B) 인간들이 의사소통하는 다른 방법들에 관해 논의할 것
(C) 다른 형태의 동물 의사소통에 대한 예를 제시할 것
(D) 다양한 의상소통 형태에 관한 리포트를 작성할 것

[해설] 화자는 담화의 마지막 문장 Can anyone suggest another form of nonverbal communication used by animals?에서 학생들에게 동물들의 비언어적인 의사소통의 다른 예를 제시해 보라고 요청했다. 따라서 (C)가 정답이다.

– 본문 p.72

Structure

1. (D)	2. (B)	3. (D)	4. (B)	5. (A)
6. (C)	7. (B)	8. (A)	9. (B)	10. (D)
11. (B)	12. (C)	13. (B)	14. (D)	15. (D)

Written Expression

16. A	17. B	18. C	19. C	20. D
21. A	22. A	23. D	24. B	25. B
26. C	27. B	28. C	29. C	30. A
31. B	32. D	33. C	34. C	35. A
36. D	37. A	38. A	39. C	40. A

Structure

1. Simple photographic lenses cannot ------- sharp, undistorted images over a wide field.

(A) to form
(B) are formed
(C) forming
(D) form

[해석] 카메라 단렌즈로 넓은 들판에 대해서 선명하고 왜곡되지 않은 상을 잡아낼 수 없다.

[어휘] sharp 선명한, 뚜렷한   undistorted 왜곡되지 않은, 뒤틀리지 않은

[해설] 조동사 can이나 부정형인 cannot 뒤에는 동사원형이 와야 한다. 따라서 (D)가 정답이다.

2. Of all the factors affecting agricultural yields, weather is the one ------- the most.

(A) it influences farmers
(B) that influences farmers
(C) farmers that it influences
(D) why farmers influence it

[해석] 농업 생산량에 영향을 미치는 요인들 중에서 날씨가 농부들에게 가장 영향을 많이 주는 요인이다.

[어휘] affect 영향을 미치다   agricultural 농업의   yield 생산량, 산출액

CHAPTER 5

[해설] 빈칸에는 앞의 the one을 수식하는 말이 필요한데, 관계대명사절 that influences farmers the most가 the one을 수식할 수 있다. 따라서 (B)가 정답이다.

3. Beverly Sills, -------, assumed directorship of the New York City Opera in 1979.

(A) be a star soprano

(B) was a star soprano

(C) a star soprano and

(D) a star soprano

[해석] 스타 소프라노인 비벌리 실스가 1979년에 뉴욕 시 오페라의 감독직을 맡았다.

[어휘] assume (책임을) 지다, (임무·역할 등을) 떠맡다 directorship 감독직, 이사직

[해설] Beverly Sills, _____이 문장의 주어이고, assumed가 동사인 문장이다. 빈칸에는 주어인 Beverly Sills의 동격 어구가 들어가야 하므로, 명사구 (D)가 정답이다.

4. ------- of tissues is known as histology.

(A) Studying scientific

(B) The scientific study

(C) To study scientifically

(D) That is scientific studying

[해석] 조직에 대한 과학적인 연구는 조직학으로 알려져 있다.

[어휘] tissue 조직 be known as ~로 알려지다 histology 조직학

[해설] _____ of tissues가 문장의 주어이므로, 빈칸에는 문장의 주어 역할을 할 수 있는 명사구가 들어가야 한다. 따라서 (B)가 정답이다.

5. With the exception of mercury, ------- at standard temperature and pressure.

(A) the metallic elements are solid

(B) which is a solid metallic element

(C) metallic elements being solid

(D) since the metallic elements are solid

[해석] 수은을 제외하고, 금속 원소들은 표준 온도와 압력에서 고체 상태이다.

[어휘] with the exception of ~을 제외하고 mercury 수은 standard temperature 표준 온도 cf. absolute temperature 절대 온도 pressure 압력 metallic 금속의 element 원소; 구성요소 solid 고체

[해설] With the exception of mercury는 전치사구이며, 빈칸에는 주어와 동사가 들어가야 완전한 문장이 된다. 따라서 (A)가 정답이다.

6. Dehydration is ------- that a land animal faces.

(A) the often greatest hazard

(B) the greatest often hazard

(C) often the greatest hazard

(D) often the hazard greatest

[해석] 탈수 증상은 육상 동물들이 종종 직면하는 가장 큰 위험 요소이다.

[어휘] dehydration 탈수(증) face 직면하다, 대담하게 맞서다 hazard 위험, 위험 요소

[해설] 어순을 묻는 문제이다. 빈도부사 often은 be동사 뒤에 와야 하며, 정관사 the와 최상급 형용사 greatest는 명사 hazard 앞에 와야 한다. 따라서 (C)가 정답이다.

7. By tracking the eye of a hurricane, forecasters can determine the speed at which -------.

(A) is a storm moving

(B) a storm is moving

(C) is moving a storm

(D) a moving storm

[해석] 기상 통보관들은 태풍의 눈을 추적하여 태풍의 이동 속도를 판단할 수 있다.

[어휘] track 추적하다 forecaster 기상 통보관, 일기 예보관 determine 판단하다, 결정하다

[해설] 관계대명사절의 구조를 묻는 문제이다. at which 다음에 주어와 동사가 와야 하므로 (B)가 정답이다.

8. The publication of *Adventures of Huckleberry Finn* helped make Mark Twain one of America's ------- literary figures.

(A) most famous

(B) the most famous

(C) are most famous

(D) and most famous

[해석] 〈허클베리 핀의 모험〉의 출판으로 마크 트웨인은 미국에서 가장 유명한 문학인들 중의 한 사람이 되었다.

[어휘] **publication** 출판, 발행 **literary** 문학의, 문학적인 **figure** 인물

[해설] 빈칸 뒤의 literary figures를 수식하는 형용사구가 들어가야 하므로 (A)가 정답이다. 소유격(America's) 뒤에는 정관사 the를 쓸 수 없으므로 (B)는 정답이 될 수 없다.

9. Technology will play a key role in ------- future lifestyles.

(A) to shape

(B) shaping

(C) shape of

(D) shaped

[해석] 과학 기술은 미래의 생활 방식들을 형성하는 데 중요한 역할을 할 것이다.

[어휘] **technology** 과학 기술 **play a key role** 중요한 역할을 하다 **shape** 형성하다

[해설] 전치사 뒤에 동사가 올 때는 -ing 형태(동명사)가 와야 하므로 (B)가 정답이다.

10. The computer has dramatically affected ------- many products are designed.

(A) is the way

(B) that the way

(C) which way do

(D) the way

[해석] 컴퓨터는 많은 제품들이 디자인되는 방식에 아주 큰 영향을 미쳐 왔다.

[어휘] **dramatically** 극적으로, 크게 **affect** 영향을 미치다 **product** 제품, 생산품

[해설] 빈칸에는 동사 affected의 목적어가 필요하므로 명사구 (D)가 정답이다. many products are designed는 관계사절로 앞의 선행사 the way를 수식한다.

11. The early railroads were ------- the existing arteries of transportation : roads, turnpikes, and canals and other waterways.

(A) those short lines connected

(B) short lines that connected

(C) connected by short lines

(D) short connecting lines

[해석] 초기의 철도는 기존 운송의 동맥이었던 도로와 유료 고속도로, 운하, 다른 수로들에 연결된 짧은 노선이었다.

[어휘] **artery** 동맥; (도로·철도 등의) 간선 **turnpike** 유료 고속도로 **canal** 운하 **waterway** 수로

[해설] The early railroads가 문장의 주어, were가 동사로, 빈칸에는 were의 보어가 되는 명사구가 적절하다. 따라서 (B)가 정답이다. that connected에서 that은 주격 관계대명사, connected는 관계대명사절의 동사로, that 이하는 short lines를 수식한다.

12. ------- as a masterpiece, a work of art must transcend the ideals of the period in which it was created.

(A) Ranks

(B) The ranking

(C) To be ranked

(D) For being ranked

[해석] 걸작으로 평가되려면, 예술 작품은 제작된 시대의 이상을 초월해야 한다.

[어휘] **masterpiece** 걸작, 명작 **work of art** 예술 작품, 미술품 **transcend** 초월하다, 능가하다 **ideal** 이상, 전형 **rank** (등급·등위·순위를) 매기다, 평가하다

[해설] 빈칸에 to부정사구가 들어가야 문장이 문법적으로 완성된다. 따라서 (C)가 정답이다. 참고로, 여기서 to는 in order to(~하기 위해서)의 의미를 나타낸다.

13. Jackie Robinson, ------- to play baseball in the major leagues, joined the Brooklyn Dodgers in 1947.

(A) the African American who first

(B) the first African American

(C) was the first African American

(D) the first and an African American who

[해석] 재키 로빈슨은 메이저리그에서 야구를 한 최초의 흑인 선수로 1947년 브루클린 다저스에 입단했다.

[해설] Jackie Robinson과 _____ to play baseball in the major leagues는 동격 어구로, 빈칸에는 주어를 보충 설명하는 명사구가 들어가야 한다. 따라서 (B)가 정답이다.

14. During the flood of 1927, the Red Cross, ------- out of emergency headquarters in Mississippi, set up temporary shelters for the homeless.

(A) operates
(B) is operating
(C) has operated
(D) operating

[해석] 1927년 홍수가 났을 때, 미시시피에 비상 본부를 운영했던 적십자는 집 없는 사람들을 위해 임시 대피소를 설치했다.

[어휘] **flood** 홍수   **emergency** 비상용의, 긴급의   **headquarters** 본부, 본사   **set up** 설치하다   **temporary shelter** 임시 대피소   **the homeless** 집 없는 사람들(= homeless people)   **operate** 운영하다

[해설] the Red Cross가 주어이고, set up이 동사인 문장으로 빈칸에는 the Red Cross를 수식하여 형용사 역할을 하는 분사가 들어가야 한다. 따라서 (D)가 정답이다.

15. In bacteria and in other organisms, ------- is DNA that provides the genetic information.

(A) both
(B) which
(C) and
(D) it

[해석] 박테리아와 다른 유기체에서 유전 정보를 제공하는 것은 바로 DNA이다.

[어휘] **organism** 유기체   **genetic** 유전적인

[해설] It ~ that 강조 구문으로, 문장의 주어 DNA를 강조하고 있다. 따라서 빈칸에는 (D) it이 들어가야 한다.

Written Expression

16. Twenty to **thirty year** after a mature forest is
  (A) .... (is)
cleared away, a nearly impenetrable thicket of
  B   C
trees and shrubs develops.
                      D

[해석] 다 자란 산림이 개간된 후 20~30년이 지나야 햇빛이 거의 통하지 않을 만큼 우거진 덤불과 관목들이 조성된다.

[어휘] **mature** 성숙한, 완전히 자란   **clear away** 개간하다, 개척하다   **impenetrable** 꿰뚫을 수 없는, 광선이 통하지 않는   **thicket** 덤불, 잡목 숲   **shrub** 관목

[해설] thirty는 복수이므로 그 뒤에는 단수형 year가 아니라 복수형 years가 와야 한다. 따라서 (A)가 정답이다.

17. The first national park **in world**, Yellowstone
  A   B
National Park, was established in 1872.
                C   D

[해석] 전 세계적으로 최초의 국립 공원인 옐로스톤 국립 공원은 1872년에 설립되었다.

[어휘] **establish** 설립하다

[해설] 일반적으로 유일무이한 천체나 방위를 나타내는 명사 앞에는 정관사 the를 붙인다. 따라서 in world가 아니라 in the world가 되어야 하므로 (B)가 정답이다.

18. Because it does not have a blood supply, the
  A   B
cornea takes **their** oxygen directly from the air.
                C   D

[해석] 각막에는 혈액이 공급되지 않기 때문에 공기에서 직접 산소를 흡수한다.

[어휘] **cornea** 각막   **oxygen** 산소

[해설] 주어 the cornea는 단수이므로, 소유격은 their가 아닌 its가 되어야 한다. 따라서 (C)가 정답이다.

19. Magnificent mountains and coastal scenery is
                A   B   C
British Columbia's chief tourist attractions.
                      C

[해석] 웅장한 산과 해안 경치는 브리티시 컬럼비아 주의 주요 관광 명소이다.

[어휘] **magnificent** 장대한, 웅장한   **scenery** 경치   **tourist attraction** 관광 명소

[해설] 주어가 Magnificent mountains and coastal scenery(복수)이므로 동사는 is가 아닌 are가 되어야 한다. 따라서 (C)가 정답이다.

20. Scientists at <u>universities</u> are <u>often</u> more <u>involved</u>
                     A   B   C
in theoretical research than in **practically**
                               (D)
research.

[해석] 대학의 과학자들은 종종 실용적인 연구보다 이론적인 연구에 더 몰두한다.

[어휘] **be involved in** ~에 몰두하다, 연루되다
theoretical 이론적인, 이론상의 **research** 연구, 탐구

[해설] 명사 research를 수식할 수 있는 품사는 부사가 아니라 형용사이므로 부사 practically가 아니라 형용사인 practical이 와야 한다. 따라서 (D)가 정답이다.

21. John Rosamond Johnson **he composed**
                               (A)
numerous <u>songs</u>, <u>including</u> *Lift Every Voice*
            B   C
and Sing, <u>for which</u> his brother, James Weldon
              D
Johnson, wrote the words.

[해석] 존 로저먼드 존슨은 형인 제임스 웰던 존슨이 작사를 한 〈모두 소리 높여 노래하자〉를 포함해 수많은 노래를 작곡했다.

[어휘] **compose** 작곡하다 **numerous** 매우 많은, 무수한
words 가사

[해설] John Rosamond Johnson이 문장의 주어, composed가 동사인 문장으로 주격 인칭대명사 he는 필요하지 않다. 따라서 (A)가 정답이다.

22. Nylon, a synthetic material **done** from a
                              (A)
<u>combination</u> of water, air, and a by-product <u>of</u>
    B   C
<u>coal</u>, was first <u>introduced</u> in 1938.
                 D

[해석] 물과 공기, 석탄 부산물을 혼합해 만들어진 합성섬유인 나일론은 1938년에 처음 소개되었다.

[어휘] **synthetic** 합성의, 인조의 **combination** 혼합, 화합물 **by-product** 부산물 **coal** 석탄

[해설] 문맥상 '물, 공기와 석탄 부산물의 혼합으로 만들어진 합성 섬유'라는 의미가 되어야 하므로 done이 아니라 made가 되어야 한다. 따라서 (A)가 정답이다.

23. Ornithology, the study of birds, is one of the <u>major</u>
                                            A
scientific <u>fields</u> in which amateurs <u>play</u> a role in
          B   C
accumulating, researching, and **publish** data.
                                  (D)

[해석] 새를 연구하는 조류학은 비전문가들이 자료를 모으고, 연구하고, 공표하는 역할을 하는 주요 과학 분야들 중의 하나이다.

[어휘] **ornithology** 조류학 **field** 분야, 영역 **amateur** 아마추어, 비전문가 **play a role** 역할을 하다 **accumulate** 모으다, 축적하다

[해설] and 앞에 있는 accumulating, researching과 병렬 구조를 이루어야 하므로, publish가 아니라 publishing이 되어야 한다. 따라서 (D)가 정답이다.

24. Animation is a <u>technique</u> for **creativity** the illusion
                        A   **(B)**
of <u>life</u> in inanimate <u>things</u>.
    C   D

[해석] 애니메이션은 생명이 없는 것들을 생명이 있는 것처럼 착각하도록 만드는 기법이다

[어휘] **technique** 기술, 기법 **illusion** 착각, 환상
inanimate 생명이 없는, 죽은, 무생물의

[해설] 전치사 for의 목적어인 동시에 the illusion이라는 목적어를 취하고 있으므로, 명사 creativity가 아닌 동명사 creating이 되어야 한다. 따라서 (B)가 정답이다.

25. The nonviolent protest <u>advocated</u> by Dr. Martin
                                  A
Luther King, Jr., **proving** highly effective in an age
                  (B)
of <u>expanding</u> television news <u>coverage</u>.
    C   D

[해석] 마틴 루터 킹이 지지한 비폭력 저항 운동은 TV 뉴스 보도가 확대된 시대에 아주 효과적인 것으로 입증되었다.

[어휘] **nonviolent** 비폭력(주의)의 **protest** 항의
advocate 지지하다, 옹호하다 **effective** 유효한, 효과적인 **expand** 확장하다, 넓히다 **coverage** 보도, 취재 범위

[해설] The nonviolent protest (advocated by Dr. Martin Luther King, Jr.)가 문장의 주어로 뒤에는 동사가 와야 한다. 따라서 proving을 proved로 고쳐야 한다. (B)가 정답이다.

26. On December 7, 1787, Delaware became **a** first
    A   B   **C**
state to ratify the United States Constitution.
      D

[해석] 1787년 12월 7일에 델라웨어 주는 미합중국 헌법을 승인한
첫 번째 주가 되었다.

[어휘] **ratify** 승인하다, 비준하다, 인가하다   **constitution**
헌법

[해설] 서수(first) 앞에는 정관사 the를 써야 하므로, a가 아니라
the가 되어야 한다. 따라서 (C)가 정답이다.

27. Nutritionists believe **what** diet affects how one
        A   **B**   C
feels physically and emotionally.
      D

[해석] 영양학자들은 식단에 따라 사람이 신체적 · 감정적으로 어
떻게 느끼는지 영향을 받는다고 믿는다.

[어휘] **nutritionist** 영양학자, 영양사   **affect** 영향을 미치다
physically 육체적으로, 물리적으로   **emotionally**
감정적으로

[해설] Nutritionists가 문장의 주어, believe가 동사이며, what
이하는 동사 believe의 목적어 역할을 하고 있다. 따라서
what이 아니라 명사절을 이끄는 접속사 that이 되어야 하
므로, (B)가 정답이다.

28. Mealii Kalama, creator of over 400 Hawaiian
                        A
quilts, was granted a National Heritage Fellowship
      B
in 1985 for **herself** contributions to folk art.
           C   D

[해석] 400여 개 이상의 하와이안 퀼트를 창시한 미알리 칼라마는
민속 예술에 대한 공헌으로 1985년에 내셔널 헤리티지 펠로
십을 수여받았다.

[어휘] **creator** 창시자, 고안자   **quilt** 퀼트   **grant** 주다,
수여하다   **contribution** 공헌, 기여

[해설] herself가 있는 자리는 뒤의 명사 contributions를 수식
하는 형용사 역할을 하고 있으므로, 재귀대명사 herself가
아닌 소유격 her가 와야 한다. 따라서 (C)가 정답이다.

29. A jetty serves to define and deepen a channel,
           A   B
improve **navigate**, or protect a harbor.
          C   D

[해석] 방파제는 해협의 경계를 분명히 나타내고 강화하며, 항해를
증진시키거나 항구를 보호하는 역할을 한다.

[어휘] **jetty** 둑, 방파제, 부두   **define** (한계나 범위를) 분명히
나타내다, 정의하다   **deepen** 깊게 하다, 강화하다
channel 해협, 수로   **navigate** 항해하다
cf. navigation 항해   **harbor** 항구, 항만

[해설] improve의 목적어이자 channel이나 harbor와 병
렬 구조를 이뤄야 하므로 navigate이 아니라 명사형
navigation이 되어야 한다. 따라서 (C)가 정답이다.

30. Minoru Yamasaki achieved a reputation as an

architect **which** works departed from the austerity
         A   B
frequently associated with architecture after the
      C   D
Second World War.

[해석] 미노루 야마사키는 건축가로서의 명성을 얻었는데, 그의 작
품은 제2차 세계대전 후의 건축 양식에서 흔히 연상되는 엄
격성에서 탈피했다.

[어휘] **reputation** 평판, 명성   **architect** 건축가   **depart**
벗어나다, 빗나가다; 출발하다   **austerity** 준엄, 엄격
associate 연상하다, 관련시키다   **architecture**
건축학, 건축 양식

[해설] 선행사가 an architect(사람)이고, 명사 works를 수식해
야 하므로, 주격 관계대명사 which가 아니라 소유격 관계
대명사 whose가 되어야 한다. 따라서 정답은 (A)이다.

31. Chemical research provides information
                    A
that is useful **when** the textile industry in the
          B   C
development of new fabrics.
      D

[해석] 화학 연구는 섬유 산업에서 새로운 직물을 개발하는 데 유
용한 정보를 제공한다.

[어휘] **chemical** 화학의, 화학적인   **research** 연구, 조사
textile 직물, 섬유   **fabric** 옷감, 직물

[해설] the textile industry (in the development of new
fabrics)는 명사구로 절이 아니기 때문에 접속사 when은
맞지 않다. 또한 앞의 useful과 함께 어울려 쓸 수 있어야
하므로 전치사 for가 적절하다. 따라서 (B)가 정답이다.

32. Because of <u>its</u> vast tracts of <u>virtually</u> uninhabited

　　　_A　　　　　　　_B

northern forest, Canada has <u>one</u> of the lowest

　　　　　　　　　　　_C

population **density** in the world.

　　　　　D

[해석] 캐나다는 사실상 사람이 살지 않는 북부 산림 지대의 광대
한 지역으로 인해 전 세계에서 인구 밀도가 가장 낮은 나라
중의 하나이다.

[어휘] **vast** 굉장히 넓은, 광대한　**tract** 넓은 공간; 지방, 지역
virtually 사실상, 실질적으로는, 거의　**uninhabited**
사람이 없는, 사람이 살지 않는　**population density**
인구 밀도

[해설] '가장 ~한 것 중의 하나'라고 할 때는 〈one of the+최상급
형용사+복수명사〉의 형태가 되어야 한다. 따라서 단수형인
density가 아니라 복수형인 densities가 되어야 하므로,
(D)가 정답이다.

33. Bromyrite crystals <u>have</u> a diamond-like luster

　　　　　　　_A

and are usually <u>colorless</u>, but they **dark** to brown

　　　　　　_B　　　　　**C**

when <u>exposed</u> to light.

　　　_D

[해석] 취은광 결정은 다이아몬드 같은 광채가 나며 보통 무색이
지만, 빛에 노출되면 갈색으로 색이 짙어진다.

[어휘] **bromyrite** 취은광　**crystal** 결정(체), 수정　**luster**
광택, 광채　**colorless** 빛깔이 없는, 무색의　**expose**
노출시키다

[해설] 주어 they(= Bromyrite crystals) 뒤에는 동사가 와야 하
므로 형용사인 dark가 아니라 동사인 darken이 되어야
한다. 따라서 (C)가 정답이다.

34. <u>Stars</u> in our universe vary <u>in</u> temperature, color,

　　_A　　　　　　　_B

bright, size, and <u>mass</u>.

　C　　　　　_D

[해석] 우주의 별들은 온도, 색깔, 밝기, 크기 및 질량이 다양하다.

[어휘] **temperature** 온도, 기온　**mass** 질량; 집단, 덩어리

[해설] bright은 전치사 in의 목적어이며, temperature, color,
size, mass와 병렬 구조를 이뤄야 하므로 명사형인
brightness가 되어야 한다. 따라서 (C)가 정답이다.

35. Ice is less **denser** than the liquid <u>from which</u> <u>it</u> is

　　　　　A　　_B　　　　_C　　_D

formed.

[해석] 얼음은 액체에서 형성되는데 액체보다 그 밀도가 더 낮다.

[어휘] **dense** (물질이) 고밀도의　**liquid** 액체

[해설] less 뒤에는 비교급이 아닌 원급이 와야 하므로 denser가
아닌 dense가 되어야 한다. 따라서 (A)가 정답이다.

36. The 1983 Nobel Prize in Medicine <u>was awarded</u>

　　　　　　　　　　　　　　　　_A

to Barbara McClintock for her <u>experiments with</u>

　　　　　　　　　　　　　_B

maize and her <u>discoveries</u> **regardless** the nature

　　　　　　_C　　　　**D**

of DNA.

[해석] 1983년 노벨 의학상은 옥수수 실험과 DNA의 특성에 대한
발견으로 바바라 맥클린톡에게 수여되었다.

[어휘] **award** 상을 주다, 수여하다　**experiment** 실험, 시험
maize 옥수수　**regardless** 개의치 않고　**nature**
성질, 특징

[해설] 문맥상 '~에 관한'이라는 의미가 되어야 하므로
regardless가 아니라 regarding이 되어야 한다. 따라서
(D)가 정답이다.

37. **In** 1866 to 1883, the bison population in North

　　A

America <u>was reduced</u> from an <u>estimated</u> 13

　　　　_B　　　　　　_C

million to a few <u>hundred</u>.

　　　　　　_D

[해석] 1866년부터 1883년까지 북아메리카에서 들소의 개체 수는
어림잡아 1,300만 마리에서 수백 마리로 감소되었다.

[어휘] **bison** 들소(아메리카들소(buffalo)와 유럽들소(wisent)
의 총칭)　**population** 인구, 주민 수, 개체군
reduce 감소시키다　**estimated** 어림의, 추측의

[해설] 'A부터 B까지'라는 의미로 기간을 나타낼 때는 from A to
B라고 표현하므로, In이 아니라 From이 되어야 한다. 따
라서 (A)가 정답이다.

38. Most of the **damage property** attributed <u>to</u> the

　　　　　　A　　　　　　　　　_B

San Francisco earthquake <u>of</u> 1906 resulted from

　　　　　　　　　　　_C

the fire <u>that followed</u>.

　　　　_D

CHAPTER 5

[해석] 1906년에 일어난 샌프란시스코 지진으로 인한 대부분의 재산 피해는 지진에 이어 일어난 화재 탓이었다.

[어휘] **property** 재산, 자산　**attribute** (원인을) ~에 돌리다, (~의) 탓으로 하다 *cf.* be attributed to ~에 기인하다　**earthquake** 지진　**result from** ~의 결과로 생기다

[해설] '재산 피해'라는 표현인 property damage를 알면 쉽게 풀 수 있는 문제이다. 만약 이 표현을 모른다면, 어순을 살펴본다. 여기서는 property가 damage를 수식하는 역할을 하고 있으므로, 어순이 damage property가 아니라 property damage가 되어야 한다. 따라서 (A)가 정답이다.

39. James Baldwin's plays and short stories, which (A) are to some degree (B) autobiographical, established them (C) as a leading (D) figure in the United States civil rights movement.

[해석] 어느 정도는 자전적인 희곡과 단편 소설들로 제임스 볼드윈은 미국 민권 운동의 지도자로 자리잡게 되었다.

[어휘] **play** 연극, 희곡　**to some degree** 어느 정도　**autobiographical** 자서전적인, 자서전체의　**leading figure** 지도자, 거물, 큰 인물　**civil rights movement** 민권 운동

[해설] 동사 established 뒤에는 James Baldwin을 가리키는 지시대명사가 와야 하므로, them이 아니라 him이 되어야 한다. 따라서 (C)가 정답이다.

40. Thunder can be listened (A) from a maximum (B) distance of about ten miles except (C) under unusual (D) atmospheric conditions.

[해석] 천둥 소리는 이례적인 대기 조건이 아닌 경우를 제외하고는 최대 10마일 정도 떨어진 거리에서도 들릴 수 있다.

[어휘] **thunder** 천둥, 우레　**maximum** 최대의, 최고의　**except** ~ 이외에는, ~을 제외하고는　**unusual** 예외적인, 이례적인　**atmospheric** 대기의, 대기 속의, 공기의

[해설] listen과 hear의 의미 차이를 묻는 문제로, listen은 '자신이 원해서 의도적으로 듣다'라는 의미이고, hear는 '의지와 관계없이 저절로 들리다'라는 의미이다. 따라서 listened가 아니라 heard가 되어야 하므로 (A)가 정답이다.

Section 3 Reading Comprehension – 본문 p.80

1. (A)	2. (D)	3. (A)	4. (C)	5. (C)
6. (B)	7. (D)	8. (D)	9. (B)	10. (C)
11. (D)	12. (B)	13. (C)	14. (D)	15. (A)
16. (D)	17. (B)	18. (D)	19. (C)	20. (C)
21. (A)	22. (C)	23. (A)	24. (A)	25. (A)
26. (B)	27. (B)	28. (C)	29. (D)	30. (A)
31. (C)	32. (A)	33. (C)	34. (D)	35. (A)
36. (D)	37. (C)	38. (B)	39. (A)	40. (B)
41. (A)	42. (C)	43. (B)	44. (C)	45. (D)
46. (C)	47. (C)	48. (B)	49. (C)	50. (B)

Questions 1–10

[1]In past centuries, Native Americans living in the arid areas of what is now the southwestern United States relied on a variety of strategies to ensure the success of their agriculture. First and foremost, [10]water was the critical factor. The soil was rich because there was little rain to leach out the minerals, but the low precipitation caused its own problems. Long periods of drought could have made agriculture impossible; on the other hand, a sudden flood could just as easily have destroyed a crop.

Several techniques were developed to [2]solve the water problem. [3]The simplest was to plant crops in the floodplains and wait for the annual floods to water the young crops. A less dangerous technique was to build dikes or dams to control the flooding. These dikes both protected the plants against excessive flooding and prevented the water from escaping too quickly once it had arrived. The Hopi people designed their fields in a checkerboard pattern, with many small dikes, each [4]enclosing only one or two stalks of maize (corn), while other groups built a series of dams to control the floods. A third technique was to dig irrigation ditches to bring water from the rivers. Water was sometimes carried to the fields in jars, particularly if the season was dry. Some crops were planted where [5]they could be watered directly by the runoff from cliff walls.

200

⁶Another strategy Native Americans used to ensure a continuous food supply was to plant their crops in more than one place, hoping that if one crop failed, another would survive. ⁸However, since the soil was rich and not easily exhausted, the same ⁷patch of ground could be cultivated year after year, whereas in the woodlands of the eastern United States it was necessary to abandon a plot of ground after a few years of farming. In the Southwest, often two successive crops were planted each year.

¹⁰It was a common southwestern practice to grow enough food so that some could be dried and stored for emergencies. ⁹If emergency supplies ran low, the people turned to the local wild plants. If these failed, they moved up into the mountains to gather the wild plants that might have survived in the cooler atmosphere.

[해석] 지난 세기 동안, 오늘닐 미국의 남시부 지역인 불모지에 살던 아메리카 원주민들은 농사를 성공시키기 위해 다양한 전략에 의존했다. 무엇보다도 먼저, 물이 결정적으로 중요한 요인이었다. 비가 거의 내리지 않아 무기질이 침출되지 않았기 때문에 토양은 비옥했지만, 적은 강수량으로 인한 문제가 발생했다. 오랜 기간의 가뭄으로 인해 농사를 짓는 것이 불가능했다. 반면에 갑작스런 홍수로 인해 농작물을 쉽게 망칠 수도 있었다.

물 문제를 해결하기 위해 몇 가지 기술들이 개발되었다. 가장 간단한 것은 범람원에 농작물을 심고 해마다 있는 홍수가 어린 농작물에 물을 대도록 기다리는 것이었다. 덜 위험한 기술은 제방이나 댐을 만들어 홍수를 조절하는 것이었다. 이런 제방들은 과도한 홍수에 대비해 작물을 보호했고 일단 내린 비가 너무 빨리 빠져나가는 것을 막았다. 호피족 사람들은 자신들의 밭을 한두 개의 옥수수대로 둘러싸인 많은 작은 제방으로 바둑판 모양으로 만든 반면에 다른 부족들은 홍수를 조절하기 위해 일련의 댐을 건설했다. 세 번째 기술은 강으로부터 물을 끌어올 관개용 수로를 파는 것이었다. 특히 건조한 계절에는 항아리에 물을 담아 밭으로 운반했다. 일부 농작물들은 절벽에서 흘러나오는 빗물로 직접 물을 댈 수 있는 곳에 심어졌다.

지속적인 식량 공급을 확실히 하기 위해 아메리카 원주민들이 사용했던 또 다른 전략은 작물을 한 장소가 아니라 여러 장소에 심는 것이었는데, 만약 한 농작물이 실패하더라도 다른 농작물이 살아남기를 바라는 것이었다. 그러나 토양이 비옥하고 (영양분이) 쉽게 고갈되지 않았기 때문에 매년 동일한 부지에 경작할 수 있었다. 반면에 미국 동부 지역의 삼림지대에서는 몇 년간 경작한 후에는 그 부지를 버려야 했다. 남서부 지역에서는 매년 연속해서 두 가지 농작물을 심었다.

충분한 식량을 재배하여 그 중 일부를 비상시에 대비해 건조 저장하는 것은 남서부 지역에서 흔히 볼 수 있는 관행이었다. 만약 비상 식량이 모자라게 되면 사람들은 그 지역의 야생 식물에 의존했다. 만약 이 방법도 실패하면 그들은 더 서늘한 대기에서도 생존할 수 있는 야생 식물을 채집하기 위해 산속으로 이동했다.

[어휘] **arid** 불모의, 건조한　**rely on** ~에 의존하다, 믿다
strategy 전략　**agriculture** 농업, 농사　**first and foremost** 무엇보다 먼저　**critical** 결정적인, 중대한
factor 요인, 요소　**leach out** (액체가 토양에서 광물질 등을) 침출시키다, 걸러내다　**precipitation** 강수량
drought 가뭄　**on the other hand** 다른 한편으로는, 반면에　**flood** 홍수　**crop** 농작물　**floodplain** (홍수의) 범람원　**annual** 연례의, 일년마다의　**dike** 제방　**excessive** 과도한　**checkerboard** 바둑판[격자] 무늬의　**enclose** 둘러싸다, 에워싸다　**stalk** 줄기
maize 옥수수　**irrigation ditch** 관개용 수로　**jar** 단지, 항아리　**runoff** 범람, 흐르는 빗물　**cliff** 벼랑, 절벽
survive (사고ㆍ재해ㆍ위기ㆍ곤란 등을) 이기고 살아남다
exhausted 고갈된, 물이 마른　**patch** 작게 구획된 땅, 좁은 땅　**cultivate** 경작하다, 개간하다　**abandon** 포기하다, 버리고 떠나다　**plot** 작은 땅, 부지　**successive** 연속하는, 잇따르는　**practice** 관행, 관례　**emergency** 비상[긴급] 사태; 비상용의　**run low** 고갈되다, 모자라게 되다
atmosphere 대기, 공기

1. What does the passage mainly discuss?

(A) Agricultural methods of Native Americans
(B) Irrigation techniques used by the Hopi
(C) Soil quality in the American Southwest
(D) Native American methods of storing emergency food supplies

[해석] 주로 무엇에 관한 글인가?
　　(A) 아메리카 원주민들의 농사법
　　(B) 호피족이 사용했던 관개 기술
　　(C) 미국 남서부 지역 토양의 품질
　　(D) 아메리카 원주민들의 비상 식량 저장법

[해설] 지문의 주제를 묻는 문제로, 각 단락에서 아메리카 원주민들의 농사법에 대해 자세히 설명하고 있다. 따라서 (A)가 정답이다.

2. The word "solve" in line 7 is closest in meaning to

(A) advance toward

(B) protect from

(B) keep in

(D) deal with

[해석] 7행에 언급된 "solve"와 의미상 가장 가까운 것은 무엇인가?
(A) 앞으로 나아가다
(B) ~로부터 보호하다
(C) ~을 가두다
(D) ~을 해결하다

[해설] 어휘 문제이다. solve the water problem은 '물 문제를 해결하다'라는 의미로 여기에서 solve는 deal with와 바꿔 쓸 수 있다. 따라서 (D)가 정답이다.

3. Planting in the floodplains was not ideal because

(A) the amount of water could not be controlled

(B) the crops could be eaten by wild animals

(C) the floodplains were too remote to be cultivated frequently

(D) corn grows better at high elevations

[해석] 범람원에 농작물을 심는 것이 이상적이지 않았던 이유는 무엇인가?
(A) 물의 양을 조절할 수 없어서
(B) 야생 동물이 농작물을 먹을 수 있어서
(C) 범람원이 너무 멀어서 자주 경작할 수 없어서
(D) 옥수수는 높은 지대에서 더 잘 자라서

[어휘] remote 먼, 외딴   elevation 높이, 고도

[해설] 두 번째 단락의 두 번째 문장 The simplest was to plant crops in the floodplains and wait for the annual floods to water the young crops.에서 범람원에 농작물을 심는다고 했고, 이어서 A less dangerous technique was to build dikes or dams to control the flooding. These dikes both protected the plants against excessive flooding and prevented the water from escaping too quickly once it had arrived.에서 제방과 댐을 만들어 홍수에 대비하고 필요한 물을 가둬 두는 덜 위험한 방법에 대해 설명하고 있다. 따라서 (A)가 정답이다.

4. The word "enclosing" in line 12 is closest in meaning to

(A) defending

(B) measuring

(C) surrounding

(D) extending

[해석] 12행에 언급된 "enclosing"과 의미상 가장 가까운 것은 무엇인가?
(A) 방어하는
(B) 측정하는
(C) 둘러싸는
(D) 연장하는

[해설] 어휘 문제이다. each enclosing only one or two stalks of maize (corn)은 '한두 개의 옥수수대로 둘러싸다'라는 의미이므로, enclosing은 '둘러싸는'이라는 의미의 surrounding과 바꿔 쓸 수 있다. 따라서 (C)가 정답이다.

5. The word "they" in line 15 refers to

(A) fields

(B) jars

(C) crops

(D) walls

[해석] 15행에 언급된 "they"가 가리키는 것은 무엇인가?
(A) 들판들
(B) 항아리들
(C) 농작물들
(D) 벽들

[해설] 지시 대상을 찾는 문제이다. Some crops were planted where they could be watered directly by the runoff from cliff walls.에서 they는 Some crops를 가리킨다. 따라서 (C)가 정답이다.

6. Why did farmers in the Southwest plant crops in several places at the same time?

(A) They moved frequently from one place to another.

(B) They feared that one of the crops might fail.

(C) The size of each field was quite limited.

(D) They wanted to avoid overusing the soil.

[해석] 남서부 지역의 농부들이 동시에 여러 곳에 농작물을 심었던 이유는 무엇인가?

(A) 한 장소에서 다른 장소로 자주 이동해서

(B) 한 작물이 실패할까 두려워서

(C) 각각 밭의 크기가 아주 작아서

(D) 토양 오용을 피하길 원해서

[어휘] **at the same time** 동시에 **limited** 제한된, 한정된, 좁은 **overuse** 혹사하다, 남용하다

[해설] 세 번째 단락의 첫 문장 Another strategy Native Americans used to ensure a continuous food supply was to plant their crops in more than one place, hoping that if one crop failed, another would survive.에서 한 농작물이 실패하더라도 다른 농작물이 살아남기를 바라는 마음에서 여러 곳에 농작물을 심었다고 했다. 따라서 (B)가 정답이다.

---

7. The word "patch" in line 19 is closest in meaning to

(A) type

(B) level

(C) group

(D) piece

[해석] 19행에 언급된 "patch"와 의미상 가장 가까운 것은 무엇인가?

(A) 종류

(B) 수준

(C) 집단

(D) 조각

[해설] 어휘 문제이다. the same patch of ground에서 patch 는 '땅 조각, 작게 구획된 땅'을 의미하므로 piece와 바꿔 쓸 수 있다. 따라서 (D)가 정답이다.

---

8. Why did farmers in the eastern woodlands periodically abandon their fields?

(A) Seasonal flooding made agriculture impossible.

(B) They experienced water shortages.

(C) They wanted a longer growing season.

(D) The minerals in the soil were exhausted.

[해석] 동부 삼림 지역의 농부들이 주기적으로 밭을 버린 이유는 무엇인가?

(A) 계절적인 홍수로 농사가 불가능해서

(B) 물 부족을 경험해서

(C) 더 긴 생장기를 원해서

(D) 토양의 무기질이 고갈되어서

[어휘] **periodically** 주기적으로, 정기적으로 **seasonal** 계절적인, 계절마다의 **shortage** 부족 **growing season** (식물·농작물의) 발육 시기, 생장 시기

[해설] 사실적인 정보 파악 문제이다. 세 번째 단락 두 번째 문장 However, since the soil was rich and not easily exhausted, the same patch of ground could be cultivated year after year, whereas in the woodlands of the eastern United States it was necessary to abandon a plot of ground after a few years of farming.에서 동부 삼림 지역의 농부들은 토양이 비옥하지 않고 토양의 영양분이 쉽게 고갈되어 몇 년간 경작한 후에는 그 부지를 버려야 했음을 알 수 있다. 따라서 (D)가 정답이다.

---

9. What did farmers in the Southwest do when a crop failed?

(A) They planted in the eastern woodlands.

(B) They gathered food from wild plants.

(C) They moved away from the mountains.

(D) They redesigned their fields for the next season.

[해석] 남서부 지역의 농부들은 농작물이 실패했을 때 어떻게 했는가?

(A) 그들은 동부 삼림 지역에서 작물을 재배했다.

(B) 그들은 야생 식물에서 식량을 채취했다.

(C) 그들은 산으로부터 멀리 이동했다.

(D) 그들은 다음 계절을 위해 논을 새롭게 재설계했다.

[해설] 마지막 단락 두 번째 문장 If emergency supplies ran low, the people turned to the local wild plants. If these failed, they moved up into the mountains to gather the wild plants that might have survived in the cooler atmosphere.에서 비상 식량이 모자라게 되면 사람들은 그 지역의 야생 식물에 의존했고 그 방법도 실패하면 산속으로 이동해 산에서 야생 식물을 채집했다고 했다. 따라서 (B)가 정답이다.

10. Farmers in the Southwest would have benefited most from which of the following?

(A) Steeper cliff walls
(B) More sunshine
(C) **Regular rain**
(D) Smaller dikes

[해석] 남서부 지역의 농부들은 다음 중 어떤 혜택을 가장 많이 받는가?
 (A) 더 가파른 절벽
 (B) 더 많은 햇빛
 (C) **일정한 강수량**
 (D) 더 작은 제방들

[어휘] **benefit** 도움이 되다   **steep** 험준한, 가파른

[해설] 너무 많거나 적은 강수량이 농사의 문제를 야기시킨다고 했으므로, 일정한 강수량이 농부들에게 보탬이 되었다는 것을 추론할 수 있다. 따라서 (C)가 정답이다.

Questions 11–20

[11]Marianne Moore (1887–1972) once said that [12]her writing could be called poetry only because there was no other name for it. Indeed her poems appear to be extremely compressed essays that happen to be printed in jagged lines on the page. [13]Her subjects were varied : animals, laborers, artists, and the craft of poetry. From her general reading came quotations that she found striking or insightful. She included these in her poems, scrupulously enclosed in quotation marks, and sometimes identified in footnotes. Of this practice, she wrote, "'Why the many quotation marks?' I am asked ... When a thing has been said so well that it could not be said better, why paraphrase it? Hence my writing is, if not a cabinet of fossils, a kind of collection of [14]flies in amber." Close observation and concentration on detail are the methods of her poetry.

Marianne Moore grew up in Kirkwood, Missouri, near St. Louis. After graduation from Bryn Mawr College in 1909, [15]she taught commercial subjects at the Indian School in Carlisle, Pennsylvania. [15]Later she became a librarian in New York City. [15]During the 1920s she was editor of *The Dial*, an important literary magazine of the [16]period. [17]She lived quietly all her life, mostly in Brooklyn, New York. She spent a lot of time at the Bronx Zoo, fascinated by animals. Her admiration of the Brooklyn Dodgers baseball team—before the team moved to Los Angeles—was widely known.

Her first book of poems was published in London in 1921 by a group of friends associated with the Imagist movement. From that time on her poetry has been read with interest by [18]succeeding generations of poets and readers. In 1952 she was awarded the Pulitzer Prize for her *Collected Poems*. She wrote that she did not write poetry "for money or fame. To earn a living is needful, but [19]it can be done in routine ways. [20]One writes because one has a burning desire to objectify what it is indispensable to one's happiness to express."

[해석] 메리앤 무어(1887~1972)는 자신의 작품에 다른 이름이 없기 때문에 시라고 불릴 수 있다고 말한 적이 있다. 사실 그녀의 시는 페이지에 들쭉날쭉하게 인쇄된 아주 간결한 에세이처럼 보인다. 그녀의 주제는 다양했다. 동물과 근로자, 예술가, 시의 기교가 그 주제였다. 그녀는 인상적이거나 통찰력 있다고 생각한 인용구를 일반적으로 읽는 글에서 가져왔다. 그녀는 자신의 시에 이 인용구들을 포함했는데, 양심적으로 인용 부호로 표시했고 때로는 각주로 표시하기도 했다. 이러한 관행에서 그녀는 "'왜 이렇게 인용 부호가 많은가?'라는 질문을 받으면… 너무 잘 표현해서 그보다 더 잘 표현할 수 없는데, 왜 그것을 바꿔서 표현해야 하는가? 그래서 내 글은 화석 진열장은 아니더라도 호박 속 파리 화석 같은 소장품의 일종이다."라고 썼다. 세부사항에 대한 면밀한 관찰과 집중이 그녀가 시를 쓰는 방법이다.

메리앤 무어는 미주리 주 세인트루이스 시 근처의 커크우드 시에서 자랐다. 1909년에 브린 모어 대학을 졸업한 후에, 펜실베이니아 주 칼라일 시의 인디언 학교에서 상업 과목을 가르쳤다. 그 후에 그녀는 뉴욕 시에서 사서가 되었다. 1920년대에는 그 시대의 중요한 문학 잡지였던 〈더 다이얼〉의 편집자였다. 그녀는 일생 동안 주로 뉴욕 시의 브룩클린에서 조용하게 살았다. 그녀는 동물에 매료되어 브롱크스 동물원에서 많은 시간을 보냈다. 브룩클린 다저스 야구팀이 로스앤젤레스로 이동하기 전에 그녀가 그 팀에 열광했다는 것은 널리 알려져 있다.

그녀의 첫 번째 시집은 심상파 운동에 가담한 몇몇 친구들에 의해 1921년 런던에서 발간되었다. 그 이후로 계속 그녀의 시를 다음 세대의 시인들과 독자들이 관심을 갖고 읽었다. 1952년에 그녀는 자신의 〈시 모음집〉으로 퓰리처상을 수상했다. 그녀는 "돈과 명예를 위해 시를 쓰지 않았다. 생계비를 버는 것도 필요하지만, 그것은 일상적인 방법으로 해결될 수 있다. 사람은 자신의 행복에 꼭 필요한 것을 구체화해 표현하려는 불타는 욕구를 가졌기 때문에 시를 쓴다."고 썼다.

[어휘] **poetry** 시, 운문 **extremely** 극단적으로, 극도로; 대단히 **compressed** 압축된, 간결한 **jagged** 들쭉날쭉한, 다듬지 않은 **subject** 주제, 제목 **craft** 솜씨, 기술 **quotation** 인용, 인용구[문] **striking** 두드러진, 현저한 **insightful** 통찰력 있는 **scrupulously** 양심적으로, 용의주도하게 **enclose** 둘러싸다 **quotation mark** 인용부호, 따옴표 **identify** 확인하다 **footnote** 각주 **paraphrase** 바꿔 쓰다, 의역하다 **fossil** 화석 **a fly in amber** 호박 속의 파리 화석, 구태의연한 것, 원형대로 남은 유물 **observation** 관찰 **concentration** 집중 (연구) **detail** 상세한 내용 **commercial** 상업의, 무역의 **librarian** 사서, 도서관원 **editor** 편집자, 교정자 **fascinate** ~을 황홀하게 하다, 매혹하다 **admiration** 감탄, 탄복 **publish** 발행하다, 출판하다 **associate** 가담하다, 연합하다, 제휴하다 **Imagist movement** 심상파 운동 **succeeding generation** 다음 세대 **earn a living** 생계를 꾸리다, 생활비를 벌다 **needful** 필요한, 소용되는 **routine** 일상적인, 일과의 **objectify** 객관화하다, 구체화하다 **indispensable** 필수적인, 꼭 필요한

11. What is the passage mainly about?

(A) The influence of the Imagists on Marianne Moore

(B) Essayists and poets of the 1920s

(C) The use of quotations in poetry

(D) Marianne Moore's life and work

[해석] 지문은 주로 무엇에 관한 글인가?
(A) 메리앤 무어에게 미친 심상파주의의 영향
(B) 1920년대의 수필가와 시인들
(C) 시에서 인용문의 사용
(D) 메리앤 무어의 삶과 작품

[어휘] **influence** 영향(력) **essayist** 수필가, 평론가

[해설] 글의 주제를 묻는 문제로, 지문에서는 메리앤 무어의 일생과 작품에 관해 주로 설명하고 있다. 따라서 (D)가 정답이다. 나머지 보기는 깊이 언급되지 않은 내용이다.

12. Which of the following can be inferred about Moore's poems?

(A) They are better known in Europe than the United States.

(B) They do not use traditional verse forms.

(C) They were all published in *The Dial*.

(D) They tend to be abstract.

[해석] 다음 중 무어의 시에 대해 추론할 수 있는 것은 무엇인가?
(A) 미국보다 유럽에서 더 잘 알려져 있다.
(B) 전통적인 운문 형식을 사용하지 않는다.
(C) 〈더 다이얼〉 지에 모두 출판되었다.
(D) 추상적인 경향이 있다.

[어휘] **verse** 시, 운문 **abstract** 추상적인

[해설] 첫 단락의 her writing could be called poetry only because there was no other name for it. Indeed her poems appear to be extremely compressed essays 등에서 무어 시의 독특한 형식을 설명하고 있다. 따라서 (B)가 정답이다.

13. According to the passage, Moore wrote about all of the following EXCEPT

(A) artists

(B) animals

(C) fossils

(D) workers

[해석] 지문에 따르면, 다음 중 무어의 작품 주제가 아닌 것은 무엇인가?
(A) 예술가
(B) 동물
(C) 화석
(D) 근로자

[해설] 첫 단락 세 번째 문장 Her subjects were varied: animals, laborers, artists, and the craft of poetry. 에 무어의 작품 주제가 잘 나타나 있다. 따라서 언급되지 않은 (C) fossils가 정답으로, 화석은 그녀의 작품 스타일에 대한 은유적 표현으로 언급된 것이지 작품의 주제는 아니다.

14. What does Moore refer to as "flies in amber" (line 9)?

(A) A common image in her poetry

(B) Poetry in the twentieth century

(C) Concentration on detail

(D) Quotations within her poetry

[해석] 무어가 "flies in amber"(9행)라고 부른 것은 무엇인가?
(A) 그녀 시에 있는 흔한 이미지
(B) 20세기의 시
(C) 세부사항에 대한 집중
(D) 그녀 시 안의 인용구

[해설] 무어는 자신의 시 안에 있는 인용구를 flies in amber(호박 속 파리 화석)로 비유하고 있다. 따라서 (D)가 정답이다. 호박(amber)이나 시(poetry) 둘 다 원형 그대로 보존한다는 점에서 단서를 찾을 수 있다.

15. The author mentions all of the following as jobs held by Moore EXCEPT

(A) commercial artist

(B) teacher

(C) magazine editor

(D) librarian

[해석] 다음 중 글쓴이가 무어의 직업으로 언급하지 않은 것은 무엇인가?
(A) 상업 예술가
(B) 교사
(C) 잡지 편집자
(D) 사서

[어휘] **commercial artist** 상업 예술가

[해설] 지문에서 언급되지 않은 직업을 고르는 문제로, 두 번째 단락에 무어의 다양한 직업이 제시되어 있다. (B)는 she taught commercial subjects at the Indian School in Carlisle, Pennsylvania에, (C)는 During the 1920s she was editor of *The Dial*, an important literary magazine of the period.에, (D)는 Later she became a librarian in New York City.에 언급되어 있다. 따라서 언급되지 않은 (A)가 정답이다.

16. The word "period" in line 14 is closest in meaning to

(A) movement

(B) school

(C) region

(D) time

[해석] 14행에 언급된 "period"와 의미상 가장 가까운 것은 무엇인가?
(A) 운동
(B) 학교
(C) 지역
(D) 시간

[해설] 어휘 문제이다. During the 1920s she was editor of *The Dial*, an important literary magazine of the period.에서 "period"는 '시기, 시대'라는 의미로 쓰였으므로, (D) time과 바꿔 쓸 수 있다.

17. Where did Moore spend most of her adult life?

(A) In Kirkwood

(B) In Brooklyn

(C) In Los Angeles

(D) In Carlisle

[해석] 무어는 대부분 어디에서 성인 시절을 보냈는가?
(A) 커크우드에서
(B) 브룩클린에서
(C) 로스앤젤레스에서
(D) 칼라일에서

[해설] 두 번째 단락 중반부 She lived quietly all her life, mostly in Brooklyn, New York.에서 무어는 브룩클린에서 대부분의 시간을 보냈다고 했다. 따라서 (B)가 정답이다.

18. The word "succeeding" in line 20 is closest in meaning to

(A) inheriting

(B) prospering

(C) diverse

(D) later

[해석] 19행에 언급된 "succeeding"과 의미상 가장 가까운 것은 무엇인가?
(A) 상속하는
(B) 번영하는
(C) 다양한
(D) 나중의

[어휘] **inherit** 물려받다, 상속하다 **prosper** 번영하다, 발전하다

[해설] From that time on her poetry has been read with interest by succeeding generations of poets and readers.에서 succeeding generations는 '다음 세대'라는 의미로, succeeding은 (D) later와 바꿔 쓸 수 있다.

19. The word "it" in line 22 refers to

(A) writing poetry

(B) becoming famous

(C) earning a living

(D) attracting readers

[해석] 22행에 언급된 "it"이 가리키는 것은 무엇인가?
(A) 시를 쓰는 것
(B) 유명해지는 것
(C) 생계비를 버는 것
(D) 독자의 마음을 끄는 것

[어휘] **attract** 끌다, 유혹하다

[해설] 지시 대상을 찾는 문제이다. To earn a living is needful, but it can be done in routine ways.에서 it은 To earn a living을 가리키고 있으므로 (C)가 정답이다.

20. It can be inferred from the passage that Moore wrote because she

(A) wanted to win awards

(B) was dissatisfied with what others

(C) felt a need to express herself

(D) wanted to raise money for the Bronx Zoo

[해석] 이 지문을 통해 무어가 글을 쓴 이유로 추론할 수 있는 것은 무엇인가?
(A) 상을 받기를 원했다.
(B) 다른 사람들이 쓴 것에 만족하지 못했다.
(C) 자신을 표현하고 싶은 욕구를 느꼈다.
(D) 브롱크스 동물원을 위해 기금을 모금하길 원했다.

[어휘] **dissatisfied** 불만인, 만족하지 못한 **raise** (돈을) 모으다

[해설] 세 번째 단락 마지막 문장 One writes because one has a burning desire to objectify what it is indispensable to one's happiness to express.에서 무어는 자신을 표현하고 싶어서 글을 썼다는 것을 알 수 있다. 따라서 (C)가 정답이다.

Questions 21–30

Different fish species swim in different ways. ³⁰Beginning in the 1920s, careful efforts have been made to classify and measure these various means of locomotion. Although the nomenclature and mathematics used to describe fish locomotion have become quite complex, the basic classification system is still largely the same as it was first outlined.

The simplest type of swim is "eel-form" (technically, "anguilliform," after the common eel *Anguilla*). As the name ²¹suggests, this swimming motion involves undulations, or wavelike motions, of the whole length of the fish's body, the amplitude of the undulation increasing toward the tail. These undulating motions generate a backward thrust of the body against the water, thereby driving ²²it forward. ²³Eel-form swimming is effective but not particularly efficient because the undulations increase the drag, or resistance in the water. ²⁵It is ²⁴employed, therefore, mostly by bottom dwellers that do not move quickly or efficiently. Not only eels but also ²⁵blennies swim this way, as do flounders, which undulate vertically, top to bottom, rather than horizontally, and certain slow-moving sharks, such as the nurse and wobbegong shark.

Most roaming predators display "jack-form" swimming (technically, "carangiform," after the Carangidae family, which includes jacks, scads, and pompanos). Although there is some variation, in general they have certain features in common: a head like the nose of an aircraft, often sloping down on the top, and a tapered posterior that ends in a forked tail. That portion of the body that connects with the forked tail is narrowed. A jack, like other carangiform swimmers, is adapted for acceleration. It thrusts its rather stiff body from side to side, creating propulsion without much waving of the body, encountering less resistance than eel-form undulations produce. The forked pattern of the tail reduces drag; the narrowed portion of the body connected to the tail ²⁶minimizes recoil, and thus helps keep the body still. ²⁷Jack-form fish are efficient swimmers, as they must be to catch their prey.

The least efficient swimmers are those that move trunkfish style (technically, "ostraciform," after the family Ostraciidae, which includes trunkfishes and cowfishes). Like the jacks, they use their tails for propulsion, but in so inept and clumsy a manner as to make it clear that speed is not their ²⁸objective. Puffer fish and porcupine fish swim in trunkfish style. ²⁹Lacking speed, they must depend on body armor or the secretion of toxic substances for protection.

[해석] 다른 물고기 어종은 다른 방식으로 헤엄친다. 1920년대 초에 이런 다양한 유영 방식을 분류하고 측정하기 위한 주의 깊은 노력이 펼쳐졌다. 물고기의 유영을 설명하는 데 사용된 학명과 수학이 아주 복잡해지기는 했지만 기본적인 분류법은 제일 처음에 잡힌 체계와 거의 같다.

가장 간단한 유영 방식은 "장어형"(전문 용어로는 일반적으로 알려진 장어 Anguilla의 이름을 딴 "anguilliform")이다. 이름에서 알 수 있듯이, 이 유영법은 물고기 몸 전체의 파동, 즉 파도 같은 움직임을 수반하는데, 꼬리쪽으로 갈수록 파동의 진폭이 더 증가한다. 이 파동의 움직임은 물에 대항하여 몸의 뒤쪽으로 추진력이 발생하도록 하여 그 결과 몸이 앞으로 나아가게 한다. 장어형 유영은 효과적이기는 하지만, 파동이 장애나 물의 저항을 증가시키기 때문에 그다지 효율적이지는 않다. 그래서 이 유영 방식은 재빠르게 움직이지 않거나 효율적으로 움직이지 않는 심해에 사는 어류들이 사용한다. 장어뿐만 아니라 베도라치도 이런 방식으로 유영하는데, 수평이라기보다는 수직으로, 위에서 아래로 파동을 치는 도다리와 수염 상어와 얼룩 상어 같이 느리게 움직이는 상어도 마찬가지이다.

대부분의 배회하는 포식자들은 "전갱이형" 유영(전문 용어로는 "전갱이, 갈고등어, 빨판매가리를 포함한 전갱이과의 이름을 딴 "carangiform")을 보여준다. 약간의 차이가 있기는 하지만, 대체로 어떤 공통적인 특징들이 있다. 즉 종종 위에서 아래로 경사진 항공기 기수 모양의 머리와 두 갈래로 갈라진 꼬리 부분이 있다. 갈라진 꼬리에 연결된 몸통 부분은 폭이 좁다. 전갱이형으로 유영하는 다른 물고기들과 마찬가지로 전갱이는 가속도에 적합하다. 전갱이는 다소 뻣뻣한 몸을 좌우로 움직여서 나아가는데, 몸을 많이 흔들지 않고도 추진력을 내서, 장어형 파동이 만드는 것보다 더 적은 저항을 맞게 된다. 두 갈래로 갈라진 꼬리도 장애를 줄여준다. 즉, 꼬리에 연결된 몸통 부분이 좁아서 반동을 최소화시켜서, 그로 인해 몸이 움직이지 않고 가만히 있게 돕는다. 전갱이형 물고기는 먹이를 잡아야 하므로 효율적으로 유영하는 물고기들이다.

가장 비효율적으로 유영하는 물고기들은 거북복형 유형(전문 용어로는 거북복류를 포함하는 거북복과의 이름을 딴 "ostraciform")으로 이동하는 물고기들이다. 전갱이들과 마찬가지로, 그들은 추진력을 위해 꼬리를 사용하지만, 속도가 자신들의 목표가 아님을 명백히 하려는 듯 아주 서툴고 볼품이 없다. 복어와 가시복은 거북복형으로 유영한다. 그들은 속도가 느려서, (자신들을) 보호하기 위해 비늘이나 유독물질 분비에 의존해야 한다.

[어휘] species (동·식물 분류상의) 종　classify 분류하다 cf. classification 분류　means 방법, 수단　locomotion 이동　nomenclature 학명, 명명법　complex 복잡한 largely 대부분, 주로　outline 개요를 말하다　eel 뱀장어 anguilliform 뱀장어 같은, 뱀장어 모양의　undulation 파동, 물결 모양　amplitude 진폭, 크기　generate 일으키다, 발생시키다　thrust 추진력　effective 유효한, 효력이 있는, 효과적인　efficient 능률적인, 효율적인　drag 질질 끌기, 지연; 장애물　resistance 저항　bottom dweller 심해에서 사는 어류　blenny 베도라치　flounder 도다리　undulate 물결치다; 파도처럼 움직이다　vertically 수직적으로　horizontally 수평으로　nurse shark 수염상어　wobbegong shark 얼룩 상어　roam 돌아다니다, 배회하다　predator 포식자　jack 전갱이　Carangidae family 전갱이과　scad 갈고등어　pompano 빨판매가리 variation 다양함, 변형　in general 일반적으로, 대체로 feature 특징　in common 공통으로　nose (항공기의) 기수　slope 비탈지다, 비스듬히 내려가다　tapered 뾰족한 posterior 꼬리 부분, 엉덩이 둔부　forked 두 갈래진, 포크 비슷한　connect 연결하다　adapt 맞추다, 적응시키다 acceleration 가속　thrust 밀다, 밀어내다　stiff 뻣뻣한 propulsion 추진력　encounter 우연히 만나다, ~에 부닥치다, 직면하다　minimize 최소 한도로 하다, 되도록 적게 하다　recoil 반동　still 움직이지 않는, 정지한　prey 먹이 trunkfish 거북복류　Ostraciidae 거북복과　cowfish 거북복어　inept 서투른　clumsy 볼품없는　objective 목적, 목표　puffer (fish) 복어　porcupine 가시복 armor 호신 기관(물고기의 비늘 따위); 갑옷　secretion 분비 toxic 유독한, 독성의

21. The word "suggests" in line 6 is closest in meaning to

(A) implies
(B) demands
(C) describes
(D) compares

[해석] 6행에 언급된 "suggests"와 의미상 가장 가까운 것은 무엇인가?
(A) 암시하다
(B) 요구하다
(C) 묘사하다
(D) 비교하다

[해설] 어휘 문제이다. As the name suggests에서 suggests는 '암시하다, 넌지시 말하다'라는 의미로 쓰였으므로, (A) implies와 바꿔 쓸 수 있다.

22. The word "it" in line 9 refers to

(A) tail
(B) thrust
(C) body
(D) water

[해석] 9행에 언급된 "it"이 가리키는 것은 무엇인가?
(A) 꼬리
(B) 추진력
(C) 몸
(D) 물

[해설] 지시 대상을 찾는 문제이다. These undulating motions generate a backward thrust of the body against the water, thereby driving it forward.에서 it은 the body를 가리키므로 (C)가 정답이다.

23. Which of the following does the author mention as the cause of the eel's inefficient swimming style?

(A) The increased drag produced by the movement of the body
(B) The eel's habit of usually swimming near the bottom of the water
(C) The simple structure of the eel's body
(D) The weakness of the backward thrust of the eel's tail

[해석] 다음 중 글쓴이가 장어의 비효율적인 유영 스타일의 이유로 언급한 것은 무엇인가?
(A) 몸의 움직임으로 인한 장애 증가
(B) 주로 심해 근처에서 유영하는 장어의 습관
(C) 장어의 단순한 몸 구조
(D) 장어 꼬리의 뒤로 미는 추진력의 약점

CHAPTER 5

[해설] 두 번째 단락 중반부의 Eel-form swimming is effective but not particularly efficient because the undulations increase the drag, or resistance in the water.에서 장어형 유영은 파동이 장애나 물의 저항력을 증가시키기 때문에 비효율적이라고 했다. 따라서 (A)가 정답이다.

24. The word "employed" in line 10 is closest in meaning to

(A) used

(B) occupied

(C) developed

(D) provided

[해석] 10행에 언급된 "employed"와 의미상 가장 가까운 것은 무엇인가?
  (A) 사용되는
  (B) 점령되는
  (C) 개발되는
  (D) 제공되는

[해설] 어휘 문제이다. It is employed, therefore, mostly by bottom dwellers that do not move quickly or efficiently.에서 employed는 '사용된'의 의미로 쓰였으므로, (A) used와 바꿔 쓸 수 있다.

25. It can be inferred from the passage that blennies (line 12) are

(A) bottom dwellers

(B) sharks

(C) predators

(D) a type of eel

[해석] 이 지문을 통해 (12행의) 베도라치에 대해 추론할 수 있는 것은?
  (A) 심해에 사는 물고기들이다
  (B) 상어들이다
  (C) 포식자들이다
  (D) 장어의 한 종류이다

[해설] 두 번째 단락 마지막 문장 Not only eels but also blennies swim this way, as do flounders, which undulate vertically, top to bottom, rather than horizontally, and certain slow-moving sharks, such as the nurse and wobbegong shark.에서 베도라치는 장어와 마찬가지로 유영한다고 했으며, 바로 앞의 문장 It(= Eel-form swimming) is employed, therefore, mostly by bottom dwellers that do not move quickly or efficiently.에서 심해에서 사는 물고기들이 장어형 유영을 한다고 했다. 따라서 베도라치는 심해에서 사는 물고기임을 추론할 수 있으므로 (A)가 정답이다.

26. The word "minimizes" in line 22 is closest in meaning to

(A) prevents

(B) reduces

(C) determines

(D) repeats

[해석] 22행에 언급된 "minimizes"와 의미상 가장 가까운 것은 무엇인가?
  (A) 방지하다
  (B) 줄이다
  (C) 결정하다
  (D) 반복하다

[해설] 어휘 문제이다. the narrowed portion of the body connected to the tail minimizes recoil에서 minimizes는 '최소화시키다'라는 의미로 쓰였으므로 (B) reduces와 바꿔 쓸 수 있다.

27. What does the author mention about fish that are "jack-form" swimmers?

(A) They usually prey on bottom-dwelling fish.

(B) Their swimming style lets them catch prey effectively.

(C) They have tails similar to those of eels.

(D) Their highly flexible skeletal structure allows them to swim efficiently.

[해석] 글쓴이는 전갱이형으로 유영하는 물고기들에 대해 뭐라고 언급하는가?
  (A) 심해에서 사는 물고기를 잡아먹고 산다.
  (B) 그들의 유영 스타일로 인해 먹이를 효과적으로 잡을 수 있다.
  (C) 장어의 꼬리와 비슷한 꼬리를 갖고 있다.
  (D) 아주 유연한 골격 구조로 인해 효율적으로 유영할 수 있다.

[어휘] **flexible** 유연한　**skeletal** 골격의

[해설] 세 번째 단락에 전갱이형으로 유영하는 물고기들의 특징이 언급되어 있다. 특히, 세 번째 단락 마지막 문장 Jack-form fish are efficient swimmers, as they must be to catch their prey.에서 전갱이형으로 유영하는 물고기들은 먹이를 효과적으로 잡을 수 있다는 것을 알 수 있다. 따라서 (B)가 정답이다.

28. The word "objective" in line 27 is closest in meaning to

(A) ability

(B) preference

(C) purpose

(D) method

[해설] 27행에 언급된 "objective"와 의미상 가장 가까운 것은 무엇인가?
(A) 능력
(B) 선호
(C) 목적
(D) 방법

[해설] 어휘 문제이다. speed is not their objective에서 objective는 '목적, 목표'의 의미로 쓰였으므로 (C) purpose와 바꿔 쓸 수 있다.

29. Which of the following fish would most likely emit a poisonous substance?

(A) A nurse shark

(B) A jack

(C) A pompano

(D) A puffer fish

[해설] 다음 물고기들 중 독성 물질을 내뿜을 것 같은 물고기는 무엇인가?
(A) 수염 상어
(B) 전갱이
(C) 빨판매가리
(D) 복어

[어휘] **emit** 방출하다, 내뿜다　**poisonous** 독성의, 유해한

[해설] 네 번째 단락 마지막 문장 Lacking speed, they (=puffer fish and porcupine fish) must depend on body armor or the secretion of toxic substances for protection.에서 복어와 가시복은 속도가 느려서, 비늘이나 유독물질 분비로 자신들을 보호한다고 했다. 따라서 (D)가 정답이다.

30. Which of the following statements does the passage support?

(A) A scientist today would use a system of classification for fish locomotion similar to that used in the 1920s.

(B) Scientists today still do not understand the mechanics of fish locomotion.

(C) Mathematical analysis of fish locomotion has remained largely unaltered since the 1920s.

(D) The classification of fish locomotion has been simplified since it was devised in the 1920s.

[해설] 다음 중 이 지문에서 지지하는 것은 무엇인가?
(A) 오늘날의 과학자는 1920년대에 사용되었던 것과 유사한 물고기의 이동에 따른 분류법을 사용하려고 한다.
(B) 오늘날의 과학자들은 여전히 물고기의 이동 방법을 이해하지 못한다.
(C) 물고기 이동의 수학적 분석은 1920년대 이후로 크게 변하지 않은 채 그대로 유지되고 있다.
(D) 물고기 이동 분류가 1920년대에 연구된 이후로 단순화되었다.

[어휘] **mechanics** 역학, 방법　**unaltered** 바뀌지 않은, 변하지 않은　**devise** 연구하다, 고안하다

[해설] 오답 소거법을 이용해 이 지문의 내용에서 지지하는 보기를 고르면 된다. (B), (C), (D)는 모두 이 지문의 내용과 맞지 않는 내용이므로, 오답이 된다. 첫 단락의 Beginning in the 1920s, careful efforts have been made to classify and measure these various means of locomotion. Although the nomenclature and mathematics used to describe fish locomotion have become quite complex, the basic classification system is still largely the same as it was first outlined.에서 (A)가 정답임을 알 수 있다.

³¹People appear to be born to compute. The numerical skills of children develop so early and so inexorably that it is easy to imagine an internal clock of mathematical maturity guiding their growth. ³²Not long after learning to walk and talk, they can set the table with impressive accuracy—one plate, one knife, one spoon, one fork, for each of the five chairs. Soon they are capable of noting that they have placed five knives, spoons, and forks on the table and, a bit later, that this amounts to fifteen pieces of silverware. Having thus mastered addition, they move on to subtraction. It seems almost reasonable to expect that ⁴⁰if a child were secluded on a desert island at birth and retrieved seven years later, he or she could enter a second-grade mathematics class without any serious problems of intellectual adjustment.

Of course, the truth is not so simple. In the twentieth century, the work of cognitive psychologists ³³illuminated the subtle forms of daily learning on which intellectual progress depends. Children were observed ³⁴as they slowly grasped—or, as the case might be, bumped into—concepts that adults take for granted, as they refused, for instance, to concede that quantity is unchanged as water pours from a short stout glass into a tall thin one. ³⁵Psychologists have since demonstrated that young children, asked to count the pencils in a pile, readily report the number of blue or red pencils but must be coaxed into finding the total. ³⁹Such studies have suggested that the rudiments of mathematics are mastered gradually and with effort. ³⁶They have also suggested that the very concept of abstract numbers—the idea of a oneness, a twoness, a threeness that applies to any class of objects and is a ³⁷prerequisite for doing anything more mathematically demanding than setting a table—is ³⁸itself far from innate.

[해석] 사람들은 계산 능력을 갖고 태어나는 것처럼 보인다. 아이들의 계산 능력은 아주 이른 시기에 멈춤 없이 발달해서 그들의 성장을 이끄는 수학 성숙도라는 생체 시계를 짐작하기 쉽다. 걷고 말하기를 배운 후로 얼마 지나지 않아 아이들은 아주 놀라울 정도로 정확하게 테이블을 세팅할 수 있는데, 즉 다섯 개 각각의 의자 앞에 접시 한 개, 나이프 한 개, 스푼 한 개, 포크 한 개를 차려 놓을 수 있다. 그들은 머지않아 테이블 위에 나이프와 스푼, 포크가 5개씩 놓였다는 것을 알아차릴 수 있으며, 조금 더 나중에는 은식기가 총 15개에 이르게 된다는 것을 알아차릴 수 있게 된다. 그렇게 덧셈이 숙달되면, 뺄셈으로 넘어간다. 만일 한 아이가 태어나자마자 무인도에 격리되었다가 7년 후에 구출된다면, 그 아이는 지적인 적응에 아무런 큰 문제 없이 2학년 수학반에 들어갈 수 있을 것이라고 예상하는 것도 거의 무리가 아니다.

물론, 진실은 그리 간단하지 않다. 20세기에 인지 심리학자들은 지적 발달이 결정되는 일상 학습의 미묘한 형태를 밝혔다. 아이들은 어른들이 당연시 여기는 개념들을 서서히 파악하거나 경우에 따라 (문제에) 봉착하는 것으로 관찰되었다. 예를 들어, 길이가 짧고 넓은 유리잔에서 길이가 길고 가는 유리잔에 물을 부어도 양은 변하지 않는다는 것을 인정하려고 하지 않았다. 심리학자들은 어린 아이들에게 무더기로 있는 연필을 세어 보라는 요청했을 때 아이들이 파란색 연필의 개수나 빨간색 연필의 개수는 쉽게 말하지만 총 개수는 알아내도록 유도해야만 한다는 것을 입증했다. 그러한 연구들은 수학의 원리는 서서히 노력해서 습득되는 것임을 암시해 왔다. 또한 그 연구들은 추상적인 숫자들의 개념이 선천적인 것과는 거리가 멀다는 것도 암시했다. 추상적인 숫자들의 개념, 즉 사물의 분류에 적용되며 식탁을 차리는 것보다 수학적으로 더 까다로운 뭔가를 하는 데 필요한 단일성, 이중성, 삼중성 같은 개념은 선천적인 것과는 거리가 멀다는 것을 암시하는 것이다.

[어휘] compute 계산하다   numerical skill 계산 능력   inexorably 가차없이, 멈춤 없이   internal clock 생체[체내] 시계(생물체에 존재한다고 추정되는 시간 측정 기구)   maturity 성숙   impressive 강한 인상을 주는, 인상인   accuracy 정확도   amount to (발전·성장하고 있는 상태로) 되다, 이르다   silverware (식탁용) 은식기류   addition 덧셈   subtraction 뺄셈   reasonable 합당한, 과하지 않은   secluded 격리된   desert island 무인도   retrieved 구출된   adjustment 조정, 조절, 적응, 순응   cognitive 인지의   psychologist 심리학자   illuminate 밝히다, 명확히 하다   subtle 미묘한, 섬세한   grasp 파악하다, 이해하다   bump into ~와 부딪치다, 우연히 만나다   take ~ for granted ~을 당연한 일로 생각하다   concede 인정하다   stout 굵직한   coax 유도해 내다   rudiment 원리, 기본   gradually 차츰, 서서히   abstract 추상적인   apply to ~에 적용되다   prerequisite 필요 조건   demanding (시간·노력·주의 등이) 많이 드는, 힘든, 고된   innate 타고난, 선천적인

31. What does the passage mainly discuss?

(A) Trends in teaching mathematics to children

(B) The use of mathematics in child psychology

(C) The development of mathematical ability in children

(D) The fundamental concepts of mathematics that children must learn

[해석] 주로 무엇에 관한 글인가?
(A) 아이들에게 수학을 가르치는 경향
(B) 아동 심리학에서 수학의 사용
(C) 아이들의 수학 능력 발달
(D) 아이들이 배워야 하는 수학의 기본 개념

[어휘] **fundamental** 기본적인

[해설] 아이들의 수학 능력 발달에 대해 설명하고 있다. 따라서 (C)가 정답이다.

32. It can be inferred from the passage that children normally learn simple counting

(A) soon after they learn to talk

(B) by looking at the clock

(C) when they begin to be mathematically mature

(D) after they reach second grade in school

[해석] 이 지문을 통해 아이들은 보통 언제/어떻게 간단한 계산을 배운다고 추론할 수 있는가?
(A) 말을 배운 바로 직후에
(B) 시계를 보는 것에 의해서
(C) 그들이 수학적으로 성숙하기 시작할 때
(D) 그들이 학교에서 2학년이 된 후에

[어휘] **mature** 성숙한

[해설] 첫 단락의 세 번째 문장 Not long after learning to walk and talk, they can set the table with impressive accuracy—one plate, one knife, one spoon, one fork, for each of the five chairs.에서 걷고 말하기를 배운 후 얼마 되지 않아 간단한 계산을 배운다는 것을 알 수 있다. 따라서 (A)가 정답이다.

33. The word "illuminated" in line 11 is closest in meaning to

(A) illustrated

(B) accepted

(C) clarified

(D) lighted

[해석] 11행에 언급된 "illuminated"와 의미상 가장 가까운 것은 무엇인가?
(A) 예를 들어 설명했다
(B) 수용했다
(C) 명확히 했다
(D) 불을 밝혔다

[어휘] **illustrate** 설명하다, 예시하다; 삽화를 넣다

[해설] 어휘 문제이다. the work of cognitive psychologists illuminated the subtle forms of daily learning on which intellectual progress depends에서 illuminate은 '밝히다, 명확히 하다'라는 의미로 쓰였으므로, (C) clarified가 정답이다. illustrate에 '밝게 하다, 비추다'라는 의미도 있으나, 여기에서는 그런 의미로 쓰인 것이 아니므로 (D)는 정답이 될 수 없다.

34. The author implies that most small children believe that the quantity of water changes when it is transferred to a container of a different

(A) color

(B) quality

(C) weight

(D) shape

[해석] 글쓴이에 따르면 대부분의 어린 아이들은 물의 양이 무엇이 다른 용기에 옮겼을 때 바뀐다고 생각하는가?
(A) 색깔
(B) 품질
(C) 무게
(D) 모양

[어휘] **transfer** 옮기다 **container** 용기, 그릇

[해설] 추론 문제이다. 두 번째 단락의 중반부 ~ as they refused, for instance, to concede that quantity is unchanged as water pours from a short stout glass into a tall thin one에서 아이들은 길이가 짧고 넓은 유리잔에서 길이가 길고 가는 유리잔에 물을 부으면 양이 변한다고 생각한다는 것을 알 수 있다. 여기에서 short stout와 tall thin은 용기의 모양을 가리키므로 (D)가 정답이다.

35. According to the passage, when small children were asked to count a pile of red and blue pencils they

(A) counted the number of pencils of each color

(B) guessed at the total number of pencils

(C) counted only the pencils of their favorite color

(D) subtracted the number of red pencils from the number of blue pencils

[해석] 지문에 따르면, 어린 아이들은 한 더미의 빨강색 연필과 파란색 연필을 세라는 요청을 받았을 때 어떻게 했는가?
(A) 각 색깔 별로 연필의 개수를 세었다
(B) 연필의 총 개수를 추측했다
(C) 자신들이 좋아하는 색깔의 연필만 세었다
(D) 파란색 연필의 개수에서 빨간색 연필의 개수를 뺐다

[어휘] **a pile of** ~ 더미, 많은 ~   **subtract** 빼다

[해설] 사실적인 정보 파악 문제이다. 두 번째 단락의 Psychologists have since demonstrated that young children, asked to count the pencils in a pile, readily report the number of blue or red pencils but must be coaxed into finding the total. 에서 무더기로 있는 연필을 세어 보라는 요청을 받았을 때 어린 아이들은 파란색 연필의 개수와 빨간색 연필의 개수를 쉽게 말했다고 했다. 따라서 연필을 색깔별로 셌다는 것을 알 수 있으므로 (A)가 정답이다.

36. The word "They" in line 18 refers to

(A) mathematicians

(B) children

(C) pencils

(D) studies

[해석] 18행에 언급된 "They"가 가리키는 것은 무엇인가?
(A) 수학자들
(B) 아이들
(C) 연필들
(D) 연구

[어휘] **mathematician** 수학자

[해설] 지시 대상을 찾는 문제이다. They have also suggested that ~.에서 They는 바로 앞 문장의 Such studies를 가리킨다. 따라서 (D)가 정답이다.

37. The word "prerequisite" in line 19 is closest in meaning to

(A) reason

(B) theory

(C) requirement

(D) technique

[해석] 19행에 언급된 "prerequisite"과 의미상 가장 가까운 것은 무엇인가?
(A) 이유
(B) 이론
(C) 요건
(D) 기술

[해설] 어휘 문제이다. ~ a prerequisite for doing anything more mathematically demanding than setting a table에서 prerequisite은 '필요 조건'이라는 의미로 쓰였으므로 (C) requirement가 정답이 된다.

38. The word "itself" in line 20 refers to

(A) the total

(B) the concept of abstract numbers

(C) any class of objects

(D) setting a table

[해석] 20행에 언급된 "itself"가 가리키는 것은 무엇인가?
(A) 합계
(B) 추상적인 숫자의 개념
(C) 사물의 종류
(D) 상을 차리기

[해설] 지시 대상을 묻는 문제이다. They have also suggested that the very concept of abstract numbers—the idea of a oneness, a twoness, a threeness that applies to any class of objects and is a prerequisite for doing anything more mathematically demanding than setting a table—is itself far from innate.에서 the very concept of abstract numbers에 대해 보충 설명하고 있는 부분을 빼면 They have also suggested that the very concept of abstract numbers is itself far from innate."이 된다. 따라서 itself는 that절의 주어인 the very concept of abstract numbers를 가리킨다는 것을 알 수 있으므로 (B)가 정답이다.

39. With which of the following statements would the author be LEAST likely to agree?

(A) **Children naturally and easily learn mathematics.**

(B) Children learn to add before they learn to subtract.

(C) Most people follow the same pattern of mathematical development.

(D) Mathematical development is subtle and gradual.

[해석] 다음 문장 중 글쓴이가 가장 동의할 것 같지 않은 것은 무엇인가?
    (A) 아이들은 선천적으로 쉽게 수학을 배운다.
    (B) 아이들은 빼기를 배우기 전에 더하기를 배운다.
    (C) 대부분의 사람들이 수학 발달에 동일한 패턴을 따른다.
    (D) 수학 발달은 감지하기 힘들고 점차적이다.

[어휘] **naturally** 자연적으로, 선천적으로   **subtle** 감지하기 힘든, 인식하기 어려운

[해설] LEAST로 미루어 글에 언급된 내용에 반대되는 것을 묻는 문제이다. 두 번째 단락 마지막 두 문장 Such studies have suggested that the rudiments of mathematics are mastered gradually and with effort. They have also suggested that the very concept of abstract numbers ~ is itself far from innate.에서 수학의 원리는 서서히 노력해서 습득해야 하는 것이며, 선천적인 것과는 거리가 멀다고 했다. 따라서 이와 반대로 아이들은 선천적으로 쉽게 수학을 배운다는 (A)가 정답이 된다.

40. Where in the passage does the author give an example of a hypothetical experiment?

(A) Lines 3–6

(B) **Lines 7–9**

(C) Lines 11–14

(D) Lines 18–21

[해석] 이 지문에서 글쓴이가 가상 실험의 일례를 제시한 부분은 어디인가?
    (A) 3–6행
    (B) 7–9행
    (C) 11–14행
    (D) 18–21행

[어휘] **hypothetical** 가설의, 가상의   **experiment** 실험

[해설] 글쓴이가 가상 내용을 언급한 부분을 찾는 문제이다. 여기서는 가정법 문장(if a child were secluded on a desert island at birth and retrieved seven years later, he or she could enter a second-grade mathematics class without any serious problems of intellectual adjustment)이 문제 해결의 단서가 된다. 따라서 (B)가 정답이다.

Botany, the study of plants, occupies a [42]peculiar position in the history of human knowledge. [41]For many thousands of years, it was the one field of awareness about which humans had anything more than the vaguest of insights. It is impossible to know today just what our Stone Age ancestors knew about plants, but from what we can observe of preindustrial societies that still exist, a detailed learning of plants and their properties must be extremely ancient. [43]This is logical. Plants are the basis of the food pyramid for all living things, even for other plants. [50]They have always been enormously important to the welfare of people, not only for food, but also for clothing, weapons, tools, dyes, medicines, shelter, and a great many other purposes. [41]Tribes living today in the jungles of the Amazon recognize literally hundreds of plants and know many [44]properties of each. To them botany, as such, has no name and is probably not even recognized as a special branch of knowledge at all.

[45]Unfortunately, the more industrialized we become the farther away we move from direct contact with plants, and the less distinct our knowledge of botany grows. Yet everyone comes unconsciously on an amazing amount of botanical knowledge, and [41]few people will fail to recognize [46]a rose, an apple, or an orchid. [47]When our Neolithic ancestors, living in the Middle East about 10,000 years ago, discovered that certain grasses could be harvested and their seeds planted for richer yields the next season, the first great step in a new association of plants and humans was taken. Grains were discovered and from them flowed the marvel of agriculture: cultivated crops. [49]From then on, humans would increasingly take their living from the [48]controlled production of a few plants rather than getting a little here and a little there from many varieties that grew wild—and the accumulated knowledge of tens of thousands of years of experience and intimacy with plants in the wild would begin to fade away.

[해석] 식물을 연구하는 식물학은 인간 지식의 역사에서 특별한 부분을 차지한다. 수천 년 동안 식물학은 인간에게 가장 막연한 통찰력 그 이상이 있다고 인식했던 한 분야였다. 석기시대 조상들이 식물에 관해 무엇을 알고 있었던지 아는 것은 불가능하지만, 여전히 존재하는 산업화 이전의 사회를 관찰한 것에서 미뤄보면 식물과 그 특성에 대한 상세한 지식은 아주 오래되었음이 틀림없다. 이 추측은 이치에 맞는다. 식물은 모든 생명체의 먹이사슬의 토대이며, 심지어 다른 식물들에게도 마찬가지이다. 식물들은 식량뿐만 아니라 옷과 무기, 도구, 염료, 약품, 주거, 아주 많은 다른 용도로 사람들의 복지에 극히 중요했다. 오늘날 아마존 정글 지역에 사는 부족들은 말 그대로 수백 가지의 식물을 식별하며 각 식물의 특성에 대해서도 많이 알고 있다. 그들에게 식물학을 뜻하는 이름도 없거니와 특별한 지식의 한 분야로 인식되지도 않는다.

안타깝게도, 우리는 산업화되면 될수록 식물과의 직접적인 접촉에서 더 멀어지고, 식물학에 대한 우리의 지식도 점점 덜 명확해진다. 그러나 모든 사람들이 많은 양의 식물학 지식에는 무감각해지더라도 장미와 사과, 난초를 식별하지 못하는 사람들은 거의 없을 것이다. 1만년 전에 중동 지역에서 살았던 신석기 시대의 우리 조상들이 어떤 풀들을 수확할 수 있으며 그 씨앗들을 심으면 다음 계절에는 더 많이 수확한다는 것을 알게 되었을 때, 식물과 인간의 새로운 조합에서 이뤄낸 위대한 첫 단계였다. 곡식이 발견되었고 그로 인해 농업이라는 경이로움, 즉 경작된 수확물이 생겨났다. 그때부터 점차적으로 인간들은 야생에서 자라는 많은 다양한 식물들에서 먹을 것을 여기에서 조금 저기에서 조금 얻기보다는 몇몇 식물을 관리해 수확으로 생계를 유지했으며, 수만 년 동안의 경험에서 축적된 지식과 야생 식물과의 친숙함은 사라져가기 시작했다.

[어휘] **botany** 식물학 *cf.* **botanical** 식물학의, 식물에 관한 **peculiar** 특이한, 독특한 **awareness** 알고 있음, 자각, 인식 **vague** 모호한, 애매한 **insight** 통찰력 **Stone Age** 석기시대 **ancestor** 조상, 선조 **preindustrial** 산업화 이전의 **detailed** 자세한, 상세한 **property** 속성, 특성 **logical** 논리적인, 필연적인 **food pyramid** (피라미드형) 먹이사슬 **enormously** 거대하게, 막대하게, 엄청나게 **welfare** 복지, 행복 **dye** 물감, 염료 **shelter** 피난처, 대피소 **literally** 문자 그대로, 말 그대로 **branch** (학문 등의) 부문, 분과 **industrialize** 공업화하다, 산업화하다 **distinct** 독특한, 분명한 **unconsciously** 무의식적으로 **orchid** 난초 **Neolithic** 신석기 시대의 **yield** 산출하다, 수확하다 **association** 교제, 친밀한 관계 **flow** 생기다, 우러나다 **marvel** 놀라움, 경이로움 **cultivate** 경작하다 **accumulate** 모으다, 축적하다 **intimacy** 친밀함 **fade away** 사라지다, 없어지다

41. Which of the following assumptions about early humans is expressed in the passage?

(A) **They probably had extensive knowledge of plants.**

(B) They divided knowledge into well-defined fields.

(C) They did not enjoy the study of botany.

(D) They placed great importance on ownership of property.

[해석] 다음 초기 인간들에 관한 가정들 중 지문에 언급된 것은 무엇인가?
(A) **아마도 식물에 대한 해박한 지식을 갖고 있었다.**
(B) 지식을 명확한 분야로 분류했다.
(C) 식물학 공부를 좋아하지 않았다.
(D) 재산 소유권을 중요하게 생각했다.

[어휘] **assumption** 가정, 추측   **extensive** 광범위한, 해박한   **divide A into B** A를 B로 분류하다   **well-defined** (정의가) 명확한, (윤곽이) 뚜렷한   **place great importance on** ~을 매우 중요하게 생각하다   **ownership** 소유; 소유권   **property** 재산, 자산, 부동산

[해설] 글 전체에서 인간들이 아주 오랫동안 식물에 대해 많은 지식을 갖고 있었다는 사실을 강조하고 있다. 따라서 (A)가 정답이다. 특히, 첫 단락의 For many thousands of years, it was the one field of awareness about which humans had anything more than the vaguest of insights.나 Tribes living today in the jungles of the Amazon recognize literally hundreds of plants and know many properties of each.와, 두 번째 단락의 few people will fail to recognize a rose, an apple, or an orchid 등에서 단서를 찾을 수 있다.

42. The word "peculiar" in line 1 is closest in meaning to

(A) clear

(B) large

(C) **unusual**

(D) important

[해석] 1행에 언급된 "peculiar"와 의미상 가장 가까운 것은 무엇인가?
(A) 분명한
(B) 커다란
(C) **특이한**
(D) 중요한

[해설] 어휘 문제이다. Botany, the study of plants, occupies a peculiar position in the history of human knowledge.에서 peculiar는 '독특한, 특이한'의 의미로 쓰였다. 따라서 (C) unusual과 바꿔 쓸 수 있다.

43. What does the comment "This is logical" in line 6 mean?

(A) There is no clear way to determine the extent of our ancestors' knowledge of plants.

(B) **It is not surprising that early humans had a detailed knowledge of plants.**

(C) It is reasonable to assume that our ancestors behaved very much like people in preindustrial societies.

(D) Human knowledge of plants is well organized and very detailed.

[해석] 6행에 언급된 "This is logical"이 의미하는 것은 무엇인가?
(A) 우리 조상들이 식물에 대해 알고 있는 지식의 정도를 알아낼 명확한 방법이 없다.
(B) **초기 인간들이 식물에 대한 상세한 지식을 갖고 있었다는 것은 놀랄 일이 아니다.**
(C) 우리 조상들이 산업화 이전 사회의 사람들과 아주 유사하게 행동했다고 추측하는 것은 합당하다.
(D) 식물에 대해 알고 있는 인간의 지식은 잘 정리되어 있고 아주 상세하다.

[어휘] **determine** 알아내다, 밝히다   **extent** 정도, 범위   **reasonable** 합리적인, 합당한   **organized** 정리된, 계획된

[해설] This is logical.은 앞에서 언급한 정보, 즉 식물은 아주 중요했기 때문에 우리 조상들이 식물에 대한 세부 지식을 많이 갖고 있었다는 추측이 논리적이라는 뜻이다. 따라서 (B)가 정답이다.

44. The phrase "properties of each" in line 10 refers to each

(A) tribe

(B) hundred

(C) **plant**

(D) purpose

[해석] 10행에 언급된 "properties of each"가 가리키는 것은 무엇인가?
(A) 부족
(B) 100
(C) **식물**
(D) 목적

45. According to the passage, why has general knowledge of botany declined?

(A) People no longer value plants as a useful resource.

(B) Botany is not recognized as a special branch of science.

(C) Research is unable to keep up with the increasing number of plants.

(D) Direct contact with a variety of plants has decreased.

[해석] 지문에 따르면 식물학에 대한 전반적인 지식이 감소한 이유는 무엇인가?
    (A) 사람들이 더 이상 식물을 유용한 자원으로 중요하게 생각하지 않아서
    (B) 식물학이 특별한 과학 분야로 인식되지 않아서
    (C) 연구가 증가하는 식물의 수를 따라갈 수 없어서
    (D) 다양한 식물들과 직접 접할 기회가 감소해서

[어휘] **value** 중요시하다, 소중히 하다　**keep up with** ～을 따라잡다, ～에 뒤떨어지지 않다

[해설] 두 번째 단락 첫 번째 문장 Unfortunately, the more industrialized we become the farther away we move from direct contact with plants, and the less distinct our knowledge of botany grows.에서 산업화되면 될수록 식물과의 직접적인 접촉이 줄어서 식물학에 대한 지식도 감소한다고 했다. 따라서 (D)가 정답이다.

46. In line 15, what is the author's purpose in mentioning "a rose, an apple, or an orchid"?

(A) To make the passage more poetic

(B) To cite examples of plants that are attractive

(C) To give botanical examples that most readers will recognize

(D) To illustrate the diversity of botanical life

[해석] 15행에서 글쓴이가 "a rose, an apple, or an orchid"를 언급한 목적은 무엇인가?
    (A) 글을 더 시적으로 만들려고
    (B) 매력적인 식물의 예를 들려고
    (C) 대부분의 독자들이 식별할 식물의 예를 제시하려고
    (D) 식물 생명의 다양성을 설명하려고

[어휘] **poetic** 시적인　**cite** 인용하다, 언급하다　**attractive** 매력적인, 멋진　**illustrate** 설명하다; 삽화를 넣다　**diversity** 다양(성)

[해설] 글쓴이가 "a rose, an apple, or an orchid"를 언급한 이유는 장미와 사과와 난초가 대부분 사람들에게 친숙한 흔한 식물이기 때문이다. 따라서 (C)가 정답이다.

47. According to the passage, what was the first great step toward the practice of agriculture?

(A) The invention of agricultural implements and machinery

(B) The development of a system of names for plants

(C) The discovery of grasses that could be harvested and replanted

(D) The changing diets of early humans

[해석] 지문에 따르면, 농업을 시작하게 된 위대한 첫 단계는 무엇이었는가?
    (A) 농기구의 발명
    (B) 식물 명칭 체계의 발달
    (C) 수확하고 이식할 수 있는 식물의 발견
    (D) 초기 인간들의 변화하는 식단

[어휘] **practice** 관습, 관례　**implement** 연장, 도구　**replant** 옮겨 심다, 이식하다

[해설] 사실 정보 파악 문제이다. 두 번째 단락 중반부의 When our Neolithic ancestors, living in the Middle East about 10,000 years ago, discovered that certain grasses could be harvested and their seeds planted for richer yields the next season, the first great step in a new association of plants and humans was taken.에서 어떤 풀들을 수확할 수 있으며 그 씨앗들을 심으면 다음 계절에는 더 많이 수확한다는 것을 알게 된 것이 농업의 첫 단계라고 했다. 따라서 (C)가 정답이다.

48. The word "controlled" in line 20 is closest in meaning to

(A) abundant

(B) managed

(C) required

(D) advanced

[해석] 20행에 언급된 "controlled"와 의미상 가장 가까운 것은 무엇인가?
　(A) 풍부한
　(B) 관리되는
　(C) 요구되는
　(D) 앞선

[해설] 어휘 문제이다. From then on, humans would increasingly take their living from the controlled production of a few plants ~에서 controlled는 '관리된, 통제된, 조절된'이라는 의미로 쓰였다. 따라서 (B) managed와 바꿔 쓸 수 있다.

49. Which of the following can be inferred from the passage about the transition to agriculture?

(A) It forced humans to study plants more carefully so that they would know how to collect and plant seeds.

(B) It led to a more narrow understanding of plants as a source of food, but not for other purposes.

(C) It had a drawback in that humans lost much of their knowledge of wild plants as a result.

(D) It led to a diet that consisted of a greater variety of plants.

[해석] 다음 중 이 지문을 통해 농업의 변천에 대해 추론할 수 있는 것은 무엇인가?
　(A) 씨앗을 채집하고 심는 방법을 알기 위해 인간들로 하여금 식물에 대해 더 주의 깊게 공부하도록 했다.
　(B) 식물을 다른 용도가 아닌 식량 공급원으로 더 제한적으로 이해하게 되었다.
　(C) 결과적으로 인간들이 야생 식물에 대한 많은 지식을 잃었다는 단점이 생겼다.
　(D) 더 많은 다양한 식물로 이루어진 식단이 생겼다.

[어휘] transition 변천, 변화　　drawback 결점, 단점

[해설] 지문의 마지막 문장 From then on, humans would increasingly take their living from the controlled production of a few plants rather than getting a little here and a little there from many varieties that grew wild—and the accumulated knowledge of tens of thousands of years of experience and intimacy with plants in the wild would begin to fade away.에서 농업으로 인해 수만 년 동안의 경험에서 축적된 지식과 야생 식물과의 친숙함은 사라져가기 시작했다고 했으므로 긍정적인 발전이 아니었음을 추론할 수 있다. 따라서 (C)가 정답이다.

50. Where in the passage does the author describe the benefits people derive from plants?

(A) Line 1

(B) Lines 7–9

(C) Lines 10–11

(D) Lines 13–15

[해석] 글쓴이가 사람들이 식물로부터 얻은 혜택에 대해 묘사한 부분은 어디인가?
　(A) 1행
　(B) 7–9행
　(C) 10–11행
　(D) 13–15행

[어휘] derive 얻다, 끌어내다, 찾다

[해설] 첫 단락의 They have always been enormously important to the welfare of people, not only for food, but also for clothing, weapons, tools, dyes, medicines, shelter, and a great many other purposes.에서 식물들은 식량뿐만 아니라 옷과 무기, 도구, 염료, 약품, 주거와 아주 많은 다른 용도로 사람들의 복지에 극히 중요하다면서 사람들이 식물로부터 얻은 혜택에 대해 언급하고 있다. 따라서 (B)가 정답이다.

Complete TOEFL ITP Practice Test

Section 1 **Listening Comprehension** – 본문 p.109

Part A

1. (C)	2. (B)	3. (A)	4. (A)	5. (A)
6. (A)	7. (C)	8. (A)	9. (C)	10. (B)
11. (A)	12. (B)	13. (B)	14. (A)	15. (A)
16. (B)	17. (D)	18. (D)	19. (C)	20. (B)
21. (C)	22. (D)	23. (D)	24. (C)	25. (D)
26. (C)	27. (C)	28. (A)	29. (C)	30. (D)

Part B

31. (A)	32. (B)	33. (D)	34. (B)	35. (B)
36. (D)	37. (C)	38. (C)		

Part C

39. (B)	40. (A)	41. (A)	42. (C)	43. (D)
44. (C)	45. (B)	46. (A)	47. (D)	48. (B)
49. (C)	50. (B)			

Part A

1. ***M*** Would you like to go to the movies with Lois and me on Friday?

W I wish I could, but I'm having dinner at my brother's.

N What will the woman do on Friday?

(A) Go to the movies with the man
(B) Take her brother to the movies
(C) Eat at her brother's home
(D) Cook dinner with Lois

[해석] *M* 금요일에 나와 로이스와 함께 영화 보러 갈래?
W 그러고 싶지만 남동생네 집에서 저녁을 먹을 거야.

N 여자는 금요일에 무엇을 할 것인가?

(A) 남자와 함께 영화를 보러 갈 것이다
(B) 자신의 남동생을 극장에 데려갈 것이다
(C) 자신의 남동생 집에서 식사를 할 것이다
(D) 로이스와 함께 저녁을 요리할 것이다.

[어휘] **take A to B** A를 B에 데리고 가다

2. ***M*** Need a hand with those boxes?

W That's OK, I can manage. They're empty.

N What does the woman mean?

(A) The man should have offered his assistance earlier.
(B) She does not need the man's help.
(C) She did not realize the boxes were empty.
(D) She wants the man to move the boxes.

[해석] *M* 그 상자들을 옮기는 거 도와줄까?
W 괜찮아. 내가 할 수 있어. 빈 상자들이야.

N 여자가 의미하는 것은 무엇인가?

(A) 남자는 더 일찍 도와주겠다고 제안했어야 했다.
(B) 여자는 남자의 도움이 필요 없다.
(C) 여자는 상자들이 비어 있다는 것을 몰랐다.
(D) 여자는 남자가 상자를 옮기기를 원한다.

[어휘] **hand** (원조의) 손길, 도움   **manage** 애를 써서 ~하다, 어떻게든 ~하다   **should have p.p.** ~했어야 했다
assistance 돕기, 원조

3. ***W*** Do you want the windows open or closed?

M I almost always prefer fresh air, if possible.

N What does the man imply?

(A) He would like to have the windows open.
(B) He rarely leaves the windows open.
(C) He thinks the air is polluted.
(D) He will help her close the windows.

W 창문을 열기를 원하세요, 아니면 닫기를 원하세요?

M 나는 거의 늘 맑은 공기가 좋아요, 가능하다면요.

N 남자가 암시하는 것은 무엇인가?

(A) 그는 창문을 열기를 원한다.

(B) 그는 창문을 거의 열어 놓지 않는다.

(C) 그는 공기가 오염되어 있다고 생각한다.

(D) 그는 그녀가 창문 닫는 것을 도와줄 것이다.

[어휘] **if possible** 가능하다면, 될 수 있다면   **rarely** 거의 ~하지 않는   **polluted** 오염된

---

4. M Hello. This is Mark Smith. I'm calling to see if my blood test results are in.

W Dr. Miller just sent them to the lab last night, so the earliest they could be back is tomorrow.

N What does the woman mean?

(A) The results might be ready tomorrow.

(B) The man needs another test tomorrow.

(C) The results were called in last night.

(D) The doctor called the lab again.

[해석] M 안녕하세요. 마크 스미스입니다. 제 혈액 검사 결과가 나왔는지 궁금해서 전화 드렸습니다.

W 밀러 박사님께서 어젯밤에 검사실에 보내셨어요. 그러니 최대한 빨라도 내일은 되어야 결과가 나올 거예요.

N 여자가 의미하는 것은 무엇인가?

(A) 결과가 내일 나올 것이다.

(B) 남자는 내일 다른 검사를 해야 한다.

(C) 결과는 어젯밤에 전화로 통보되었다.

(D) 의사가 검사실에 다시 전화를 했다.

[어휘] **blood test** 혈액 검사   **lab** 실험실, 연구실(= laboratory)   **call in** 전화로 보고하다

---

5. M I need to talk to someone who knows a lot about Portland. Someone said you lived there.

W Oh, but I was really young at the time.

N What does the woman imply?

(A) She does not remember much about Portland.

(B) She has never been to Portland.

(C) She knows someone else who could help him.

(D) She would be happy to talk to the man later.

[해석] M 포틀랜드에 대해 잘 아는 사람과 이야기를 나눠야 해요. 누군가가 당신이 거기 살았었다고 하더군요.

W 오, 하지만 그땐 아주 어릴 때였어요.

N 여자가 암시하는 것은 무엇인가?

(A) 그녀는 포틀랜드에 대해 기억이 잘 나지 않는다.

(B) 그녀는 한 번도 포틀랜드에 가 본 적이 없다.

(C) 그녀는 그를 도와줄 수 있는 누군가를 알고 있다.

(D) 그녀는 나중에 남자와 이야기하고 싶어 한다.

---

6. M Do you have to play that music so loud? I've got a test tomorrow!

W Sorry, I didn't realize you were studying.

N What will the woman probably do?

(A) Turn down the volume

(B) Help the man study for a test

(C) Play a different kind of music

(D) Speak louder

[해석] M 음악을 그렇게 시끄럽게 틀어야 하니? 나 내일 시험 있어!

W 미안해. 난 네가 공부하고 있는 줄 몰랐어.

N 여자는 어떻게 할 것 같은가?

(A) 소리를 줄일 것이다

(B) 남자가 시험 공부하는 것을 도와줄 것이다

(C) 다른 종류의 음악을 틀 것이다

(D) 더 큰 소리로 말할 것이다

[어휘] **turn down** (소리 · 밝기 · 세기 등을) 줄이다

7. *M* Pam, I don't understand the problem. You've known for months this report was due today.

W I know. But I'm afraid I need another few days. The data was harder to interpret than I thought it would be.

N What does the woman mean?

(A) She forgot when the report was due.

(B) She would like the man to help her with the report.

(C) She needs more time to finish the report.

(D) She has not included any data in her report.

[해석] *M* 팸, 난 문제를 이해할 수가 없네요. 이 보고서를 오늘까지 제출해야 한다는 것을 몇 달째 알고 있었잖아요.

W 알아요. 하지만 며칠 더 걸릴 것 같아요. 데이터를 해석하는 것이 내가 생각했던 것보다 더 어려웠어요.

N 여자가 의미하는 것은 무엇인가?

(A) 그녀는 보고서 제출일이 언제인지 잊어버렸다.

(B) 그녀는 남자가 자신의 보고서를 도와주기를 바란다.

(C) 그녀는 보고서를 완성하는 데 시간이 더 필요하다.

(D) 그녀는 보고서에 아무 데이터도 포함하지 않았다.

[어휘] **due** (지급 · 제출) 기일이 된   **interpret** 해석하다, 통역하다

8. *W* So how are you getting along with Debbie's cat?

M Well, she never comes when I call her, she spills her food, and she sheds all over the place. I can't wait till Debbie gets back.

N What does the man imply?

(A) The cat is causing him problems.

(B) The cat is quite friendly.

(C) He does not get along with Debbie.

(D) He is glad Debbie gave him the cat.

[해석] *W* 그래서 데비의 고양이와는 잘 지내고 있어?

M 글쎄, 그 고양이는 내가 불러도 오지 않고, 먹이를 쏟는데다 온 집안에 털이 빠져. 데비가 얼른 돌아오면 좋겠어.

N 남자가 암시하는 것은 무엇인가?

(A) 고양이는 그에게 문제를 일으키고 있다.

(B) 고양이가 아주 다정하다.

(C) 그는 데비와 잘 지내지 못한다.

(D) 그는 데비가 자신에게 고양이를 줘 기쁘다.

[어휘] **get along with** ~와 사이 좋게 지내다   **spill** 엎지르다, 쏟다   **shed** 털이 빠지다   **cause** 일으키다, 야기하다   **friendly** 친절한, 다정한

9. *M* This crazy bus schedule has got me completely frustrated. I can't for the life of me figure out when my bus to Cleveland leaves.

W Why don't you just go up to the ticket window and ask?

N What does the woman suggest the man do?

(A) Try to get a seat next to the window

(B) Find another passenger going to Cleveland

(C) Ask for information about the departure time

(D) Find out if there are any seats left on the bus

[해석] *M* 이 말도 안 되는 버스 시간표 때문에 정말 짜증이 나요. 아무리 애를 써도 내가 탈 클리블랜드행 버스가 언제 출발하는지 도무지 알 수 없어요.

W 그냥 매표창구에 가서 물어보지 그래요?

N 여자는 남자에게 어떻게 하라고 제안하는가?

(A) 창가 자리를 구하도록 애써 볼 것

(B) 클리블랜드에 가는 다른 승객을 찾아볼 것

(C) 출발 시간에 관한 정보를 물어볼 것

(D) 버스에 남아 있는 좌석이 있는지 알아볼 것

[어휘] **frustrated** 낙담한, 실망한, 좌절된   **not for the life of me** 아무리 해도 ~ 않다   **figure out** ~을 알아내다   **ticket window** 매표창구   **passenger** 승객   **departure time** 출발 시간

10. **M** I bought this fish to cook for my dinner tonight, but it doesn't look all that fresh to me now. Would you say it's still all right to eat?

W Let's take a look. Oh, if I were you, I wouldn't even think of it.

N What does the woman mean?

(A) She forgot to stop at the store.

(B) The man should not eat the fish.

(C) The fish is safe to eat.

(D) The food should not be reheated.

[해석] M 오늘밤 저녁 요리를 하려고 이 생선을 샀어요. 그런데 지금 보니 그렇게 싱싱해 보이지 않는군요. 그래도 먹어도 괜찮을까요?

W 어디 봐요. 이런. 내가 당신이라면 그런 생각조차 하지 않을 거예요.

N 여자가 의미하는 것은 무엇인가?

(A) 여자는 그 가게에 들르는 것을 잊어 버렸다.

(B) 남자는 생선을 먹지 말아야 한다.

(C) 생선은 먹기 안전하다.

(D) 그 음식을 다시 데우면 안 된다.

[어휘] **take a look** 한 번 슬쩍 보다   **reheat** 다시 가열하다, 새로 데우다

---

11. **M** Would you like to go with me to the airport to pick up Frank?

W I'd like to, but I have class till 2:00. And I know Frank's decided to take the early flight.

N What does the woman imply?

(A) She will not be able to go with the man.

(B) She does not think Frank is arriving until tomorrow morning.

(C) She has to pick up Frank at 2 :00.

(D) She does not know when her class will end.

[해석] M 나와 함께 공항으로 프랭크를 마중 나갈래?

W 그러고 싶은데 나는 2시까지 수업이 있어. 그런데 내가 알기로 프랭크는 이른 항공편을 타기로 했잖아.

N 여자가 암시하는 것은 무엇인가?

(A) 그녀는 남자와 함께 갈 수 없을 것이다.

(B) 그녀는 프랭크가 내일 아침은 되어야 도착할 것이라고 생각한다.

(C) 그녀는 2시에 프랭크를 마중 나가야 한다.

(D) 그녀는 자신의 수업이 언제 끝날지 모른다.

[어휘] **pick up** 태우다, 마중 나가다   **flight** 항공편, 비행기(편)

---

12. **W** Did you catch our very own Professor Stiller on TV last night?

M I almost missed it! But my mother just happened to be watching at home and gave me a call.

N What does the man mean?

(A) He watched the television program with his mother.

(B) His mother reminded him that his professor was on television.

(C) Answering the phone caused him to miss the television program.

(D) His mother missed the television program.

[해석] W 너는 어젯밤에 우리 스틸러 교수님이 TV에 출연하신 것 봤니?

M 거의 못 볼 뻔했어! 그런데 엄마가 우연히 집에서 보고 계시다가 내게 전화해 주셨어.

N 남자가 의미하는 것은 무엇인가?

(A) 그는 엄마와 함께 그 TV 프로그램을 봤다.

(B) 엄마가 그에게 교수님이 TV에 출연했다는 것을 알려줬다.

(C) 그는 전화를 받느라 그 TV 프로그램을 보지 못했다.

(D) 그의 엄마는 그 TV 프로그램을 보지 못했다.

[어휘] **miss** 놓치다, 빠뜨리다   **happen to+동사원형** 우연히 ～하다, 뜻밖에 ～하다   **remind** 상기시키다, 생각나게 하다   **answer the phone** 전화를 받다

13. **W** These summer days are getting to be more than I can take. It was even too hot to go to the pool yesterday.

M Hold on; according to the weather report we should have some relief by the end of the week.

N What does the man mean?

(A) The pool will be open all week.

(B) The weather will cool down soon.

(C) The woman should go swimming.

(D) He prefers to stay inside in hot weather.

[해석] W 이런 여름 날씨를 점점 더 견딜 수가 없어요. 어제는 너무 더워서 심지어 수영장에도 갈 수 없을 정도였어요.

M 잠깐만요, 일기예보에 따르면 이번 주말까지는 좀 나아진대요.

N 남자가 의미하는 것은 무엇인가?

(A) 수영장은 일주일 내내 개장할 것이다.
(B) 날씨가 곧 시원해질 것이다.
(C) 여자는 수영하러 가야 한다.
(D) 남자는 날씨가 더울 때는 실내에 머무는 것을 더 좋아한다.

[어휘] **take** 견디다, 감수하다   **hold on** (전화를) 끊지 않고 두다, 기다리다   **weather report** 일기예보   **relief** 경감, 완화   **cool down** 서늘해지다, 서늘하게 하다

---

14. **M** My roommate and I have decided to do our own cooking next semester.

W Then I hope you'll have a lighter schedule than this term.

N What problem does the woman think the man may have?

(A) He may not have enough time to cook.

(B) He may spend more money on food next semester.

(C) He may gain weight if he does his own cooking.

(D) He may not enjoy cooking.

[해석] M 나와 룸메이트는 다음 학기에는 우리가 직접 요리를 하기로 정했어.

W 그럼, 이번 학기보다는 일정이 좀 더 한가하기를 바랄게.

N 여자는 남자에게 무슨 문제가 있을지도 모른다고 생각하는가?

(A) 그가 요리를 할 만큼 충분한 시간이 없을지도 모른다.
(B) 그는 다음 학기에는 요리에 더 많은 돈을 쓸지도 모른다.
(C) 그는 직접 요리를 하면 체중이 늘지도 모른다.
(D) 그는 요리를 즐기지 않을지도 모른다.

[어휘] **semester** 학기   **term** 학기   **gain weight** 체중이 늘다

---

15. **W** Come on, we're almost there. I'll race you to the top of the hill.

M I'm so out of shape, I might have to crawl the rest of the way.

N What can be inferred about the man?

(A) He is tired.

(B) He lost the race.

(C) He has already been to the top of the hill.

(D) He prefers doing exercise indoors.

[해석] W 자, 거의 다 왔어요. 우리 언덕 꼭대기까지 경주해요.

M 나는 몸이 엉망이에요. 나는 이제 남은 길은 기어가야 할지도 몰라요.

N 남자에 대해 추론할 수 있는 것은 무엇인가?

(A) 그는 피곤하다.
(B) 그는 경주에서 졌다.
(C) 그는 이미 언덕 꼭대기까지 갔다 왔다.
(D) 그는 실내에서 운동하는 것을 더 좋아한다.

[어휘] **race** ~와 경주하다   **out of shape** 몸 상태가 나쁜   **crawl** 기다, 기어가다   **indoors** 실내에서 (↔ outdoors 실외에서)

---

16. **M** Yes, hello, this is Robert White calling. Could Dr. Jones see me on Tuesday morning instead of Thursday afternoon?

W Tuesday morning? Let's see ... is that the only other time you could come?

N What does the woman imply?

(A) The doctor only has time on Tuesdays.

(B) The doctor is busy on Tuesday morning.

(C) The man must come more than one time.

(D) The man must arrive on time.

[해석] M 네, 안녕하세요, 로버트 화이트입니다. 목요일 오후 대신 화요일 오전에 존스 박사님께 진료를 받을 수 있을까요?

W 화요일 아침이요? 한 번 볼게요… 그때 외에는 못 오시는 거죠?

N 여자가 암시하는 것은 무엇인가?

(A) 의사가 화요일에만 시간이 있다.

(B) 의사가 화요일 오전에 바쁘다.

(C) 남자는 한번 이상 와야 한다.

(D) 남자는 제시간에 도착해야 한다.

[어휘] **instead of** ~대신에   **on time** 정시에, 제때에

---

17. **M** I really need to make some extra money. I've practically spent my entire budget for the semester.

W You should check out the new cafeteria. I think there're a few openings left in the evening.

N What does the woman suggest the man do?

(A) Eat at the cafeteria more often

(B) Find out when the cafeteria opens

(C) Meet her in the cafeteria this evening

(D) Try to get a job at the cafeteria

[해석] M 나는 정말 돈을 더 벌어야 해. 사실 이번 학기의 예산을 다 써 버렸어.

W 새로 문을 연 카페테리아에 확인해 봐. 아마 저녁 일자리가 좀 남아 있을 거야.

N 여자는 남자에게 어떻게 하라고 제안하는가?

(A) 카페테리아에서 더 자주 식사를 할 것

(B) 카페테리아가 언제 문을 여는지 알아볼 것

(C) 오늘 저녁에 카페테리아에서 그녀를 만날 것

(D) 카페테리아에서 일자리를 찾아볼 것

[어휘] **practically** 사실상, 실제로는   **budget** 예산   **semester** 학기   **check out** ~을 확인하다   **opening** 빈자리, 일자리

---

18. **M** These long drives always wear me out. Instead of just stopping at a fast-food place, why don't we take some time out for a nice lunch?

W That's a great idea! It'll make the trip a bit longer, but at least we'll be refreshed when we get there.

N What will the speakers probably do?

(A) Cancel their trip

(B) Make a quick stop for a meal

(C) Arrive at their destination early

(D) Have a longer lunch than originally planned

[해석] M 이렇게 장거리 운전을 하면 항상 녹초가 돼요. 패스트푸드점에 들르는 대신 시간을 좀 내서 근사한 점심을 먹으러 가는 건 어때요?

W 정말 좋은 생각이에요! 그러면 여행 시간은 좀 더 걸리겠지만, 적어도 거기에 가면 기운이 날 거예요.

N 화자들은 무엇을 할 것 같은가?

(A) 여행을 취소할 것이다

(B) 식사를 위해 잠깐 정차할 것이다

(C) 목적지에 일찍 도착할 것이다

(D) 원래 계획보다 더 오랫동안 점심을 먹을 것이다

[어휘] **wear out** ~을 지치게 하다, 싫증나게 하다   **refreshed** 재충전되는, 기운이 나는   **cancel** 취소하다   **make a quick stop** 잠깐 정차하다   **destination** 목적지

---

19. **M** This notice says that all the introductory psychology classes are closed.

W That can't be true! There're supposed to be thirteen sections of it this semester.

N What does the woman mean?

(A) She does not want to take the course this semester.

(B) She thought the class would be easy.

(C) She is surprised that all the sections are filled.

(D) There are only thirteen students in the psychology class.

20. W Whoops! Did any of my coffee just spill on you?

M Just a little, but it wasn't really hot.

N What does the man imply?

(A) He does not like to drink coffee.
(B) He is not upset by the accident.
(C) The woman should apologize.
(D) The woman has spilled coffee on him before.

21. W Oh, my shirt sleeve. Must have gotten caught on that nail.

M Here, let me take a look. Hmm ... with a needle and thread, this can be mended— and look just like new.

N What does the man mean?

(A) The woman will have to buy a new sweater.
(B) The sweater looks just like the woman's new one.
(C) The sweater can be repaired easily.
(D) The woman should not put sharp objects in her sweater pocket.

22. W I'm looking for a lightweight jacket . . . navy blue ... medium ...

M Let's see. Have you checked the sales rack in the back? There were still a few there yesterday.

N What does the man mean?

(A) The jackets sold out quickly.
(B) The sale ended yesterday.
(C) He will check with the sales clerk.
(D) The woman might find a jacket on sale.

[해석] W 가벼운 재킷을 찾고 있어요… 짙은 감색의… 중간 사이즈로 요….

M 어디 보죠. 뒤쪽의 세일 상품 진열대는 보셨어요? 어제 거기에 몇 벌 있었거든요.

N 남자가 의미하는 것은 무엇인가?

(A) 재킷이 빠르게 다 팔렸다.
(B) 어제 세일이 끝났다.
(C) 남자는 판매 직원에게 확인해 볼 것이다.
(D) 여자는 할인 중인 재킷을 찾을지도 모른다.

[어휘] lightweight 가벼운, 경량의   medium 중간 사이즈(의)
sales rack 세일 상품 진열대   sell out 다 팔리다, 품절되다
on sale 할인 중인, 판매 중인

---

23. M I've figured it all out. It looks like it'll take us about six hours to drive from here to Chicago.

W It'd be more relaxing to take the train. But, I guess we should watch our expenses.

N What does the woman imply?

(A) She likes to drive when she travels.
(B) She does not want to go to Chicago.
(C) She does not know how much the train trip will cost.
(D) It is cheaper to go to Chicago by car.

[해석] M 전부 다 알아냈어요. 우리가 차로 여기서 시카고까지 가는 데 6시간 정도 걸릴 것 같아요.

W 기차를 타고 가는 게 더 편할 거예요. 하지만, 비용도 생각해 봐요죠.

N 여자가 암시하는 것은 무엇인가?

(A) 그녀는 여행할 때 차로 가는 것을 좋아한다.
(B) 그녀는 시카고에 가고 싶어하지 않는다.
(C) 그녀는 기차 여행 경비가 얼마나 들지 모른다.
(D) 시카고에 차로 가는 것이 더 저렴하다.

[어휘] figure out ~을 생각해내다, 알아내다, 이해하다   relaxing
편안한, 느긋한   watch 주의하다, 조심하다   expense
경비, 비용

---

24. M I've been working out at the gym since January … I'd been wanting to get in better shape.

W You look terrific! Seems like all your hard work has paid off.

N What does the woman mean?

(A) The man paid a lot to join the gym.
(B) The man has been working too hard.
(C) The man has improved his physical appearance.
(D) The man should find a better job.

[해석] M 난 1월부터 체육관에서 운동을 하고 있어… 좀 더 좋은 몸을 만들고 싶어서.

W 정말 멋져! 열심히 운동한 보람이 있는 것 같아.

N 여자가 의미하는 것은 무엇인가?

(A) 남자는 체육관 회원이 되려고 많은 돈을 지불했다.
(B) 남자는 너무 열심히 일해 왔다.
(C) 남자의 외모가 더 멋있어졌다.
(D) 남자는 더 좋은 직업을 찾아야 한다.

[어휘] work out 운동하다   gym 체육관(= gymnasium)   get in
shape 체력을 단련하다, 몸매를 가꾸다   pay off 성과가 있다
physical appearance 외모

---

25. M This heat is unbearable. If only we'd gone to the beach instead.

W Why, with the museums and restaurants in Washington, I'd be happy here no matter what the weather.

N What does the woman mean?

(A) She prefers hot weather.
(B) The man should visit Washington when it is cooler.
(C) She agrees that going to the beach would have been better.
(D) Visiting Washington is enjoyable despite the heat.

M 더워 죽겠어. 대신 해변에 갔더라면 좋았을 텐데.

W 아니, 워싱턴에는 박물관과 레스토랑이 있어서 난 날씨가 어떻든 여기가 좋아.

N 여자가 의미하는 것은 무엇인가?

(A) 여자는 더운 날씨를 더 좋아한다.
(B) 남자는 더 시원할 때 워싱턴을 방문해야 한다.
(C) 여자는 해변에 가는 것이 더 좋았을 것이라는 말에 동의한다.
(D) 더위에도 불구하고 워싱턴을 방문하는 것이 즐겁다.

[어휘] unbearable 참을 수 없는, 견디기 어려운 if only 오직 ~하기만 하면 (좋으련만) why (놀라거나 뜻밖의 발견에) 이런!, 아니!, 어머 no matter what 비록 무엇이 ~일지라도 despite ~에도 불구하고

---

26. M I can't believe you stayed so calm last weekend when my Mom brought my little brother to visit. He practically wrecked the dorm lounge!

W Don't be so hard on him. He's only four.

N What does the woman imply?

(A) She will help the man clean up the lounge.
(B) The mother should be more considerate.
(C) The man should be more understanding.
(D) The child is not well behaved for his age.

[해석] M 나는 지난 주에 우리 엄마가 내 동생을 데리고 왔을 때 네가 그렇게 차분했던 게 믿기지 않아. 동생이 기숙사 라운지를 엉망으로 해놓았는데도!

W 동생한테 그렇게 심하게 하지 마. 겨우 4살이잖아.

N 여자가 암시하는 것은 무엇인가?

(A) 여자는 남자가 라운지 청소하는 것을 도와줄 것이다.
(B) 엄마는 더 사려 깊어야 한다.
(C) 남자는 더 너그러워야 한다.
(D) 그 아이는 나이에 비해 예의 바르게 행동하지 않는다.

[어휘] practically 사실상, 실제로는 wreck 망가뜨리다, 부수다 dorm 기숙사(= dormitory) clean up ~을 청소하다, 깨끗이 하다 considerate 사려 깊은, 친절한 understanding 너그러운 well behaved 예의 바른, 얌전한

---

27. W When's a good time to get together to discuss our history project?

M Other than this Wednesday, one day's as good as the next.

N What does the man mean?

(A) He can meet the woman on Wednesday.
(B) He will not be ready until next week.
(C) He is available any day except Wednesday.
(D) He needs to do the history project before Wednesday.

[해석] W 우리 언제 모여서 역사 과제를 논의하는 게 좋을까?

M 이번 주 수요일만 제외하고, 언제든지 좋아.

N 남자가 의미하는 것은 무엇인가?

(A) 그는 수요일에 여자를 만날 수 있다.
(B) 그는 다음 주는 되어야 준비가 될 것이다.
(C) 그는 수요일만 빼고 언제든지 시간이 된다.
(D) 그는 수요일 전에 역사 과제를 해야 한다.

[어휘] get together 만나다, 모이다 other than ~이외에, ~를 제외하고 available 틈이 나는, 시간이 나는

---

28. M Congratulations! I heard your field hockey team is going to the mid-Atlantic championships!

W Yeah! Now we're all working hard to get ready for our game tomorrow.

N What will the woman probably do this afternoon?

(A) Prepare for an important game
(B) Try out for the field hockey team
(C) Get tickets to see the championship game
(D) Receive an award for winning a championship

---

29. M On Saturday evenings, I usually meet some friends for dinner at a café near campus. Would you like to join us?

W I'm up to my ears in work, so I'll have to take a rain check.

N What does the woman mean?

(A) She wants to check the weather before deciding.
(B) She has a problem with her hearing.
(C) **She would enjoy having dinner another time.**
(D) She wants the man to help her with some work.

[해석] M 토요일 저녁에 나는 대개 캠퍼스 근처에서 친구들을 만나서 저녁 먹어. 우리와 같이 저녁 할래?

W 난 일이 많이 밀려 있어서, 다음으로 미뤄야겠어.

N 여자가 의미하는 것은 무엇인가?

(A) 그녀는 결정하기 전에 날씨를 확인해 보고 싶어한다.
(B) 그녀는 청각에 문제가 있다.
(C) **그녀는 다음에 저녁을 했으면 한다.**
(D) 그녀는 남자가 자신의 일을 도와주기를 원한다.

[어휘] be up to one's ears in work 일이 밀려[쌓여] 있다, 일이 과도하게 많다   take a rain check 다음 번에 응하겠다고 약속하다

30. W If you rub some soap on that drawer, it might stop sticking.

M Well, maybe, but if I took out the paper that has fallen down in back, that would help, for sure.

N What is the problem?

(A) The back of the drawer has fallen off.
(B) The man does not have any soap.
(C) The cabinet is too heavy to move.
(D) **Something is blocking the back of the drawer.**

[해석] W 그 서랍에 비누칠을 좀 하면 열릴 지도 몰라.

M 글쎄, 어쩌면 뒤로 떨어져 있는 종이를 꺼내면, 분명히 도움이 될 거야.

N 무엇이 문제인가?

(A) 서랍의 뒷부분이 빠졌다.
(B) 남자는 비누를 가지고 있지 않다.
(C) 캐비닛이 너무 무거워서 옮길 수 없다.
(D) **뭔가가 서랍의 뒷부분을 막고 있다.**

[어휘] rub ~을 문질러 바르다, 문지르다   drawer 서랍   stick (~에 끼여) 꼼짝하지 않다   for sure 분명히, 확실히   fall off 떨어지다   block 막다, 방해하다

Part B
Questions 31–34

N   Listen to a discussion about the Ice Age.

M   Hey, Jane! What's so interesting?

W   What? Oh hi, Tom. I'm reading this fascinating article on the societies of the Ice Age during the Pleistocene period.

M   The Ice Age? There weren't any societies then—³¹there were just small groups of people living in caves, right?

W   That's what people used to think. But a new exhibit at the American Museum of Natural History shows that Ice Age people were surprisingly advanced.

M   Oh, really? In what ways?

W   Well, Ice Age people were the inventors of language, art, and music as we know it. And they didn't live in caves; they built their own shelters.

M   What did they use to build them? The cold weather would have killed off most of the trees, so they couldn't have used wood.

W   ³²In some of the warmer climates they did build houses of wood. In other places they used animal bones and skins or lived in natural stone shelters.

M   How did they stay warm? Animal-skin walls don't sound very sturdy.

W   Well, it says here that ³³in the early Ice Age they often faced their homes toward the south to take advantage of the sun—a primitive sort of solar heating.

M   Hey, that's pretty smart.

W   Then people in the late Ice Age even insulated their homes by putting heated cobblestones on the floor.

M   I guess I spoke too soon. ³⁴Can I read that magazine article after you're done? I think I'm gonna try to impress my anthropology teacher with my amazing knowledge of Ice Age civilization.

W   [laughing] What a show-off!

[해석] N   빙하 시대에 대한 토론을 들어 보세요.

M   안녕, 제인! 뭐가 그렇게 재미있어?

W   뭐라고? 오, 안녕, 톰. 홍적세 기간 동안 빙하 시대의 사회에 관한 아주 재미있는 기사를 읽고 있어.

M   빙하 시대? 그때는 사회라는 게 없었잖아. 다만 소규모 사람들이 동굴에서 살았지, 그렇지?

W   그렇게들 생각했었지. 하지만 미국 자연사 박물관의 새 전시회에서는 빙하 시대 사람들이 놀라울 만큼 진보했다는 것을 보여 주고 있어.

M   오, 정말. 어떤 면에서?

W   음, 빙하시대 사람들은 우리가 알고 있는 언어와 예술, 음악을 만든 사람들이었어. 그리고 그들은 동굴에서 살지 않았어. 자신들의 집을 지었어.

M   그들이 무엇으로 집을 지었는데? 추운 날씨 탓에 대부분의 나무들이 죽어서, 그들은 목재를 사용할 수도 없었을 텐데.

W   기후가 좀 더 따뜻한 일부 지역에서는 나무로 집을 지었어. 다른 곳에서는 동물의 뼈와 가죽을 이용하거나 자연 돌집에서 살았어.

M   그들은 어떻게 따뜻하게 지냈지? 동물 가죽으로 된 벽은 그리 튼튼할 것 같지 않은데.

W   글쎄, 기사에 따르면 초기 빙하 시대에는 태양열을 이용하기 위해 집을 남쪽으로 향하게 했대. 일종의 원시적인 태양열 난방이지.

M   와, 정말 똑똑했구나.

W   게다가 후기 빙하 시대 사람들은 바닥에 가열된 자갈을 놓아서 집을 단열하기까지 했어.

M   내가 잘 알지도 못하면서 함부로 말한 것 같아. 네가 그 잡지 기사를 다 읽은 후에 내가 좀 읽어볼 수 있을까? 빙하 시대의 문명에 대한 엄청난 지식으로 인류학 선생님을 놀라게 해 드려야겠어.

W   [웃으면서] 자랑이라니!

[어휘] **fascinating** 정말 재미있는, 매혹적인   **article** 기사   **Ice Age** 빙하 시대   **Pleistocene** 플라이스토세, 홍적세(신생대 제4기의 전기로 빙하가 후퇴하고 인류가 출현한 시기)   **cave** 동굴   **exhibit** 전시, 전시회   **advanced** 진보한   **inventor** 발명가   **shelter** 거처, 숙소   **kill off** ~을 멸종시키다, 대량으로 죽이다   **skin** (짐승의) 가죽   **sturdy** 억센, 튼튼한   **face** ~을 향하다   **take advantage of** ~을 이용하다   **primitive** 원시의   **solar heating** 태양열 난방   **insulate** 보온하다, 절연하다   **cobblestone** 자갈, 조약돌   **speak too soon** 잘 모르면서 함부로 말하다   **anthropology** 인류학   **civilization** 문명, 문화   **show-off** 자랑, 과시

31. N What did the man think about people of the Ice Age?

(A) **They lived in caves.**
(B) They traveled in groups.
(C) They had an advanced language.
(D) They ate mostly fruit.

[해석] N 남자는 빙하 시대 사람들에 대해 어떻게 생각했는가?

(A) **그들은 동굴에서 살았다.**
(B) 그들은 단체로 여행을 했다.
(C) 그들에게는 발달된 언어가 있었다.
(D) 그들은 대부분 과일을 먹었다.

[어휘] in groups 단체로   advanced 발달된

32. N What does the woman say about the use of wood during the Ice Age?

(A) It was unavailable because dry weather had killed the trees.
(B) **It was used to build shelters in some regions.**
(C) It was used mainly for heating and cooking.
(D) Ice Age people did not have the tools to work with wood.

[해석] N 여자는 빙하 시대 동안 나무의 이용에 대해 뭐라고 말하는가?

(A) 건조한 날씨 탓에 나무가 다 죽어서 사용할 수 없었다.
(B) **일부 지역에서 집을 짓는 데 사용되었다.**
(C) 주로 난방과 요리에 사용되었다.
(D) 빙하 시대 사람들은 나무를 사용할 도구가 없었다.

[어휘] unavailable 이용할 수 없는

33. N How did people in the early Ice Age keep warm?

(A) They wore clothing made of animal skins.
(B) They used sand as insulation.
(C) They kept fires burning constantly.
(D) **They faced their homes toward the south.**

[해석] N 초기 빙하 시대 사람들은 어떻게 따뜻하게 지냈는가?

(A) 그들은 동물 가죽으로 만든 옷을 입었다.
(B) 그들은 모래를 단열재로 이용했다.
(C) 그들은 계속 불을 피워 두었다.
(D) **그들은 집을 남쪽으로 향하게 했다.**

[어휘] insulation 보온, 단열, 절연   constantly 변함없이, 끊임없이, 빈번하게

34. N What does the man want the woman to do?

(A) Meet his anthropology teacher
(B) **Lend him her magazine when she is done with it**
(C) Help him with an assignment about the Ice Age
(D) Help him study for an anthropology test

[해석] N 남자는 여자가 어떻게 하기를 원하는가?

(A) 그의 인류학 선생님을 만날 것
(B) **그녀가 잡지를 다 읽으면 그에게 빌려 줄 것**
(C) 그가 빙하 시대에 관한 과제를 하는 것을 도와줄 것
(D) 그가 인류학 시험 공부하는 것을 도와줄 것

Questions 35-38

N Listen to a conversation between two students.

M I really appreciate your filling me in on yesterday's lecture.

W No problem, I thought you might want to go over it together. And, anyway, it helps me review. [36]Hope you're feeling better now.

M I am. Thanks. So, you said she talked about squid? Sounds a little strange.

W Well, actually, it was about [35]the evolution of sea life—a continuation from last week. The octopus and the squid descended from earlier creatures with shells. [37]They survived by shedding their shells—somewhere between 200 and 500 million years ago.

M That's a pretty long span of time.

W I know. That's what she said, though. To be precise: "Exactly when they emerged is uncertain, and why is still unexplained."

M Some squid are really huge. Can you imagine something that big if it still had a shell?

W Actually, it's because they lost their shells that they could evolve to a bigger size.

M Makes sense. I've read about fishermen who caught squid that weighed over a ton. Did she talk about how that happens?

W Not really. But she did mention some unusual cases. In 1933 in New Zealand, they caught a giant squid ... let's see here ... it was 20 meters long. Its eyes were almost 46 centimeters across. Can you imagine?

M Reminds me of all those stories of sea monsters.

W [38]Professor Simpson thinks there are probably even larger ones that haven't been found because squid are intelligent and fast—so they can easily get away from humans. Maybe some of those monster stories are true.

[해석] **N** 두 학생의 대화를 들어 보세요.

M 어제 강의 내용을 내게 설명해줘서 정말 고마워.

W 천만에. 네가 같이 살펴보길 원할 것 같았어. 그리고 그러면 내가 복습하는 데도 도움이 되고. 이제 네 몸이 좀 더 좋아지기를 바라.

M 좋아지고 있어. 고마워. 그런데 교수님께서 오징어에 대해 말씀하셨다고? 좀 이상한 것 같아.

W 글쎄, 사실 지난주 수업에 이어서 바다 생물의 진화를 다뤘어. 문어와 오징어의 기원은 딱딱한 껍데기가 있는 초기 생물이야. 2~5억 년 전 사이의 어느 시점엔가 껍데기를 탈피해 살아 남았어.

M 그건 정말 아주 오랜 기간이구나.

W 알아. 아무튼 교수님께서 그렇게 말씀하셨어. 정확히 말하자면, "그들이 정확히 언제 나타났는지 확실하지 않으며, 그 이유도 여전히 불명확해."라고.

M 어떤 오징어는 정말 크잖아. 여전히 껍데기가 있다면 그렇게 큰 오징어를 상상할 수 있겠어?

W 사실, 껍데기를 탈피했기 때문에 더 큰 크기로 진화할 수 있었던 거잖아.

M 맞는 말이야. 나는 무게가 1톤이 넘는 오징어를 잡은 어부 기사를 읽은 적이 있어. 교수님께서 어떻게 그런 일이 일어나는지도 말씀하셨어?

W 아니. 하지만 교수님께서는 몇 가지 특이한 사건들을 말씀하셨어. 1933년 뉴질랜드에서 거대한 오징어를 잡았는데… 여기 좀 봐… 길이가 20미터였어. 눈은 직경이 46cm였고. 상상이 가니?

M 그 말을 들으니 바다 괴물 얘기들이 떠올라.

W 심슨 교수님께서 오징어는 영리하고 빠르기 때문에 발견되지 않은 더 큰 것들이 있을지도 모른다고 하셨어. 사람들로부터 쉽게 도망갈 수 있을 테니 말이야. 어쩌면 그런 괴물 이야기들이 진짜일 수도 있어.

[어휘] **appreciate** 고맙게 생각하다, 감사하다   **fill ~ in on** ~에게 (…을) 알리다, 설명하다   **go over** 검토하다, 복습하다   **review** 복습하다   **squid** 오징어   **evolution** 진화   **continuation** 연속, 지속   **octopus** 낙지, 문어   **descend** 기원하다, 계통을 잇다   **survive** (이기고) 살아남다, 견뎌내다   **shed** 탈피하다, 탈모하다   **span** 기간, 동안, 범위   **to be precise** 정확히 말하자면   **emerge** 나타나다, 출현하다   **evolve** 진화하다, 발달하다   **make sense** 말이 되다, (어떤 일이) 사리에 맞다   **monster** 괴물, 도깨비   **get away from** ~로부터 도망치다

35. *N*　What topic are the man and woman
discussing?

(A) Mating habits of squid and octopus

**(B) The evolution of certain forms of
sea life**

(C) The study of marine shells

(D) Survival skills of sea creatures

[해석] *N*　남자와 여자가 논의하고 있는 주제는 무엇인가?

(A) 오징어와 문어의 짝짓기 습성

(B) 특정 형태의 바다 생물의 진화

(C) 바다 조개에 관한 연구

(D) 바다 생물의 생존 기술

[어휘]　**mating** 교배, 짝짓기

36. *N*　Why does the man need to talk to the
woman about the class?

(A) He did not understand the lecture.

(B) He wants to borrow her notes next week.

(C) He needs help preparing for an exam.

**(D) He was sick and unable to attend the
lecture.**

[해석] *N*　남자가 여자에게 수업에 대해 이야기해 줘야 하는 이유는 무엇
인가?

(A) 그가 강의를 이해하지 못해서

(B) 그가 다음 주에 그녀의 공책을 빌리기를 원해서

(C) 그가 시험 준비를 하는데 도움이 필요해서

(D) 그는 아파서 강의를 들으러 갈 수 없었기 때문에

37. *N*　According to the woman, what happened
200 to 500 million years ago?

(A) Some sea creatures developed vertebrae.

(B) The first giant squid was captured.

(C) Some sea creatures shed their shells.

(D) Sea life became more intelligent.

[해석] *N*　여자에 따르면, 2~5억 년 전에 무슨 일이 일어났는가?

(A) 일부 바다 생물의 척추가 발달했다.

(B) 처음으로 거대한 오징어가 잡혔다.

(C) 일부 바다 생물이 껍데기를 탈피했다.

(D) 바다 생물이 더 영리해졌다.

[어휘]　**vertebra** 척추 *pl.* vertebrae

38. *N*　What does the woman imply about sea
monsters?

(A) She has always believed they exist.

(B) She heard about them in New Zealand.

**(C) Stories about them may be based on
giant squid.**

(D) The instructor mentioned them in the
lecture.

[해석] *N*　여자가 바다 괴물에 대해 암시하는 것은 무엇인가?

(A) 그녀는 늘 바다 괴물들이 존재한다고 믿어 왔다.

(B) 그녀는 뉴질랜드에서 바다 괴물들에 관해 들었다.

**(C) 바다 괴물들에 대한 이야기들이 거대한 오징어에 근거한 것인
지도 모른다.**

(D) 교수님은 강의 시간에 바다 괴물들에 대해 언급했다.

Part C
Questions 39–42

N Listen to a professor talk to new students about an experiment in child development.

W [39]In our lab today, we'll be testing the hypothesis that babies can count as early as five months of age. The six babies here are all less than six months old. You'll be watching them on closed-circuit TV and measuring their responses.

The experiment is based on the well-established observation that babies stare longer if they don't see what they expect to see. First, we're going to let two dolls move slowly in front of the babies. The babies will see the two dolls disappear behind a screen. Your job is to record, in seconds, how long the babies stare at the dolls when the screen is removed.

In the next stage, two dolls will again move in front of the babies and disappear. But then a third doll will follow. When the screen is removed, the babies will only see two dolls. If we're right, [40]the babies will now stare longer because they expect three dolls but only see two.

It seems remarkable to think that such young children can count. [41]My own research has convinced me that they have this ability from birth. But whether they do or not, perhaps we should raise another question—should we take advantage of this ability by teaching children mathematics at such a young age? They have great untapped potential, but [42]is it good for parents to pressure young children?

[해석] N 신입 학생들을 대상으로 하는 아동 발달 실험에 관한 교수의 강의를 들어 보세요.

W 오늘 실험에서, 우리들은 아기들이 일찍이 5개월부터 셈을 셀 수 있다는 가정에 대해 실험할 것입니다. 여기 있는 6명의 아기들은 모두 6개월 미만입니다. 여러분은 CCTV로 아기들을 보면서 그들의 반응을 측정할 것입니다.

실험은 아기들이 보려고 기대하는 것을 보지 못하면 더 오래 쳐다본다는 확립된 관찰에 근거합니다. 첫 번째로, 우리는 두 개의 인형이 아기들 앞에서 천천히 움직이도록 할 것입니다. 아기들은 그 두 인형이 스크린 뒤로 사라지는 것을 보게 될 것입니다. 여러분이 해야 할 일은 스크린이 치워졌을 때 아기들이 그 인형들을 얼마나 오랫동안 쳐다보는지를 초 단위로 기록하는 것입니다.

다음 단계에서는 두 개의 인형이 다시 아기들 앞으로 가서 사라질 것입니다. 하지만 그때는 세 번째 인형이 뒤따라갈 것입니다. 스크린이 치워졌을 때 아기들은 두 개의 인형만 보게 될 것입니다. 만약 우리가 맞는다면, 아이들은 세 개의 인형을 기대하는데 두 개밖에 보지 못하기 때문에 더 오래 쳐다볼 것입니다.

그렇게 어린 아이들이 셀 수 있다는 생각은 놀랄만한 것입니다. 내 연구를 통해 아기들은 태어날 때부터 이런 능력을 가지고 있다는 점을 확신하게 되었습니다. 하지만 그들에게 그런 능력이 있든 있지 않든, 우리는 또 다른 의문을 제기해야 합니다. 그렇게 어린 나이에 아이들에게 수학을 가르쳐 이 능력을 활용해야 할까요? 아기들에게 개발되지 않은 위대한 잠재력이 있는데, 부모가 어린 자녀들에게 강요하는 것이 좋을까요?

[어휘] **experiment** 실험 **lab** 실험실(= laboratory) **hypothesis** 가정 **closed-circuit TV** 폐쇄 회로 TV (= CCTV) **observation** 관찰, 주시 **stare** 응시하다 **remarkable** 주목할 만한, 놀랄만한 **convince** 확신시키다, 납득시키다 **take advantage of** ~를 이용하다, 활용하다 **untapped** (자원 따위가) 이용되지 않은, 미개발의 **potential** 가능성, 잠재력

39. *N* What is the experiment designed to demonstrate?

(A) That babies understand language before they can speak

(B) That babies have simple mathematical skills

(C) That babies prefer different kinds of toys

(D) That television has a strong influence on babies

[해석] *N* 입증하고자 하는 실험은 무엇인가?

(A) 아기들은 말을 할 수 있기 전에 언어를 이해한다.
(B) 아기들은 단순한 수학 능력이 있다.
(C) 아기들은 다른 종류의 장난감을 선호한다.
(D) TV는 아기들에게 강한 영향력을 미친다.

[어휘] **demonstrate** 증명하다, 입증하다

40. *N* Which of the babies' reactions would be significant for the purposes of the experiment?

(A) Staring at the dolls longer

(B) Crying loudly

(C) Blinking their eyes rapidly

(D) Reaching for the dolls

[해석] *N* 다음 아기들의 반응 중 실험 목적에 중요한 것은 무엇인가?

(A) 인형을 더 오래 쳐다보는 것
(B) 크게 우는 것
(C) 눈을 빠르게 깜빡이는 것
(D) 인형을 잡으려고 손을 뻗는 것

[어휘] **significant** 중요한   **blink** 눈을 깜빡이다   **reach for** ~을 향하여 손을 뻗다

41. *N* How does the professor explain the babies' behavior?

(A) They are born with the ability to count.

(B) They are exceptionally intelligent.

(C) They learned to count from playing with dolls.

(D) They have learned to count from their parents.

[해석] *N* 교수는 아기들의 행동에 대해 어떻게 설명하는가?

(A) 아기들은 셀 수 있는 능력을 타고 난다.
(B) 아기들은 대단히 총명하다.
(C) 아기들은 인형을 가지고 놀면서 세는 것을 배웠다.
(D) 아기들은 부모로부터 세는 것을 배워 왔다.

[어휘] **exceptionally** 예외적으로, 이례적으로, 대단히

42. *N* What implication of her research is the professor concerned about?

(A) Language ability might be negatively affected.

(B) Babies who learn quickly might develop learning problems later.

(C) Parents might try to teach their children certain skills at too early an age.

(D) Learning math early might interfere with creativity.

[해석] *N* 자신의 연구가 암시하는 내용에서 교수가 우려하고 있는 것은 무엇인가?

(A) 언어 능력이 부정적인 영향을 받을지도 모른다.
(B) 빨리 배우는 아기들은 나중에 학습 장애를 일으킬지도 모른다.
(C) 부모들은 너무 어린 나이에 자신의 자녀들에게 어떤 기술을 가르치려고 할지도 모른다.
(D) 일찍 수학을 배우는 것은 창의력에 지장을 줄지도 모른다.

[어휘] **implication** 의미, 함축   **concerned** 걱정스러운, 염려하고 있는   **interfere** 방해하다, 지장을 주다

Questions 43-46

N Listen to part of a lecture in a geology class.

M I'm glad you brought up the question of our investigations into the makeup of Earth's interior. [43]In fact—since this is the topic of your reading assignment for next time—let me spend these last few minutes of class talking about it. There were several important discoveries that helped geologists develop a more accurate picture of Earth's interior.

[45]The first key discovery had to do with seismic waves—remember they are the vibrations caused by earthquakes. Well, [44]scientists found that they traveled thousands of miles through Earth's interior. This finding enabled geologists to study the inner parts of the Earth. You see, these studies revealed that these vibrations were of two types: compression—or P—waves and shear—or S—waves. And researchers found that P waves travel through both liquids and solids, while S waves travel only through solid matter.

In 1906 a British geologist discovered that P waves slowed down at a certain depth but kept traveling deeper. On the other hand, S waves either disappeared or were reflected back, so he concluded that [46]the depth marked the boundary between a solid mantle and a liquid core. Three years later another boundary was discovered—that between the mantle and Earth's crust.

There's still a lot to be learned about Earth. For instance, geologists know that the core is hot. Evidence of this is the molten lava that flows out of volcanoes. But we're still not sure what the source of the heat is.

[해석] N 지질학 수업 강의를 들어 보세요.

M 나는 여러분들이 지구의 내부 구조에 대한 연구에 문제를 제기해서 기쁩니다. 사실, 이 문제는 다음 수업 시간을 위한 읽기 과제의 주제이니, 몇 분 남은 수업 시간 동안에 이와 관련해 이야기해 보도록 하겠습니다. 지질학자들이 더 정확한 지구의 내부 구조를 그리는데 도움이 된 몇 가지 중요한 발견들이 있었습니다.

첫 번째 중요한 발견은 지진파와 관계가 있었는데, 지진파는 지진에 의해 생기는 진동이라는 점에 유념하세요. 음, 과학자들은 지진파가 지구의 내부를 통과해 수천 마일까지 이동한다는 것을 발견했습니다. 이 발견으로 인해 지질학자들은 지구의 내부 구조를 연구할 수 있었습니다. 저, 이런 연구들을 통해 이 진동에는 두 종류, 즉 압축파(또는 P파)와 전단파(또는 S파)가 있다는 것이 밝혀졌습니다. 그리고 연구자들은 P파는 액체와 고체를 둘 다 통과해 이동하는 반면, S파는 오직 고체 물질만을 통과해 이동한다는 것도 발견했습니다.

1906년에 한 영국 지질학자는 P파는 어떤 깊이에서 느려지지만 계속해서 더 깊이 이동한다는 것을 발견했습니다. 반면에, S파는 사라지거나 반사합니다. 그래서 그는 그 깊이가 고체인 맨틀과 액체인 핵 사이의 경계를 표시한다는 결론을 내렸습니다. 3년 후에 또 다른 경계가 밝혀졌는데, 그것은 맨틀과 지각 사이의 경계입니다.

아직도 지구에 대해 알아야 할 것들이 많이 남아 있습니다. 예를 들어, 지질학자들은 핵이 뜨겁다는 것을 알고 있습니다. 화산에서 흘러나온 녹은 용암이 이에 대한 증거입니다. 하지만 열이 어디에서 발생하는지는 여전히 확실히 알지 못합니다.

[어휘] geology 지질학 bring up (문제를) 꺼내다, 제기하다 investigation 조사, 연구 makeup 구성, 구조 interior 내부, 안쪽 assignment 숙제, 과제 geologist 지질학자 accurate 정확한 have to do with ~와 관계[관련]가 있다 seismic 지진의; 지진에 의한 cf. seismic wave 지진파 vibration 진동 reveal 드러내다, 나타내다, 보여주다 compression 압축, 압착 shear 전단 변형; 비뚤어짐, 엇갈림 liquid 액체(의) solid 고체(의) reflect 반사하다 conclude 결론을 내리다, 결론짓다 boundary 경계(선), 접점 mantle (지구의) 맨틀, 외투부 core (지구의) 중심부, 핵 crust 지각 evidence 증거, 근거, 증명 molten 열로 녹은, 용해된 lava 용암, 화산암 volcano 화산; 분화구

43. *N* What is the purpose of the talk?

(A) To review what students know about volcanic activity

(B) To demonstrate the use of a new measurement device

(C) To explain the answer to an examination question

(D) To provide background for the next reading assignment

[해석] *N* 강연의 목적은 무엇인가?

(A) 학생들이 화산 활동에 관해 알고 있는 것을 복습하려고

(B) 새로운 측정 장치 사용법을 보여 주려고

(C) 시험 문제의 답을 설명하려고

(D) 다음 수업 시간을 위한 읽기 과제에 대한 배경을 설명해 주려고

[어휘] **volcanic activity** 화산활동 **demonstrate** 설명하다, 시연하다 **measurement device** 측정 장치

44. *N* What important discovery about seismic waves does the instructor mention?

(A) They occur at regular intervals.

(B) They can withstand great heat.

(C) They travel through Earth's interior.

(D) They can record Earth's internal temperature.

[해석] *N* 강사가 지진파에 관한 중요한 발견 사항으로 언급한 것은 무엇인가?

(A) 지진파는 일정한 간격으로 발생한다.

(B) 지진파는 높은 열에 견딜 수 있다.

(C) 지진파는 지구 내부를 통과해 이동한다.

(D) 지진파는 지구의 내부 온도를 기록할 수 있다.

[어휘] **at regular intervals** 일정한 간격으로 **withstand** 견디다, 이겨내다

45. *N* What did the study of seismic vibrations help geologists learn more about?

(A) When Earth was formed

(B) The composition of the Earth's interior

(C) Why lava is hot

(D) How often a volcano is likely to erupt

[해석] *N* 지진 진동의 연구는 지질학자들이 무엇을 더 연구하는 데 도움이 되었는가?

(A) 지구의 형성 시기

(B) 지구 내부의 구성

(C) 용암이 뜨거운 이유

(D) 화산 폭발의 빈도

[어휘] **composition** 구성 **erupt** 분출하다, 폭발하다

46. *N* What did P and S waves help scientists discover about the layers of Earth?

(A) How deep they are

(B) Where earthquakes form

(C) How hot they are

(D) What purpose they serve

[해석] *N* P파와 S파는 과학자들이 지층에 관한 어떤 점을 발견하는 데 도움이 되었는가?

(A) 지층이 얼마나 깊은지

(B) 지진이 어디서 형성되는지

(C) 지층이 얼마나 뜨거운지

(D) 지층이 어떤 역할을 하는지

[어휘] **layer** 층, 지층

Questions 47–50

N Listen to part of a talk in an art history class.

W [48]You may remember that a few weeks ago we discussed the question of what photography is. Is it art, or is it a method of reproducing images? Do photographs belong in museums or just in our homes? Today I want to talk about a person who tried to make his professional life an answer to such questions.

Alfred Stieglitz went from the United States to Germany to study engineering. While he was there, he became interested in photography and began to experiment with his camera. [47]He took pictures under conditions that most photographers considered too difficult—he took them at night, in the rain, and of people and objects reflected in windows. When he returned to the United States, he continued [49]these revolutionary efforts. Stieglitz was the first person to photograph skyscrapers, clouds, and views from an airplane.

What Stieglitz was trying to do in these photographs was what he tried to do throughout his life make photography an art. He felt that photography could be just as good a form of self-expression as painting or drawing. For Stieglitz, his camera was his brush. While many photographers of the late 1800s and early 1900s thought of their work as a reproduction of identical images, [50]Stieglitz saw his as a creative art form. He understood the power of the camera to capture the moment. In fact, he never retouched his prints or made copies of them. If he were in this classroom today, I'm sure he'd say, "Well, painters don't normally make extra copies of their paintings, do they?"

[해석] **N** 예술사 수업 강의를 들어 보세요.

W 여러분은 우리가 몇 주 전에 사진술이 무엇인지에 관한 질문에 대해서 토론했던 것을 기억하고 있을 겁니다. 사진술은 예술인가요, 아니면 이미지를 복사하는 방법인가요? 사진들은 박물관에 있나요, 아니면 단지 우리 집에 있나요? 오늘은 전문적인 삶으로 그런 질문에 답하려고 애썼던 한 사람에 관해 이야기하고자 합니다.

알프레드 스티글리츠 씨는 공학을 공부하기 위해 미국에서 독일로 건너 갔습니다. 독일에 있으면서 그는 사진에 관심을 갖게 되어 자신의 사진기로 실험을 하기 시작했습니다. 그는 대부분의 사진사들이 너무 어렵다고 생각하는 상황에서 사진을 찍었습니다. 즉, 그는 밤에, 비가 내릴 때 사진을 찍었고, 창문에 비친 사람들이나 사물들을 사진 찍었습니다. 그는 미국으로 돌아와서도 계속해서 이런 획기적인 시도를 했습니다. 스티글리츠 씨는 처음으로 초고층 빌딩과 구름, 비행기에서 본 경치를 찍은 사람이었습니다.

스티글리츠 씨가 이런 사진에서 하려고 했던 시도는 평생을 통해 사진을 예술로 만들려고 했던 것이었습니다. 그는 사진이 그림이나 소묘처럼 자신을 표현하는 좋은 형식이 될 수 있다고 생각했습니다. 스티글리츠 씨에게 사진기는 붓이었습니다. 1800년대 후반과 1900년대 초기의 많은 사진가들은 자신의 일을 동일한 이미지의 재현이라고 생각한 반면, 스티글리츠 씨는 자신의 작품을 창의적인 예술 형식으로 보았습니다. 그는 순간을 포착하는 사진기의 능력을 이해했습니다. 사실, 그는 절대 인화된 사진을 다듬거나 복사하지 않았습니다. 만약 그가 오늘 이 교실에 있다면, 분명히 그는 "글쎄요, 화가들은 보통 자신들의 그림을 복사하지 않잖아요, 그렇죠?"라고 말할 것입니다.

[어휘] **reproduce** 재현하다, 복사하다 cf. reproduction 재현, 복사 **photograph** 사진; 사진을 찍다, 촬영하다 **professional** 전문의, 본업의; 전문가의, 프로의 **engineering** 공학 **experiment** 실험(하다), 시험(하다) **reflect** 비추다, 반영하다 **revolutionary** 혁명적인, 획기적인 **skyscraper** 초고층 빌딩, 마천루 **identical** 똑같은, 동일한 **capture** 붙잡다 **retouch** 손질하다, 다듬다

47. *N* What is the professor mainly discussing?

(A) Photographic techniques common in the early 1900s
(B) The early life of Alfred Stieglitz
(C) The influence of weather on Alfred Stieglitz' photography
(D) Alfred Stieglitz' approach to photography

[해석] *N* 교수는 주로 무엇에 관해 이야기하고 있는가?

(A) 1900년대 초에 흔했던 사진 기법들
(B) 알프레드 스티글리츠 씨의 어린 시절
(C) 알프레드 스티글리츠 씨의 사진에 미친 날씨의 영향
(D) 알프레드 스티글리츠 씨의 사진에 대한 접근 방식

[어휘] **photographic technique** 사진 기법 **influence** 영향 **approach** (학문 등에의) 길잡이, 입문; 접근 (방식)

48. *N* What question had the professor raised in a previous class?

(A) How to analyze photographic techniques
(B) How to classify photography
(C) How Alfred Stieglitz contributed to the history of photography
(D) Whether photography is superior to other art forms

[해석] *N* 교수가 지난 수업 시간에 제기했던 질문은 무엇이었는가?

(A) 사진 기법들을 분석하는 방법
(B) 사진을 분류하는 방법
(C) 알프레드 스티글리츠 씨가 사진술의 역사에 얼마나 기여했는지
(D) 사진이 다른 예술 장르보다 우월한지 여부

[어휘] **analyze** 분석하다 **classify** 분류하다 **contribute** 기여하다 **be superior to** ~보다 뛰어나다

49. *N* What does the professor imply about the photographs Stieglitz took at night?

(A) They were influenced by his background in engineering.
(B) They were very expensive to take.
(C) They were among the first taken under such conditions.
(D) Most of them were of poor quality.

[해석] *N* 교수가 스티글리츠 씨가 밤에 찍은 사진에 관해 암시하는 것은 무엇인가?

(A) 그 사진들은 그의 공학적 배경 지식에 영향을 받았다.
(B) 그 사진들은 찍기 아주 비쌌다.
(C) 그러한 상황에서 처음 찍힌 사진들이다.
(D) 대부분의 사진들은 질이 좋지 않았다.

50. *N* Why did Stieglitz choose to not make copies of the photographs?

(A) He thought that the copying process took too long.
(B) He considered each photograph to be an individual work of art.
(C) He did not have the necessary equipment for reproduction.
(D) He did not want them to be displayed outside of his home.

[해석] *N* 스티글리츠 씨가 자신의 사진을 복사하지 않기로 결정한 이유는 무엇인가?

(A) 그는 복사 과정이 너무 오래 걸린다고 생각했다.
(B) 그는 각각의 사진이 개별적인 예술품이라고 생각했다.
(C) 그는 복사에 필요한 장비를 갖고 있지 않았다.
(D) 그는 사진들이 자신의 집 밖에서 전시되는 것을 원하지 않았다.

[어휘] **process** 과정, 절차 **individual** 개인적인, 개별적인 **work of art** 예술품

Structure

1. (A)	2. (A)	3. (B)	4. (B)	5. (B)
6. (D)	7. (D)	8. (A)	9. (C)	10. (D)
11. (C)	12. (C)	13. (D)	14. (D)	15. (A)

Written Expression

16. C	17. B	18. B	19. A	20. D
21. C	22. D	23. D	24. C	25. A
26. C	27. D	28. B	29. D	30. C
31. A	32. D	33. A	34. C	35. B
36. A	37. C	38. B	39. A	40. C

Structure

1. Tourism is ------- leading source of income for many coastal communities.

(A) a
(B) at
(C) then
(D) none

[해석] 관광 산업은 많은 해안 지역 사회의 주요 수입원이다.

[어휘] **tourism** 관광 (산업) **leading** 주요한 **income** 수입, 소득 **coastal** 해안의 **community** 공동 사회, 지역 사회

2. Although thunder and lightning are produced at the same time, light waves travel faster -------, so we see the lightning before we hear the thunder.

(A) than sound waves do
(B) than sound waves are
(C) do sound waves
(D) sound waves

[해석] 천둥과 번개는 동시에 생성되지만, 광파는 음파보다 빨리 이동한다. 그래서 우리는 천둥소리를 듣기 전에 번개를 본다.

[어휘] **thunder** 천둥 **lightning** 번개 **at the same time** 동시에 **light wave** 광파 **sound wave** 음파

3. Beef cattle ------- of all livestock for economic growth in the North American economy.

(A) the most are important
(B) are the most important
(C) the most important are
(D) that are the most important

[해석] 육우는 북미 경제에서 경제적 성장을 위해 모든 가축들 중에서 가장 중요하다.

[어휘] **beef cattle** 육우 **livestock** 가축 **economic growth** 경제 성장

4. The discovery of the halftone process in photography in 1881 made it ------- photographs in books and newspapers.

(A) the possible reproduction
(B) possible to reproduce
(C) the possibility of reproducing
(D) possibly reproduced

[해석] 1881년 사진에서 망판 공정의 발견으로 인해 책과 신문에 사진을 게재할 수 있게 되었다.

[어휘] **halftone** 망판의, 망판으로 만든; 중간색의, 반색조의 **process** 공정, 과정 **reproduce** 복사하다, 재현하다

5. Flag Day is a legal holiday only in the state of Pennsylvania, -------, according to tradition, Betsy Ross sewed the first American flag.

(A) which
(B) where
(C) that
(D) has

[해석] 미국 국기 제정 기념일은 펜실베이니아 주에서만 법정 공휴일인데, 전설에 따르면 펜실베이니아 주에서 베시 로스가 첫 성조기를 바느질했다고 한다.

[어휘] **Flag Day** 미국 국기 제정 기념일(6월 14일) **legal holiday** 법정 휴일 **tradition** 전통, 관습; 전설, 구비 **sew** 바느질하다, 꿰매다

6. ------- vastness of the Grand Canyon, it is difficult to capture it in a single photograph.

(A) While the

(B) The

(C) For the

(D) Because of the

[해석] 그랜드 캐니언의 광대함 때문에 그랜드 캐니언을 한 장의 사진에 담기는 어렵다.

[어휘] **vastness** 광대(함), 막대(함)   **capture** ~을 표현[포착]하다, 담다

7. Speciation, -------, results when an animal population becomes isolated by some factor, usually geographic.

(A) form biological species

(B) biological species are formed

(C) which forming biological species

(D) the formation of biological species

[해석] 종의 형성, 즉 생물 종의 형성은 동물 개체군이 어떤 요인, 대개 지리적 요인에 의해 격리될 때 생긴다.

[어휘] **speciation** 종의 형성; 신종으로의 분화   **isolated** 분리된, 격리된   **geographic** 지리상의, 지리적인

8. In its pure state antimony has no important uses, but ------- with other substances, it is an extremely useful metal.

(A) when combined physically or chemically

(B) combined when physically or chemically

(C) the physical and chemical combination

(D) it is combined physically and chemically

[해석] 안티몬은 순수한 상태에서는 중요한 쓰임새가 없지만, 물리적으로나 화학적으로 다른 물질들과 결합될 때는 상당히 유용한 금속이다.

[어휘] **antimony** 안티몬(유독성의 은백색 금속 원소)   **combine** 결합시키다, 화합시키다

9. The dawn redwood appears ------- some 100 million years ago in northern forests around the world.

(A) was flourished

(B) having to flourish

(C) to have flourished

(D) have flourished

[해석] 메타세쿼이아는 1억 년 전에 전세계적으로 북쪽 산림 지역에서 무성했던 것으로 보인다.

[어휘] **dawn redwood** 메타세쿼이아(낙엽 침엽 교목)   **flourish** 잘 자라다, 무성하다

10. Beginning in the Middle Ages, composers of Western music used a system of notating their compositions ------- be performed by musicians.

(A) will

(B) that

(C) and when to

(D) so they could

[해석] 중세 시대부터 서양 음악의 작곡가들은 음악가들이 연주할 수 있도록 자신들의 작품을 악보에 기록하는 기보법을 사용했다.

[어휘] **composer** 작곡가   **notate** 악보에 기보하다   **composition** 작곡(법), 악곡   **perform** (음악을) 연주하다

11. Civil rights are the freedoms and rights ------- as a member of a community, state, or nation.

(A) may have a person

(B) may have a person who

(C) a person may have

(D) and a person may have

[해석] 시민권은 한 사람이 지역사회, 주, 또는, 국가의 일원으로 가질 수 있는 자유와 권리이다.

[어휘] **civil rights** 시민권 cf. **rights** 권리   **community** 지역 사회

12. Richard Wright enjoyed success and influence ------- among Black American writers of his era.

(A) were unparalleled

(B) are unparalleled

(C) unparalleled

(D) the unparalleled

[해석] 리차드 라이트는 자신의 동시대 흑인 작가들 중에서 전대미문의 성공과 영향력을 누렸다.

[어휘] **era** 시대, 시절   **unparalleled** 전대미문의, 비할 데 없는

13. ------- of large mammals once dominated the North American prairies : the American bison and the pronghorn antelope.

(A) There are two species

(B) With two species

(C) Two species are

(D) Two species

[해석] 거대한 포유류 중 두 종이 한때 북미 초원을 장악했었는데, 바로 아메리카 들소와 가지 뿔 영양이었다.

[어휘] **mammal** 포유류   **dominate** 장악하다, 지배하다   **prairie** 초원   **bison** 들소   **pronghorn antelope** 가지 뿔 영양

14. Franklin D. Roosevelt was ------- the great force of radio and the opportunity it provided for taking government policies directly to the people.

(A) as the first president he understood fully

(B) the first President that, to fully understand

(C) the first President fully understood

(D) the first President to understand fully

[해석] 프랭클린 D. 루스벨트는 라디오의 엄청난 힘과 라디오로 정부 정책을 국민들에게 직접 전달하는 기회를 완벽하게 이해한 첫 대통령이었다.

[어휘] **policy** 정책, 방침   **directly** 직접, 직접적으로

15. During the late fifteenth century, ------- of the native societies of America had professions in the fields of arts and crafts.

(A) only a few

(B) a few but

(C) few, but only

(D) a few only

[해석] 15세기 후반 동안 아메리카 원주민 사회에서 오직 소수의 사람들만이 미술 공예 분야의 직업을 가졌다.

[어휘] **profession** 직업, 직종   **arts and crafts** 미술 공예, 수공예

Written Expression

16. Jane Addams, social worker, author, and

spokeswoman for the peace and women's
<u>A</u>

suffrage movements, she received the Nobel
<u>B</u>   <u>C</u>

Peace Prize in 1931 for her humanitarian
<u>D</u>

achievements.

[해석] 사회 운동가이자 작가이자 평화와 여성 참정권 운동의 대변
인인 제인 아담스는 인도주의 활동으로 1931년에 노벨 평화
상을 받았다.

[어휘] **spokeswoman** 여성 대변인, 여성 대표 **suffrage**
투표권, 선거권, 참정권 **humanitarian** 박애의,
인도주의의 **achievement** 업적, 공적

17. The public ceremonies of the North American
<u>A</u>

Plains Indians are **lesser** elaborate than those of
<u>B</u>   <u>C</u>

the Navajo in the Southwest.
<u>D</u>

[해석] 북미 평원 인디언들의 공개 의식은 남서부 지역의 나바호족
의 공개 의식들보다 덜 정교하다.

[어휘] **ceremony** 의식, 예식 **Plains Indian** 평원 인디언
elaborate 정성 들인, 공들인, 복잡한

18. In some species of fish, **such the** three-spined
<u>A</u>   <u>B</u>

stickleback, the male, not the female, performs
<u>C</u>

the task of caring for the young.
<u>D</u>

[해석] 큰가시고기처럼 일부 어종에서는 암컷이 아니라 수컷이 새
끼를 돌보는 일을 한다.

[어휘] **species** (동·식물의) 종 **three-spined
stickleback** 큰가시고기(등에 가시가 3개 있는
가시고기과의 물고기) **care for** ~을 돌보다

19. When she **retires** in September 1989, tennis
<u>A</u>   <u>B</u>

champion Christine Evert was the most famous
<u>C</u>

woman athlete in the United States.
<u>D</u>

[해석] 테니스 챔피언 크리스틴 에버트는 1989년 9월에 은퇴했을
때 미국에서 가장 유명한 여자 운동 선수였다.

[어휘] **retire** 퇴직하다, 은퇴하다 **athlete** 운동 선수

20. The ancient Romans used vessels equipped with
<u>A</u>   <u>B</u>

sails and banks of oars **to transporting** their
<u>C</u>   <u>D</u>

armies.

[해석] 고대 로마인들은 자신들의 군대를 수송하기 위해 돛이 있고
노 젓는 자리가 갖춰진 배들을 이용했다.

[어휘] **ancient** 고대의 **vessel** (대형) 배, 선박
equipped with ~을 갖춘 **sail** 돛 **bank**
노젓는 사람의 자리; 노젓는 사람; 노의 열 **oar** 노
transport 수송하다, 옮기다, 나르다

21. Dinosaurs are traditionally classified as cold-
<u>A</u>

blooded reptiles, but recent evidence based on
<u>B</u>

eating habits, posture, and skeletal **structural**
<u>C</u>

suggests some may have been warm-blooded.
<u>D</u>

[해석] 공룡들은 전통적으로 냉혈 파충류로 분류되지만, 식습관과
자세, 골격의 구조를 근거로 한 최근의 증거에서는 일부 공
룡들이 온혈 동물이었을지도 모른다는 것을 암시한다.

[어휘] **classify** 분류하다, 구분하다 **cold-blooded**
(동물이) 냉혈의 **reptile** 파충류 **evidence** 증거,
근거, 증명 **posture** (몸의) 자세 **skeletal** 골격의,
해골의 **structural** 구조(상)의, 조직(상)의 *cf.* structure
구조

22. Since the Great Depression of the 1930s,

government <u>programs</u> such as Social Security
　　　　　　　　 A

have <u>been built</u> into the economy <u>to help</u> avert
　　　 B 　　　　　　　　　　　　 C

severity business declines.
　 Ⓓ

[해석] 1930년대의 세계 대공황 이래로, 심한 경기 쇠퇴를 막는
데 도움이 되도록 경제 체제에 사회 보장 제도와 같은 정부
프로그램을 설립해 왔다.

[어휘] **Great Depression** (1929년 10월 미국에서 시작된)
세계 대공황　**Social Security** (정부가 1935년에
도입한) 사회 보장 (제도)　**avert** ~을 돌리다, 비키다;
(사고를) 피하다, 막다　**severity** 엄격, 엄함; 가혹
cf. severe 엄한, 가혹한　**decline** 쇠퇴, 몰락

23. In the 1970s, <u>consumer</u> activists <u>succeeded in</u>
　　　　　　　　　　 A　　　　　　　 B

promoting laws that set <u>safety</u> standards for
　　　　　　　　　　　 C

automobiles, children's clothing, and a **widely**
　　　　　　　　　　　　　　　　　 Ⓓ

range of household products.

[해석] 1970년대에 소비자 행동주의자들은 자동차와 아동용 의류,
다양한 종류의 가정용품에 대한 안전 기준을 마련하는 법안
을 통과시키는 데 성공했다.

[어휘] **consumer** 소비자　**activist** 적극적 행동주의자,
실천주의자　**promote** (의안을) 지지하다, 통과되도록
힘쓰다　**safety standard** 안전 기준　**household**
가정의, 가사의

24. Zoos in New Orleans, San Diego, Detroit, and

the Bronx <u>have become</u> biological parks <u>where</u>
　　　　　 A　　　　　　　　　　　　 B

animals **roams freely** and people <u>watch from</u>
　　　 Ⓒ　　　　　　　　　 D

across a moat.

[해석] 뉴올리언스와 샌디에이고, 디트로이트, 브롱크스에 있는 동
물원들은 동물들이 자유롭게 돌아다니고 사람들이 해자 너
머로 볼 수 있는 생물공원이 되었다.

[어휘] **biological** 생물학의, 생물학적인　**roam** (정처 없이)
돌아다니다, 배회하다　**moat** 호, 해자

25. In primates, as in other **mammal**, hairs <u>around</u>
　　　　　　　　　　　　 Ⓐ　　　　　 B

the eyes and ears and in the nose, <u>prevent</u> dust,
　　　　　　　　　　　　　　　　 C

insects, and other matter from <u>entering</u> these
　　　　　　　　　　　　　　 D

organs.

[해석] 다른 포유동물에서처럼 영장류들에게 있는 눈과 귀 주위의
털과 콧속의 털은 먼지와 곤충, 다른 이물질들이 이들 기관
에 들어가지 못하도록 막는다.

[어휘] **primate** 영장류　**mammal** 포유동물
prevent A from -ing A가 ~하지 못하도록 막다
organ (생물의) 기관

26. The Rocky Mountains <u>were</u> explored <u>by</u> fur
　　　　　　　　　　　 A　　　　　 B

traders during the early 1800s, in **a decades**
　　　　　　　　　　　　　　　　 Ⓒ

<u>preceding</u> the United States Civil War.
　 D

[해석] 로키 산맥은 1800년대 초에, 즉 미국 남북전쟁이 발발하기
수십 년 전에 모피 상인들에 의해 개척되었다.

[어휘] **explore** 탐험하다, 개척하다　**fur** 모피　**trader** 상인,
무역업자　**decade** 10년간　**preceding** (바로) 전의,
이전의　**Civil War** 남북전쟁

27. The works of the <u>author</u> Herman Melville are
　　　　　　　　　 A

<u>literary</u> creations of a high order, blending <u>fact</u>,
　 B　　　　　　　　　　　　　　　　　 C

fiction, adventure, and subtle **symbolic**.
　　　　　　　　　　　　　 Ⓓ

[해석] 작가 헤르만 멜빌의 작품들은 사실과 허구, 모험과 미묘한
상징주의가 혼합된 가장 수준 높은 문학 창작물이다.

[어휘] **author** 작가, 필자　**literary** 문학의, 문학적인
creation 창작물　**of a high order** 가장 높은 수준의
blend 섞다, 혼합하다

28. Each <u>chemical</u> element is characterized **to** the
　　　 A　　　　　　　　　　　　　　 Ⓑ

number of protons that <u>an atom</u> of that element
　　　　　　　　　　　 C

contains, called <u>its</u> atomic number.
　　　　　　 D

[해석] 각각의 화학 원소는 그 원소의 원자가 포함하고 있는 양자의 수, 즉 원자 번호라고 불리는 양자의 수에 의해 규정된다.

[어휘] **chemical** 화학의, 화학적인　**element** 원소
proton 양자(원자핵의 기본 성분을 이루는 소립자)
atom 원자　**atomic number** 원자 번호

29. The <u>body structure</u> that developed in birds <u>over</u>
　　　　A　　　　　　　　　　　　　　B
millions of years is <u>well designed</u> for flight, being
　　　　　　　　　　　　C
both **lightly** in weight and remarkably strong.
　　　🄓

[해석] 수백 만 년 이상에 걸쳐 새들에게 발전된 신체 구조는 무게가 가벼우면서도 매우 강하게 진화되어 비행에 적합하도록 잘 고안되었다.

[어휘] **structure** 구조, 구성　**flight** 날기, 비행
remarkably 현저하게, 주목할 만하게; 매우, 몹시

30. <u>From</u> 1905 to 1920, American novelist Edith
　A
Wharton <u>was</u> at the height of her writing career,
　　　　B
producing **of her** three <u>most</u> popular novels.
　　　　　🄒　　　　D

[해석] 1905년부터 1920년까지 미국의 소설가 에디스 아턴은 집필 경력의 절정기에 있었는데, 가장 인기 있는 소설을 세 편 출판했다.

[어휘] **at the height of** ~의 절정에서, 절정기에; 한창 ~중
career 경력, 직업

31. In the early twentieth century, there was
considerable **interesting** among sociologists in
　　　　　　　　🄐
the fact <u>that</u> in the United States <u>the family</u> was
　　　　B　　　　　　　　　　　　　C
losing its <u>traditional</u> roles.
　　　　　D

[해석] 20세기 초 사회학자들 사이에서는 미국에서 가족이 그 전통적인 역할을 잃어가고 있었다는 사실에 상당한 관심을 두고 있었다.

[어휘] **considerable** 상당한, 적지 않은　**sociologist** 사회학자　**traditional** 전통적인　**role** 역할

32. <u>Although</u> diamond is colorless and transparent
　　A
<u>when</u> pure, <u>it</u> may appear in various **color**,
　B　　　　C　　　　　　　　　　🄓
ranging from pastels to opaque black, if it is
contaminated with other material.

[해석] 다이아몬드는 순수할 때는 무색이고 투명하지만, 다른 물질로 오염될 때는 파스텔 색깔에서 불투명한 검정색에 이르기까지 다양한 색깔로 보인다.

[어휘] **transparent** 투명한　**opaque** 불투명한, 빛을 통하지 않는　**contaminated** 오염된

33. Comparative anatomy is **concerned to** the
　　　　　　　　　　　　🄐
<u>structural</u> differences <u>among</u> animal <u>forms</u>.
　　B　　　　　　　　　C　　　　　　　D

[해석] 비교 해부학은 동물 형태들 사이에서 구조상의 차이점에 관한 것이다.

[어휘] **comparative** 비교적인, 상대적인　**anatomy** 해부학
concerned 관련된, 관계하고 있는　**structural** 구조상의, 형태상의

34. A seismograph records oscillation of the ground
<u>caused by</u> seismic waves, vibrations that <u>travel</u>
　A　　　　　　　　　　　　　　　　　　B
from **its** point of origin <u>through</u> Earth or along its
　　　🄒　　　　　　　D
surface.

[해석] 지신계는 시진파, 즉 진원지로부터 지구를 통과하거나 지표를 따라 이동하는 진동에 의해 발생하는 지면의 진동 움직임을 기록한다.

[어휘] **seismograph** 지진계　**oscillation** 진동, (진동을 보이는 것의) 움직임　**seismic wave** 지진파
vibration 진동　**surface** 표면

35. Electric lamps came into widespread use during
the early 1900s and eventually <u>replaced</u> once-
　　　　　　　　　　　　　　　　A
popular **type** of fat, gas, or <u>oil</u> lamps for <u>almost</u>
　　　　🄑　　　　　　　　C　　　　　　D
every purpose.

36. Located in Canada, the Columbia Icefield **covers**
<u>(A)</u>
<u>area</u> of 120 square miles <u>and</u> is 3,300 feet <u>thick</u> in
B   C
some <u>places</u>.
D

[해석] 캐나다에 위치해 있는 컬럼비아 빙원은 120제곱 마일의 지역을 덮고 있는데, 일부 지역에서는 두께가 3,300피트이다.

[어휘] **Icefield** (극지방의) 빙원

37. Composer Richard Rodgers and lyricist Oscar

Hammerstein II <u>brought</u> to the musical *Oklahoma!*
A
<u>extensive</u> musical and theatrical backgrounds
B
as well as **familiar** with the <u>traditional</u> forms of
(C)   D
operetta and musical comedy.

[해석] 작곡가 리차드 로저스와 작사가 오스카 해머스타인 2세는 〈오클라호마〉라는 뮤지컬에 대규모의 음악적이고 극적인 배경을 가져왔을 뿐만 아니라, 전통적인 형태의 오페레타와 뮤지컬 코미디의 친숙함을 가져왔다.

[어휘] **composer** 작곡가   **lyricist** 작사가   **extensive** 광범위한, 포괄적인   **theatrical** 연극의, 연극적인   **traditional** 전통적인

38. Although traditional flutes are <u>among</u> the world's
A
oldest musical instruments, **but the** flute <u>used</u> in
(B)   C
orchestras today is <u>one of</u> the most technically
D
sophisticated.

39. Rice, **which it still** forms the staple diet of <u>much</u>
(A)   B
of the world's population, grows <u>best</u> in <u>hot</u>, wet
C   D
lands.

[해석] 여전히 전 세계 많은 인구의 주식이 되는 쌀은 덥고 습한 땅에서 가장 잘 자란다.

[어휘] **staple diet** 주식 *cf.* staple 주요한, 중요한

40. Federal funds appropriated <u>for art</u> in the 1930s
A
made possible <u>hundreds of</u> murals and statues
B
still **admiration** in small towns <u>all over</u> the United
(C)   D
States.

[해석] 1930년대에 예술에 할당된 연방 기금 덕에 수백 점의 벽화와 조각상들이 미국 전역의 작은 마을에서 여전히 사랑 받고 있다.

[어휘] **federal funds** 연방 기금   **appropriate** 할당하다, 충당하다   **mural** 벽화   **statue** 조각상   **admiration** 감탄, 탄복

1. (C)	2. (D)	3. (C)	4. (B)	5. (C)
6. (D)	7. (A)	8. (A)	9. (C)	10. (B)
11. (A)	12. (D)	13. (D)	14. (B)	15. (B)
16. (D)	17. (A)	18. (D)	19. (C)	20. (C)
21. (C)	22. (B)	23. (B)	24. (D)	25. (B)
26. (B)	27. (D)	28. (B)	29. (A)	30. (A)
31. (B)	32. (C)	33. (D)	34. (A)	35. (D)
36. (D)	37. (A)	38. (C)	39. (B)	40. (B)
41. (B)	42. (B)	43. (A)	44. (B)	45. (C)
46. (A)	47. (A)	48. (C)	49. (C)	50. (D)

Questions 1–7

Hotels were among the earliest facilities that [1]bound the United States together. [7]They were both creatures and creators of communities, as well as symptoms of the frenetic quest for community. [7]Even in the first part of the nineteenth century, Americans were already forming the habit of gathering from all corners of the nation for both public and private, business and pleasure, purposes. [7]Conventions were the new occasions, and hotels were distinctively American facilities making conventions possible. The first national convention of a major party to choose a candidate for president (that of [2]the National Republican Party, which met on December 12, 1831, and nominated Henry Clay for president) was held in Baltimore, at a hotel that was then reputed to be the best in the country. The presence in Baltimore of Barnum's City Hotel, a six-story building with two hundred apartments, helps explain why many other early national political conventions were held there.

[7]In the longer run, American hotels made other national conventions not only possible but pleasant and convivial. The growing custom of regularly [3]assembling from afar the representatives of all kinds of groups—not only for political conventions, but also for commercial, professional, learned, and avocational [4]ones—in turn supported the multiplying hotels. By the mid-twentieth century, conventions accounted for over a third of the yearly room occupancy of all hotels in the nation; about 18,000 different conventions were held annually with a total attendance of about ten million persons.

[6]Nineteenth-century American hotelkeepers, who were no longer the genial, deferential "hosts" of the eighteenth-century European inn, became leading citizens. [7]Holding a large stake in the community, they exercised power to make [5]it prosper. As owners or managers of the local "palace of the public," they were makers and shapers of a principal community attraction. Travelers from abroad were mildly shocked by this high social position.

[해석] 호텔은 미국을 결속시킨 최초의 시설들 중 하나였다. 지역사회의 산물이자 창조자일 뿐만 아니라 지역 사회를 위한 열광적인 탐구에 대한 징조이기도 했다. 심지어 19세기 초에도, 미국인들은 공적인 목적과 사적인 목적에서, 사업상 목적과 오락상 목적에서 이미 전국 각지에서 모임을 가졌다. 컨벤션은 새로운 행사였고, 호텔은 컨벤션을 가능하게 하는 독특한 미국의 시설이었다. (공화당의) 대통령 후보를 뽑기 위한 제1정당의 첫 전당 대회(1831년 12월 12일에 열렸으며, 대통령 후보로 헨리 클레이를 지명했음)는 볼티모어의 호텔에서 열렸는데, 그 호텔은 당시 그 나라에서 최고 평판의 호텔이었다. 200개의 스위트룸을 갖춘 6층 건물인 바넘 시티 호텔이 볼티모어에 있다는 것은 초기에 다른 전국 전당 대회가 왜 거기에서 많이 열렸는지 설명하는 데 도움이 된다.

결국, 미국의 호텔들은 다른 전국의 컨벤션을 가능하게 했을 뿐만 아니라 즐겁고 경쾌하게 만들었다. 정당 컨벤션뿐만 아니라 상업적 · 전문적 · 학술적 · 취미적인 목적에서 모든 종류의 단체 대표자들이 멀리서 와서 정기적으로 모이는 모임이 증가함에 따라 차례로 호텔들이 늘어나게 되었다. 20세기 중반까지 컨벤션들이 전국 모든 호텔의 연간 객실 점유의 1/3 이상을 차지하는 사유였는데, 대략 1만 8천 건의 다양한 컨벤션이 해마다 열렸으며, 총 참석 인원은 대략 약 1천 만 명이었다.

19세기 미국 호텔 경영자들은 더 이상 18세기 유럽 여관의 친절하고 공손한 "주인"들이 아니었고, 주도적인 시민들이 되었다. 그들은 지역 사회에서 큰 지분을 보유하고 있으면서, 지역사회를 번창하게 하는 데 큰 영향력을 행사했다. 그 지역의 "대중의 궁전" 소유주들이거나 관리자들로서, 그들은 지역 사회의 주요 관광 명소를 만들고 실현하는 사람들이었다. 해외에서 온 관광객들은 이런 높은 사회적인 지위에 다소 놀랐다.

[어휘] **facility** 시설, 설비　**creature** 산물, 소산　**creator**
창조자, 창시자　**symptom** 징후, 조짐; 증상　**frenetic**
열광적인　**quest** 탐구　**convention** 대회, 회의,
협약　**occasion** (특별한) 행사　**distinctively** 독특하게,
특별하게　**major party** 제1당, 대정당, 다수당　**candidate**
후보자　**nominate** 지명하다, 추천하다　**reputed** 평판이
있는　**presence** 존재　**apartment** (객실의 호화) 스위트룸
political convention 전당 대회　**in the longer run**
결국에는　**convivial** 명랑한, 유쾌한　**custom** 관행, 관례
regularly 정기적으로　**assemble** 모이다　**from afar**
멀리서　**representative** 대표자　**commercial** 상업의,
무역의　**learned** 학식이 있는, 학문적인　**avocational**
부업의, 취미 삼아 하는　**in turn** 교대로; 순서대로,
다음에는　**multiplying** 증가하는　**account for** ～의
이유가 되다; ～을 차지하다　**room occupancy** 객실
점유　**annually** 매년, 해마다　**hotelkeeper** 호텔 경영자,
호텔 직원　**genial** 친절한　**deferential** 공손한　**stake**
지분　**prosper** 번영하다, 발전하다　**principal** 주요한
attraction 명소　**mildly** 다소, 약간

1. The word "bound" in line 1 is closest in meaning to

(A) led

(B) protected

(C) tied

(D) strengthened

[해석] 1행에 언급된 "bound"와 의미상 가장 가까운 것은 무엇인가?
　　(A) 이끌었다
　　(B) 보호했다
　　(C) 묶었다
　　(D) 강화했다

2. The National Republican Party is mentioned in line 7 as an example of a group

(A) from Baltimore

(B) of learned people

(C) owning a hotel

(D) holding a convention

[해석] 7행에 언급된 공화당은 어떤 단체의 예로 언급되는가?
　　(A) 볼티모어에서 온 단체
　　(B) 학자 단체
　　(C) 호텔 소유자 단체
　　(D) 컨벤션을 개최하는 단체

3. The word "assembling" in line 13 is closest in meaning to

(A) announcing

(B) motivating

(C) gathering

(D) contracting

[해석] 13행에 언급된 "assembling"과 의미상 가장 가까운 것은 무엇인가?
　　(A) 발표하는
　　(B) 동기를 주는
　　(C) 모이는
　　(D) 계약하는

[어휘] **motivate** 동기를 주다, 자극하다　**contract** 계약하다

4. The word "ones" in line 15 refers to

(A) hotels

(B) conventions

(C) kinds

(D) representatives

[해석] 15행에 언급된 "ones"가 가리키는 것은 무엇인가?
　　(A) 호텔
　　(B) 컨벤션
　　(C) 종류
　　(D) 대표자

5. The word "it" in line 21 refers to

(A) European inn

(B) host

(C) community

(D) public

[해석] 21행에 언급된 "it"이 가리키는 것은 무엇인가?
　　(A) 유럽 여관
　　(B) 주인
　　(C) 지역사회
　　(D) 대중

6. It can be inferred from the passage that early hotelkeepers in the United States were

(A) active politicians
(B) European immigrants
(C) professional builders
(D) influential citizens

[해석] 지문을 통해 초기 미국의 호텔 경영자들에 대해 추론할 수 있는 것은 무엇인가?
(A) 활동적인 정치가들이었다
(B) 유럽 이민자들이었다
(C) 전문 건축가들이었다
(D) 영향력 있는 시민들이었다

[어휘] **immigrant** 이민자, 입국자   **influential** 영향력 있는

7. Which of the following statements about early American hotels is NOT mentioned in the passage?

(A) Travelers from abroad did not enjoy staying in them.
(B) Conventions were held in them.
(C) People used them for both business and pleasure.
(D) They were important to the community.

[해석] 다음 중 초기 미국 호텔들에 관한 설명으로 지문에서 언급되지 않은 것은 무엇인가?
(A) 외국에서 온 여행자들은 호텔에서 묵고 싶어 하지 않았다.
(B) 호텔에서 컨벤션들이 열렸다.
(C) 사람들은 사업상과 오락상의 목적에서 호텔을 이용했다.
(D) 호텔은 지역사회에 중요했다.

Questions 8–15

With Robert Laurent and William Zorach, direct carving enters into the story of modern sculpture in the United States. [11]Direct carving—in which the sculptors themselves carve stone or wood with mallet and chisel—must be recognized as something more than just a technique. Implicit in it is an aesthetic principle as well : that the [8]medium has certain qualities of beauty and expressiveness with which sculptors must bring their own aesthetic sensibilities into harmony. [9]For example, sometimes the shape or veining in a piece of stone or wood suggests, perhaps even [10]dictates, not only the ultimate form, but even the subject matter.

[11]The technique of direct carving was a break with the nineteenth-century tradition in which the making of a clay model was considered the creative act and the work was then turned over to studio assistants to be cast in plaster or bronze or carved in marble. Neoclassical sculptors seldom held a mallet or chisel in their own hands, readily conceding that the assistants they employed were far better than they were at carving the finished marble.

With the turn-of-the-century Arts and Crafts movement and the discovery of nontraditional sources of inspiration, such as wooden African figures and masks, there arose a new urge for hands-on, personal execution of art and an interaction with the medium. Even as early as the 1880s and 1890s, nonconformist European artists were attempting direct carving. By the second decade of the twentieth century, Americans—Laurent and Zorach most notably—had adopted it as their primary means of working.

Born in France, Robert Laurent (1890–1970) was a prodigy who received his education in the United States. [13]In 1905 he was sent to Paris as an apprentice to an art dealer, and in the years that followed he [12]witnessed the birth of

Cubism, discovered primitive art, and learned the techniques of woodcarving from a frame maker.

Back in New York City by 1910, Laurent began carving pieces such as *The Priestess*, which reveals his fascination with African, pre-Columbian, and South Pacific art. Taking a walnut plank, [15]the sculptor carved the expressive, stylized design. It is one of the earliest examples of direct carving in American sculpture. [15]The plank's form dictated the rigidly frontal view and the low relief. Even its irregular shape must have appealed to Laurent as [14]a break with a long-standing tradition that required a sculptor to work within a perfect rectangle or square.

[어휘] **direct carving** (조각) 직접 새기기   **sculpture** 조각
sculptor 조각가   **mallet** 나무망치   **chisel** 정   **implicit**
함축적인, 은연 중의   **aesthetic** 미적인   **principle**
원리, 원칙   **medium** 매개물, 매체   **expressiveness**
표현력   **sensibility** 감각, 감성   **veining** (목재 · 대리석의)
불규칙한 줄, 결   **dictate** 지시하다; 결정하다, 영향을 끼치다
ultimate 최종의, 궁극적인   **subject matter** 주제;
소재   **break** 단절, 중단   **clay** 진흙, 점토   **assistant**
조수, 보조자   **cast** 주조하다, 틀에 넣어 만들다   **plaster**
석고   **bronze** 청동   **marble** 대리석   **Neoclassical**
신고전주의의   **concede** 인정하다   **nontraditional**
비전통적인   **inspiration** 영감   **figure** (그림 · 조각 등의)
인물상   **urge** 촉구   **hands-on** 실제의, 직접의, 손으로
행하는   **execution** 실행   **interaction** 상호작용, 관련
nonconformist (관습에) 따르지 않는   **decade** 10년간
notably 명백히, 특히   **adopt** 채택하다   **prodigy** 천재,
신동   **apprentice** 견습생, 도제   **dealer** 판매인, 거래인
reveal 보여주다, 드러내다   **fascination** 매혹, 집착,
흥미   **plank** 널빤지, 판자   **stylized** 양식화된, 정형화된
rigidly 엄격히, 완고하게   **frontal** 정면의   **low relief**
얕은 돋을새김   **irregular** (모양이) 가지런하지 않은, 불규칙한
long-standing 오랫동안에 걸친, 다년간의   **rectangle**
직사각형   **square** 정사각형

[해석] 로버트 로랑과 윌리엄 조라크와 더불어, 직접 새기기가 미국 현대 조각의 이야기로 들어선다. 직접 새기기는 조각가 자신이 나무망치와 정으로 돌이나 나무에 직접 새기는 것으로, 단순히 한 가지 기법 이상의 특별한 것으로 인식되어야 한다. 그 안에는 미적 원리도 내재되어 있다. 즉, 매체에는 미와 표현의 어떤 특성이 있는데, 이 특성들로 조각가들은 자신들의 미적 감각을 조화롭게 만들어야 한다. 예를 들어, 때때로 돌이나 나무 조각의 형태나 결이 궁극적인 형태뿐만 아니라 주제까지도 제시하거나 심지어 결정하기도 한다.

직접 새기기 기법은 점토 모형을 만드는 것이 창의적인 예술 행위로 간주되었으며 그 다음 일을 작업실의 조수에게 넘겨서 석고나 청동에 주조하거나 대리석에 조각하도록 했던 19세기 전통과의 단절이었다. 신고전주의 조각가들은 자신의 손에 나무 망치나 정을 거의 들지 않았으며, 자신들이 고용한 조수들이 완성된 대리석을 조각하는 데 자신들보다 훨씬 더 낫다는 것을 기꺼이 인정했다.

20세기 초의 미술 공예 운동과 아프리카의 나무 조각상과 나무 탈 같은 비전통적인 영감의 원천에 대한 발견으로 인해, 개인이 직접 예술을 실행하고 매체와 교감하고자 하는 새로운 욕구가 일어났다. 일찍이 1880년대와 1890년대에도 개혁주의 유럽 미술가들은 직접 새기기를 시도했었다. 20세기 초 20년까지(1920년대까지) 미국인들, 특히 로랑과 조라크는 직접 새기기를 자신들의 주요 작업 수단으로 채택했다.

프랑스에서 태어난 로버트 로랑(1890–1970)은 미국에서 교육을 받았던 천재였다. 1905년에 그는 파리에 한 미술상의 도제로 보내졌고, 그 후 몇 년 동안 입체파의 탄생을 목격했고, 원시미술을 발견했으며, 한 틀 제조업자에게서 목재 조각 기법을 배웠다.

로랑은 1910년에 뉴욕 시로 다시 돌아와 〈여사제〉와 같은 작품을 조각하기 시작했고, 그 작품에는 그가 아프리카 미술과 콜럼버스 이전 시대의 미술, 남태평양 미술에 빠져 있었다는 것이 드러난다. 그 조각가는 호두나무 판자를 택해 표현력 있고 정형화된 디자인을 조각했다. 그것은 미국 조각에서 직접 새기기 기법을 쓴 가장 초기의 사례들 중 하나이다. 그 판자의 형태로 엄격한 정면도와 얕은 돋을새김을 할 수밖에 없었다. 심지어 그 판자의 불규칙한 모양조차도 로랑이 조각가에게 완벽한 직사각형이나 정사각형 안에서만 작업하도록 요구했던 오랫동안 지속되어 온 전통과 단절하는데 자극이 되었음에 틀림없다.

8. The word "medium" in line 4 could be used to refer to

(A) **stone or wood**

(B) mallet and chisel

(C) technique

(D) principle

[해석] 4행에 언급된 "medium"은 무엇을 가리키기 위해 사용되었는가?

(A) **돌 또는 나무**

(B) 나무 망치와 정

(C) 기술

(D) 원리

9. What is one of the fundamental principles of direct carving?

(A) A sculptor must work with talented assistants.

(B) The subject of a sculpture should be derived from classical stories.

(C) **The material is an important element in a sculpture.**

(D) Designing a sculpture is a more creative activity than carving it.

[해석] 직접 새기기의 기본 원리들 중 하나는 무엇인가?
(A) 조각가는 유능한 조수와 일해야 한다.
(B) 조각의 주제는 고전적인 이야기들에서 유래한 것이어야 한다.
(C) 재료는 조각에서 중요한 요소이다.
(D) 조각을 디자인하는 것은 조각을 하는 것보다 더 창조적인 활동이다.

[어휘] **fundamental** 기본적인 **talented** 유능한
derive 유래하다

10. The word "dictates" in line 7 is closest in meaning to

(A) reads aloud
(B) determines
(C) includes
(D) records

[해석] 7행에 언급된 "dictates"와 의미상 가장 가까운 것은 무엇인가?
(A) 큰 소리로 읽다
(B) 결정하다
(C) 포함하다
(D) 기록하다

11. How does direct carving differ from the nineteenth-century tradition of sculpture?

(A) Sculptors are personally involved in the carving of a piece.
(B) Sculptors find their inspiration in neoclassical sources.
(C) Sculptors have replaced the mallet and chisel with other tools.
(D) Sculptors receive more formal training.

[해석] 직접 새기기는 19세기의 전통적인 조각과 어떻게 다른가?
(A) 조각가들이 직접 조각을 하는 데 관여한다.
(B) 조각가들이 신고전주의의 원천에서 영감을 발견한다.
(C) 조각가들이 나무망치와 정을 다른 도구로 대체했다.
(D) 조각가들이 더 정식 교육을 받는다.

[어휘] **personally** 몸소, 직접 **involve** 참여하다
replace 대체하다, 교체하다

12. The word "witnessed" in line 22 is closest in meaning to

(A) influenced
(B) studied
(C) validated
(D) observed

[해석] 22행에 언급된 "witnessed"와 의미상 가장 가까운 것은 무엇인가?
(A) 영향을 미쳤다
(B) 공부했다
(C) 입증했다
(D) 목격했다

[어휘] **validate** 입증하다, 비준하다

13. Where did Robert Laurent learn to carve?

(A) New York
(B) Africa
(C) The South Pacific
(D) Paris

[해석] 로버트 로랑은 어디에서 조각을 배우기 시작했는가?
(A) 뉴욕
(B) 아프리카
(C) 남태평양
(D) 파리

14. The phase "a break with" in line 28 is closest in meaning to

(A) a destruction of
(B) a departure from
(C) a collapse of
(D) a solution to

[해석] 28행에 언급된 "a break with"와 의미상 가장 가까운 것은 무엇인가?
(A) ~의 파괴
(B) ~로부터의 이탈
(C) ~의 붕괴
(D) ~에 대한 해결책

[어휘] **departure** 이탈, 벗어남 **collapse** 붕괴

15. The piece titled *The Priestess* has all of the following characteristics EXCEPT:

(A) The design is stylized.

(B) It is made of marble.

(C) The carving is not deep.

(D) It depicts the front of a person.

[해석] 다음 중 〈여사제〉라는 작품의 특징이 아닌 것은 무엇인가?
    (A) 디자인이 정형화되었다.
    (B) 대리석으로 만들어졌다.
    (C) 조각이 깊지 않다.
    (D) 사람의 정면을 묘사한다.

[어휘] **depict** 묘사하다, 표현하다

Questions 16–26

[16]Birds that feed in flocks commonly retire together into roosts. The reasons for roosting communally are not always obvious, but there are some likely benefits. In winter especially, it is important for birds to keep warm at night and [17]conserve precious food reserves. One way to do this is to find a sheltered roost. Solitary roosters shelter in dense vegetation or enter a cavity—horned larks dig holes in the ground and [18]ptarmigan burrow into snow banks—but the effect of sheltering is [19]magnified by several birds huddling together in the roosts, as wrens, swifts, brown creepers, bluebirds, and anis do. [24]Body contact reduces the surface area exposed to the cold air, so the birds keep each other warm. Two [20]kinglets huddling together were found to reduce their heat losses by a quarter, and three together saved a third of their heat.

[24]The second possible benefit of communal roosts is that they act as information centers. During the day, parties of birds will have spread out to [21]forage over a very large area. When they return in the evening some will have fed well, but others may have found little to eat. Some investigators have observed that when the birds set out again next morning, those birds that did not feed well on the previous day appear to follow those that did. The behavior of common and lesser kestrels may illustrate different feeding behaviors of similar birds with different roosting habits. The common kestrel hunts vertebrate animals in a small, familiar hunting ground, whereas the very similar lesser kestrel feeds on insects over a large area. [22]The common kestrel roosts and hunts alone, but the lesser kestrel roosts and hunts in flocks, possibly so that one bird can learn from others where to find insect swarms.

²⁴Finally, there is safety in numbers at communal roosts since there will always be a few birds awake at any given moment to give the alarm. ²⁵But this increased protection is partially ²³counteracted by the fact that mass roosts attract predators and are especially vulnerable if ²⁶they are on the ground. Even those in trees can be attacked by birds of prey. The birds on the edge are at greatest risk since predators find it easier to catch small birds perching at the margins of the roost.

[해석] 떼를 지어 먹이를 먹는 새들은 일반적으로 함께 둥지에 든다. 공동으로 둥지에 드는 이유들이 항상 분명한 것은 아니지만, 그럴듯한 이점들이 좀 있다. 특히 겨울에 새들에게 밤에 따뜻하게 지내고 소중한 먹이를 보관하는 것은 중요하다. 이렇게 하는 한 가지 방법은 보호가 되는 둥지를 찾는 것이다. 혼자 지내는 수새들은 무성한 초목에 숨거나 구멍에 들어가는데, 두뿔종다리는 땅에 구멍을 파고 들꿩은 눈 더미 속에 굴을 파지만, 굴뚝새와 칼새, 갈색 나무발바리, 블루버드, 아니처럼 둥지에 함께 모여 있는 몇몇 새들에게 둥지에서 지내는 효과는 증대된다. 신체 접촉은 차가운 공기에 노출된 표면을 줄여서, 새들은 서로 온기를 유지한다. 함께 붙어 있는 상모솔새 두 마리는 열 손실을 1/4로 줄이고, 함께 붙어 있는 세 마리는 열의 1/3을 저장하는 것으로 알려졌다.

공동 둥지의 두 번째로 가능한 혜택은 그곳이 정보 센터의 역할을 한다는 것이다. 낮 동안에 새 무리는 넓은 지역으로 먹이를 찾아 다니기 위해 흩어진다. 저녁에 돌아올 때 몇몇 새들은 잘 먹었지만 다른 새들은 먹을 것을 많이 찾지 못했을 수도 있다. 몇몇 연구자들은 새들이 다음날 아침에 다시 출발할 때, 전날 잘 먹지 못한 새들은 잘 먹은 새들을 따라가는 것을 관찰했다. 황조롱이와 작은 황조롱이의 행동은 다른 둥지 습성을 지닌 유사한 새들이 다른 먹이를 먹는 행동을 보여줄 지도 모른다. 황조롱이는 좁고 익숙한 사냥 지역에서 척추동물을 사냥하는 반면, 아주 유사한 작은 황조롱이는 넓은 지역에서 곤충을 잡아 먹고 산다. 황조롱이는 혼자 살고 사냥하지만, 작은 황조롱이는 아마도 한 마리의 새가 다른 새들로부터 곤충 떼를 찾을 수 있는 장소를 배울 수 있도록 떼를 지어 살고 사냥한다.

마지막으로, 경고를 하기 위해 어떤 순간에라도 깨어 있는 몇몇 새들이 늘 있기 때문에 공동 둥지에서는 다수의 새들이 안전하다. 하지만 많은 둥지들은 약탈자들을 유인하고, 특히 땅에 있을 때는 취약하다는 점에서 이런 향상된 보호는 일부 불리하게 작용하기도 한다. 심지어 나무에 있는 새들도 맹금들의 공격을 받을 수 있다. 약탈자들이 둥지의 가장자리에 앉아 있는 작은 새들을 잡는 것이 더 쉽다는 것을 알기 때문에 가장자리에 있는 새들이 가장 큰 위험에 처해 있다.

[어휘] in flocks 떼를 지어, 무리를 이루어　retire 자다, 잠자리에 들다　roost 새장, 보금자리; 보금자리에 들다　communally 공동으로 cf. communal 공동의　likely 있을 법한, 그럴싸한　benefit 이점, 이익　conserve 보존하다　reserve 축적, 예비, 보존　shelter 보호하다, 숨기다　solitary 혼자의　rooster 새의 수컷　dense 무성한, 우거진, 밀집한　vegetation 식물, 초목　cavity 구멍, 빈곳　horned lark 두뿔종다리　ptarmigan 뇌조, 들꿩　burrow 굴을 파다　snow bank 눈더미　magnify 확대하다, 증대하다　huddle 밀집하다, 모이다; 몸을 웅크리다　wren 굴뚝새　swift 칼새　creeper 나무발바리　bluebird 블루버드(북미산 푸른 날개의 명금)　ani 아니(두견이과 뻐꾸기속의 새)　expose 노출시키다　kinglet 상모솔새　party (동물의) 무리　spread out 넓히다, 전개하다　forage (먹이를) 찾아 돌아다니다　investigator 연구자, 조사자　set out 시작하다, 출발하다　kestrel 황조롱이　illustrate 설명하다, 예시하다　vertebrate animal 척추 동물　swarm (곤충의) 떼　partially 부분적으로, 불완전하게, 불공평하게　counteract 반대로 작용하다, 방해하다　predator 약탈자　vulnerable 취약한　bird of prey 맹금　perch 앉다, 자리잡다　margin 가장자리

16. What does the passage mainly discuss?

(A) How birds find and store food

(B) How birds maintain body heat in the winter

(C) Why birds need to establish territory

(D) Why some species of birds nest together

[해석] 주로 무엇에 관해 이야기하고 있는가?
(A) 새들이 먹이를 찾고 저장하는 방법
(B) 새들이 겨울에 체온을 유지하는 방법
(C) 새들이 영역을 확립하는 이유
(D) 몇몇 새들이 함께 둥지를 짓는 이유

[어휘] establish 확립하다　territory 영토, 영역　nest 둥지를 짓다, 둥지에 들다

17. The word "conserve" in line 3 is closest in meaning to

(A) retain

(B) watch

(C) locate

(D) share

CHAPTER 6

18. Ptarmigan keep warm in the winter by

(A) huddling together on the ground with other birds

(B) building nests in trees

(C) burrowing into dense patches of vegetation

(D) **digging tunnels into the snow**

19. The word "magnified" in line 6 is closest in meaning to

(A) caused

(B) modified

(C) **intensified**

(D) combined

20. The author mentions kinglets in line 8 as an example of birds that

(A) protect themselves by nesting in holes

(B) nest with other species of birds

(C) **nest together for warmth**

(D) usually feed and nest in pairs

21. The word "forage" in line 11 is closest in meaning to

(A) fly

(B) assemble

(C) **feed**

(D) rest

22. Which of the following statements about lesser and common kestrels is true?

(A) The lesser kestrel and the common kestrel have similar diets.

(B) **The lesser kestrel feeds sociably, but the common kestrel does not.**

(C) The common kestrel nests in larger flocks than does the lesser kestrel.

(D) The common kestrel nests in trees; the lesser kestrel nests on the ground.

23. The word "counteracted' in line 22 is closest in meaning to

(A) suggested

(B) negated

(C) measured

(D) shielded

[해석] 22행에 언급된 "counteracted"와 의미상 가장 가까운 것은 무엇인가?
(A) 제안되는
(B) 무효화하는
(C) 정확히 재는
(D) 보호되는

[어휘] **negate** 무효화하다, 부정하다   **shield** 보호하다

24. Which of the following is NOT mentioned in the passage as an advantage derived by birds that huddle together while sleeping?

(A) Some members of the flock warn others of impending dangers.

(B) Staying together provides a greater amount of heat for the whole flock.

(C) Some birds in the flock function as information centers for others who are looking for food.

(D) Several members of the flock care for the young.

[해석] 다음 중 새들이 떼로 모여 자는 것에서 얻을 수 있는 이점으로 지문에서 언급되지 않은 것은 무엇인가?
(A) 무리 중 일부 새들은 다른 새들에게 임박한 위험을 경고한다.
(B) 함께 머무르는 것은 전체 무리에 더 많은 양의 열을 제공한다.
(C) 무리의 일부 새들은 먹이를 찾는 다른 새들에게 정보 센터의 기능을 한다.
(D) 무리의 몇몇 새들은 어린 새들을 돌본다.

[어휘] **derive** 얻다, 끌어내다, 찾다   **impending** 절박한, 임박한   **function** 기능을 다하다, 구실을 하다   **care for** ~을 돌보다

25. Which of the following is a disadvantage of communal roosts that is mentioned in the passage?

(A) Diseases easily spread among the birds.

(B) Groups are more attractive to predators than individual birds are.

(C) Food supplies are quickly depleted.

(D) Some birds in the group will attack the others.

[해석] 다음 중 지문에서 공동 둥지의 불리한 점으로 언급된 것은 무엇인가?
(A) 새들 사이에서 질병이 쉽게 퍼진다.
(B) 무리는 개별적인 새들보다 약탈자들에게 더 매력적이다.
(C) 먹이 공급이 빨리 고갈된다.
(D) 무리의 몇몇 새들이 다른 새들을 공격할 것이다.

[어휘] **deplete** 다 써버리다, 고갈시키다

26. The word "they" in line 23 refers to

(A) a few birds

(B) mass roosts

(C) predators

(D) trees

[해석] 23행에 언급된 "they"가 가리키는 것은 무엇인가?
(A) 몇 마리의 새들
(B) 공동 둥지들
(C) 약탈자들
(D) 나무들

²⁷Perhaps the most striking quality of satiric literature is its freshness, its originality of perspective. Satire rarely offers original ideas. Instead, it presents the familiar in a new form. Satirists do not offer the world new philosophies. What they do is look at familiar conditions from a perspective that makes these conditions seem foolish, harmful, or affected. ³²Satire jars us out of complacence into a pleasantly shocked ²⁸realization that many of the values we unquestioningly accept are false. ²⁹*Don Quixote* makes chivalry seem absurd; ²⁹*Brave New World* ridicules the pretensions of science; ²⁹*A Modest Proposal* dramatizes starvation by advocating cannibalism. None of these ideas is original. Chivalry was suspect before Cervantes, humanists objected to the claims of pure science before Aldous Huxley, and people were aware of famine before Swift. It was not the originality of the idea that made these satires popular. It was the manner of expression, the satiric method, that made them interesting and entertaining. Satires are read because they are ³⁰aesthetically satisfying works of art, not because they are morally wholesome or ethically instructive. ³¹They are stimulating and refreshing because with commonsense briskness ³⁷they brush away illusions and secondhand opinions. With spontaneous irreverence, satire rearranges perspectives, scrambles familiar objects into incongruous juxtaposition, and speaks in a personal idiom instead of abstract platitude.

Satire exists because there is need for it. ³⁶It has lived because readers appreciate a ³³refreshing stimulus, an irreverent reminder that they live in a world of platitudinous thinking, cheap moralizing, and foolish philosophy. ³⁷Satire serves to prod people into an awareness of truth, though rarely to any action on behalf of truth. ³²Satire tends to remind people that much of what ³⁴they see, hear, and read in popular media is sanctimonious, sentimental, and only partially true. Life resembles in only a slight degree the popular image of it. Soldiers rarely hold the ideals that movies attribute to them, nor do ordinary citizens ³⁵devote their lives to unselfish ³⁸service of humanity. Intelligent people know these things but tend to forget them when they do not hear them expressed.

[해석] 풍자 문학의 가장 두드러진 특징은 아마도 신선함, 즉 관점의 독창성일 것이다. 풍자는 거의 독창적인 아이디어를 제공하지 않는다. 그 대신, 그것은 친숙한 것을 새로운 형태로 제시한다. 풍자가들은 세상에 새로운 철학을 제공하지 않는다. 그들은 친숙한 상황들을 어리석거나 해롭거나 꾸며진 것 같이 만드는 관점에서 바라보게 한다. 풍자는 우리에게 충격을 줘서 자기 만족의 태도에서 벗어나, 우리가 당연히 받아들이는 많은 가치관이 거짓임을 기분 좋은 충격 속에 깨닫게 한다. 〈돈키호테〉는 기사도를 우스꽝스럽게 보이게 만들고, 〈멋진 신세계〉는 과학의 가식을 조롱하며, 〈겸손한 제안〉은 식인을 옹호하여 기아를 극화하고 있다. 이 아이디어들 중 어느 것도 독창적인 것은 없다. 기사도는 세르반테스 이전에도 의심을 받았고, 인도주의자들은 올더스 헉슬리 이전에도 순수 과학의 주장에 반대했으며, 사람들은 스위프트 이전에도 기근을 알고 있었다. 이러한 풍자들을 인기 있게 만든 것은 아이디어의 독창성이 아니었다. 그것들을 흥미 있고 재미있게 만든 것은 바로 표현 방식, 즉 풍자 방법이었다. 풍자 문학들은 미적으로 만족스러운 예술 작품이기 때문에 읽는 것이지, 도덕적으로 건전하다든지 또는 윤리적으로 교훈적이기 때문에 읽는 것이 아니다. 이 풍자들은 상식적인 활기로 망상과 전해 들은 의견을 떨쳐 버리기 때문에 자극적이고 신선하다. 자연스럽게 우러난 무례함으로, 풍자는 관점을 재정리하고, 친숙한 사물들을 휘저어 앞뒤가 맞지 않게 나란히 늘어놓고, 추상적인 상투어 대신 개인적인 어법으로 이야기한다.

풍자는 그 필요성 때문에 존재한다. 독자들이 참신한 자극, 즉 자신들이 진부한 사고와 값싼 도덕과, 어리석은 철학의 세상에 살고 있다는 것을 불손하게 상기시키는 것의 가치를 인정하기 때문에 존재해왔다. 풍자는 사람들을 자극하여 진실을 깨닫도록 하지만, 진실을 위해 어떤 행동을 취하게까지 하는 경우는 드물다. 풍자는 사람들에게 대중매체에서 보고 듣고 읽는 많은 것이 경건한 척하고 감상적이고 부분적으로만 옳다는 점을 상기시키는 경향이 있다. 인생은 그것에 대해 일반적으로 믿고 있는 이미지와 아주 미미한 정도로만 비슷하다. 군인들은 영화에서 자신들에게 부여하는 이상들을 거의 갖고 있지 않으며, 일반 시민들도 사심없이 인류를 위해 봉사하는 데 헌신하지도 않는다. 지성인들은 이러한 점들을 알고 있지만, 그 점들이 겉으로 들리지 않을 때는 그런 점들을 잊어버리는 경향이 있다.

[어휘] **striking** 두드러진, 놀랄만한　**satiric** 풍자적인
originality 독창성　**perspective** 시각, 관점　**satire**
풍자; 풍자극, 풍자 문학　**satirist** 풍자가　**affected** 가장된,
꾸며진　**jar** 충격을 주다; (신경을) 거슬리다　**complacence**
자기 만족　**unquestioningly** 의문을 품지 않고, 망설임 없이
chivalry 기사도　**absurd** 터무니없는, 황당한　**ridicule**
조롱하다　**pretension** 거짓, 허식　**dramatize**
극화하다　**starvation** 기아, 아사　**advocate**
옹호하다, 지지하다　**cannibalism** 동족끼리 잡아먹음,
인육　**suspect** 미심쩍은, 의심스러운, 수상한, 용의자, 요주의
인물　**famine** 기근　**aesthetically** 미적으로　**morally**
도덕적으로　**wholesome** 건강에 좋은; 유익한, 도움이
되는　**ethically** 윤리적으로　**instructive** 교훈적인
stimulating 자극적인　**refreshing** 참신한, 기운을
돋우는, 개운한, 상쾌한　**commonsense** 상식적인, 양식
있는　**briskness** 활발함, 활기　**brush away** 털어 버리다,
떨쳐 버리다　**illusion** 환상, 착각　**secondhand** 간접의
spontaneous 자발적인, 자연스러운　**irreverence**
불경, 무례　**rearrange** 재정리하다　**scramble** 마구
뒤섞다　**incongruous** 앞뒤가 맞지 않은; 일관성이 없는,
모순된　**juxtaposition** 병렬 관계　**platitude** 상투어,
진부　**appreciate** 진가를 알다, 인식하다　**stimulus** 자극
irreverent 불경한　**reminder** 생각나게 하는 사람[것]
platitudinous 진부한, 단조로운　**moralize** 도덕적으로
설명하다　**prod** 자극하다, 격려하다　**on behalf of** ~을
위해; ~을 대표하여, 대신하여　**sanctimonious** 신성한
체하는　**sentimental** 감상적인　**resemble** 유사하다,
닮다　**attribute** ~을 부여하다　**ordinary** 보통의, 통상의
devote 헌신하다　**unselfish** 이기적이 아닌, 사심이 없는,
이타적인

27. What does the passage mainly discuss?

(A) Difficulties of writing satiric literature

(B) Popular topics of satire

(C) New philosophies emerging from satiric
literature

(D) Reasons for the popularity of satire

> [해석] 주로 무엇에 관해 이야기하고 있는가?
> (A) 풍자 문학 저술의 어려움
> (B) 인기 있는 풍자 주제들
> (C) 풍자 문학에서 나타나는 새로운 철학
> **(D) 풍자가 인기 있는 이유**

28. The word "realization" in line 5 is closest in
meaning to

(A) certainty

(B) awareness

(C) surprise

(D) confusion

> [해석] 5행에 언급된 "realization"과 의미상 가장 가까운 것은 무
> 엇인가?
> (A) 확신
> **(B) 깨달음**
> (C) 놀람
> (D) 혼란

29. Why does the author mention *Don Quixote*, *Brave
New World*, and *A Modest Proposal* in lines 6–7?

**(A) They are famous examples of satiric
literature.**

(B) They present commonsense solutions to
problems.

(C) They are appropriate for readers of all ages.

(D) They are books with similar stories.

> [해석] 글쓴이가 6~7행에서 〈돈키호테〉와 〈멋진 신세계〉, 〈겸손
> 한 제안〉을 언급한 이유는 무엇인가?
> **(A) 풍자 문학의 유명한 사례여서**
> (B) 문제점에 대한 상식적인 해결책을 제시해서
> (C) 모든 연령대의 독자들에게 적당해서
> (D) 비슷한 줄거리를 가진 책들이어서

> [어휘] **commonsense** 상식의　**appropriate** 적당한,
> 적절한

30. The word "aesthetically" in line 12 is closest in
meaning to

(A) artistically

(B) exceptionally

(C) realistically

(D) dependably

> [해석] 12행에 언급된 "aesthetically"와 의미상 가장 가까운 것은?
> **(A) 예술적으로**
> (B) 예외적으로
> (C) 사실적으로
> (D) 신뢰할 수 있게

31. Which of the following can be found in satiric literature?

(A) Newly emerging philosophies

(B) Odd combinations of objects and ideas

(C) Abstract discussion of morals and ethics

(D) Wholesome characters who are unselfish

[해석] 다음 중 풍자 문학에서 발견할 수 있는 것은 무엇인가?
　　(A) 새롭게 나타나고 있는 철학
　　(B) 대상과 관념의 특이한 조합
　　(C) 도덕과 윤리의 추상적인 논의
　　(D) 이타적인 사람들의 건전한 특성

[어휘] **odd** 이상한, 특이한　**wholesome** (도덕적·정신적으로) 건전한

32. According to the passage, there is a need for satire because people need to be

(A) informed about new scientific developments

(B) exposed to original philosophies when they are formulated

(C) reminded that popular ideas are often inaccurate

(D) told how they can be of service to their communities

[해석] 지문에 따르면 풍자가 필요한 이유는 무엇인가?
　　(A) (사람들이) 새로운 과학 발전에 관해 정보를 얻어야 해서
　　(B) (사람들은) 철학이 체계화될 때 기존 철학에 노출되어야 해서
　　(C) (사람들에게) 통상적인 관념들이 때로는 부정확하다는 것을 상기시키려고
　　(D) (사람들이) 지역 사회에 도움이 될 수 있는 방법에 대해 알리려고

[어휘] **formulate** 체계화하다, 공식화하다　**inaccurate** 부정확한, 정확하지 않은　**be of service** 도움이 되다

33. The word "refreshing" in line 18 is closest in meaning to

(A) popular

(B) ridiculous

(C) meaningful

(D) unusual

[해석] 18행에 언급된 "refreshing"과 의미상 가장 가까운 것은 무엇인가?
　　(A) 인기 있는
　　(B) 터무니없는
　　(C) 의미 있는
　　(D) 이례적인

34. The word "they" in line 21 refers to

(A) people

(B) media

(C) ideals

(D) movies

[해석] 21행에 언급된 "they"가 가리키는 것은 무엇인가?
　　(A) 사람들
　　(B) 매체들
　　(C) 관념들
　　(D) 영화들

35. The word "devote" in line 23 is closest in meaning to

(A) distinguish

(B) feel affection

(C) prefer

(D) dedicate

[해석] 23행에 언급된 "devote"와 의미상 가장 가까운 것은 무엇인가?
　　(A) 구별하다
　　(B) 애정을 느끼다
　　(C) 선호하다
　　(D) 헌신하다

36. As a result of reading satiric literature, readers will be most likely to

(A) teach themselves to write fiction

(B) accept conventional points of view

(C) become better informed about current affairs

(D) reexamine their opinions and values

[해석] 풍자 문학을 읽은 결과 독자들은 어떠할 것 같은가?
(A) 스스로 소설 쓰는 법을 배우게 될 것이다
(B) 전통적인 관점을 수용할 것이다
(C) 시사 문제에 대해 더 잘 알게 될 것이다
(D) **자신들의 의견과 가치관을 재검토할 것이다**

[어휘] **point of view** 관점, 견지, 입장 **current affairs** 최근 사건, 시사 **reexamine** 재검토하다

37. The various purposes of satire include all of the following EXCEPT

(A) introducing readers to unfamiliar situations
(B) brushing away illusions
(C) reminding readers of the truth
(D) exposing false values

[해석] 다음 중 풍자의 다양한 목적에 포함되지 않는 것은 무엇인가?
(A) 독자들에게 낯선 상황을 소개하는 것
(B) 망상을 떨쳐 버리도록 하는 것
(C) 독자들에게 진실을 상기시키는 것
(D) 거짓된 가치관을 드러내는 것

38. Why does the author mention "service of humanity" in line 24?

(A) People need to be reminded to take action.
(B) Readers appreciate knowing about it.
(C) It is an ideal that is rarely achieved.
(D) Popular media often distort such stories.

[해석] 글쓴이가 24행에서 "service of humanity"를 언급한 이유는 무엇인가?
(A) 사람들에게 행동에 옮기도록 상기시키려고
(B) 독자들이 그것에 관해 알도록 인식시키려고
(C) 거의 성취되지 않은 관념이라서
(D) 유명한 매체들이 종종 그런 이야기를 왜곡해서

[어휘] **distort** (사실·생각 등을) 왜곡하다

Galaxies are the [39]major building blocks of the universe. A galaxy is a giant family of many millions of stars, and it is held together by its own gravitational field. Most of the material in the universe is organized into galaxies of stars, together with gas and dust.

[40]There are three main types of galaxies: spiral, elliptical, and irregular. The Milky Way is a spiral galaxy: a flattish disc of stars with two spiral arms emerging from its central nucleus. About one-quarter of all galaxies have this shape. [42]Spiral galaxies are well supplied with the interstellar gas in [41]which new stars form; as the rotating spiral pattern sweeps around the galaxy, it compresses gas and dust, triggering the formation of bright young stars in its arms. The elliptical galaxies have a [43]symmetrical, elliptical or spheroidal shape with no [44]obvious structure. [45]Most of their member stars are very old, and since ellipticals are devoid of interstellar gas, no new stars are forming in them. The biggest and brightest galaxies in the universe are ellipticals with masses of about 1013 times that of the Sun; these giants may frequently be sources of strong radio emission, [46]in which case they are called radio galaxies. About two-thirds of all galaxies are elliptical. [47]Irregular galaxies comprise about one-tenth of all galaxies, and they come in many subclasses.

Measurement in space is quite different from measurement on Earth. Some terrestrial distances can be expressed as intervals of time: the time to fly from one continent to another or the time it takes to drive to work, for example. By comparison, with these familiar yardsticks, the distances to the galaxies are incomprehensibly large, but [48]they too are made more manageable by using a time calibration, in this case, the distance that light travels in one year. [49]On such a scale, the nearest giant spiral galaxy, the Andromeda galaxy, is two million light years away. The most distant luminous objects seen by telescopes are probably ten thousand million light years away. Their light was already halfway here before the Earth even formed. The light from the nearby Virgo galaxy set out when reptiles still ⁵⁰dominated the animal world.

[해석] 은하계는 우주의 주요한 기본 구성 요소이다. 하나의 은하계는 수백 만 개의 별들로 구성된 거대한 집단으로, 그 자체의 중력장에 의해 함께 모여 있다. 우주에서 대부분의 물질은 별들의 은하계와 함께 가스 및 먼지로 구성되어 있다.

세 가지 주요 유형의 은하계가 있는데, 즉 나선형 (은하), 타원형 (은하)와 부정형 (은하)이다. 은하수는 나선형 은하로, 약간 평평한 원반 모양의 별들로 중앙의 핵에서 두 개의 나선형 팔이 나온 모양이다. 모든 은하계의 대략 1/4이 이런 모양이다. 나선형 은하는 새로운 별들이 형성되는 성간 가스가 풍족하다. 선회하는 나선형 모양이 은하계 주변을 휩쓸면서 가스와 먼지를 압축해서, 그 팔에 밝고 어린 별들의 형성을 유발한다. 타원형 은하는 뚜렷한 구조 없이 대칭적인 타원형이거나 회원체 모양이다. 타원형 은하를 구성하는 대부분의 별들은 아주 오래되었고, 타원형 은하에는 성간 가스가 없기 때문에 새로운 별들이 형성되지 않는다. 우주에서 가장 크고 밝은 은하계는 태양의 약 1013배 크기인 타원형 은하이다. 이런 거대한 은하는 종종 강한 전파 방출의 공급원이 되는데, 이 경우 그것들은 전파 은하라고 불린다. 모든 은하계의 약 2/3가 타원형이다. 부정형 은하는 전체 은하계의 약 1/10을 차지하며 많은 하위 분류로 나뉜다.

우주에서의 측량법은 지구에서의 측량법과 상당히 다르다. 지구의 거리는 시간의 간격으로 표현될 수 있다. 예를 들어 한 대륙에서 다른 대륙으로 비행하는 데 걸리는 시간이나 차로 출근하는데 걸리는 시간으로 나타낼 수 있다. 이런 익숙한 척도로 비교해 보면, 은하계까지의 거리는 상상을 초월할 정도로 광대하지만, 이런 경우 그 거리들 역시 빛이 1년에 이동하는 거리인 시간 척도를 사용하여 처리할 수 있다. 그런 척도로 가장 가까운 거대한 나선형 은하인 안드로메다 은하는 2백만 광년 떨어져 있다. 망원경으로 볼 수 있는 가장 먼 발광체들은 아마도 100억 광년 떨어져 있을 것이다. 그 빛은 심지어 지구가 생기기도 전에 이미 절반은 여기에 와 있었다. 처녀자리 은하 근처의 빛은 여전히 파충류가 동물계를 지배하던 때에 출발했다.

[어휘] **galaxy** 은하, 은하계 **building block** (복잡한 것을 구성하는) 기초 단위, 구성물 **gravitational field** 중력장 **spiral** 나선형의 **elliptical** 타원형의 **irregular** (모양·배치 등이) 가지런하지 않은, 불규칙한 **Milky Way** 은하, 은하수 **flattish** 약간 평평한, 좀 단조로운 **emerge** 나타나다, 출현하다 **nucleus** 핵 **interstellar** 별과 별 사이의, 성간의 **sweep** 휩쓸다, 청소하다 **compress** 압축하다 **trigger** 유발하다, 일으키다 **symmetrical** 대칭인 **spheroidal** 회전 타원체의, 거의 구형의 **obvious** 분명한, 명백한 **devoid of** ~이 결여된, 전혀 없는 **mass** 크기, 질량 **radio** 전파 **emission** 방사, 방출 **comprise** 구성하다, 차지하다 **subclass** 하위 분류 **measurement** 측정(법), 측량 **terrestrial** 지구의

interval 간격 **continent** 대륙 **comparison** 비교 **yardstick** (비교·판단의) 척도, 기준 **incomprehensibly** 이해할 수 없게, 상상을 초월할 정도로 **manageable** 처리할 수 있는, 관리할 수 있는 **calibration** 눈금 **scale** 규모, 척도, 기준 **light year** 광년 **luminous** 빛을 내는, 발광의 **telescope** 망원경 **halfway** 절반의, 중간의 **Virgo** 처녀자리 **set out** 시작하다, 출발하다 **reptile** 파충류 **dominate** 지배하다, 장악하다

39. The word "major" in line 1 is closest in meaning to

(A) intense

(B) principal

(C) huge

(D) unique

[해석] 1행에 언급된 "major"와 의미상 가장 가까운 것은 무엇인가?
  (A) 강렬한
  (B) 주요한
  (C) 거대한
  (D) 독특한

40. What does the second paragraph mainly discuss?

(A) The Milky Way

(B) Major categories of galaxies

(C) How elliptical galaxies are formed

(D) Differences between irregular and spiral galaxies

[해석] 두 번째 단락에서는 주로 무엇에 관해 이야기하고 있는가?
  (A) 은하수
  (B) 주요 은하의 종류
  (C) 타원형 은하의 형성 방법
  (D) 부정형 은하와 나선형 은하의 차이

41. The word "which" in line 7 refers to

(A) dust

(B) gas

(C) pattern

(D) galaxy

[해석] 7행에 언급된 "which"가 가리키는 것은 무엇인가?
  (A) 먼지
  (B) 가스
  (C) 모양
  (D) 은하

42. According to the passage, new stars are formed in spiral galaxies due to

(A) an explosion of gas

(B) the compression of gas and dust

(C) the combining of old stars

(D) strong radio emissions

[해석] 지문에 따르면, 나선형 은하에서 새로운 별들이 생성되는 이유는 무엇인가?
(A) 가스의 폭발
(B) 가스와 먼지의 압축
(C) 오래된 별들의 결합
(D) 강한 전파 방출

[어휘] explosion 폭발 compression 압축

43. The word "symmetrical" in line 9 is closest in meaning to

(A) proportionally balanced

(B) commonly seen

(C) typically large

(D) steadily growing

[해석] 9행에 언급된 "symmetrical"과 의미상 가장 가까운 것은 무엇인가?
(A) 비례하여 균형이 잡힌
(B) 흔히 보이는
(C) 전형적으로 큰
(D) 꾸준히 자라는

[어휘] proportionally 비례하여 typically 전형적으로 steadily 꾸준히, 점차

44. The word "obvious" in line 9 is closest in meaning to

(A) discovered

(B) apparent

(C) understood

(D) simplistic

[해석] 9행에 언급된 "obvious"와 의미상 가장 가까운 것은 무엇인가?
(A) 발견된
(B) 분명한
(C) 이해되는
(D) 아주 간단한

[어휘] simplistic 극단적으로 단순화한, 아주 간단한

45. According to the passage, which of the following is NOT true of elliptical galaxies?

(A) They are the largest galaxies.

(B) They mostly contain old stars.

(C) They contain a high amount of interstellar gas.

(D) They have a spherical shape.

[해석] 지문에 따르면, 다음 중 타원형 은하에 대한 설명으로 맞지 않는 것은 무엇인가?
(A) 가장 큰 은하계이다.
(B) 주로 오래된 별들이 속해 있다.
(C) 많은 양의 성간 가스가 들어 있다.
(D) 구형 모양이다.

[어휘] spherical 구형의, 둥근

46. Which of the following characteristics of radio galaxies is mentioned in the passage?

(A) They are a type of elliptical galaxy.

(B) They are usually too small to be seen with a telescope.

(C) They are closely related to irregular galaxies.

(D) They are not as bright as spiral galaxies.

[해석] 다음 중 지문에 언급된 전파 은하의 특성은 무엇인가?
(A) 타원형 은하의 한 종류이다.
(B) 보통 너무 작아서 망원경으로 볼 수 없다.
(C) 부정형 은하와 밀접한 관계가 있다.
(D) 나선형 은하만큼 밝지 않다.

47. What percentage of galaxies is irregular?

(A) 10%

(B) 25%

(C) 50%

(D) 75%

[해석] 부정형 은하의 비율은 얼마나 되는가?
(A) 10퍼센트
(B) 25퍼센트
(C) 50퍼센트
(D) 75퍼센트

48. The word "they" in line 19 refers to

(A) intervals

(B) yardsticks

(C) distances

(D) galaxies

[해석] 19행에 언급된 "they"가 가리키는 것은 무엇인가?
    (A) 간격
    (B) 척도
    (C) 거리
    (D) 은하

49. Why does the author mention the Virgo galaxy and the Andromeda galaxy in the third paragraph?

(A) To describe the effect that distance has on visibility

(B) To compare the ages of two relatively young galaxies

(C) To emphasize the vast distances of the galaxies from Earth

(D) To explain why certain galaxies cannot be seen by a telescope

[해석] 글쓴이가 세 번째 단락에서 처녀자리 은하와 안드로메다 은하를 언급한 이유는 무엇인가?
    (A) 거리가 시계에 미치는 영향을 설명하려고
    (B) 두 개의 비교적 젊은 은하를 비교하려고
    (C) 지구로부터 은하까지의 광대한 거리를 강조하려고
    (D) 특정 은하를 망원경으로 볼 수 없는 이유를 설명하려고

[어휘] **visibility** 시계, 보이는 범위   **emphasize** 강조하다   **vast** 광대한

50. The word "dominated" in line 24 is closest in meaning to

(A) threatened

(B) replaced

(C) were developing in

(D) were prevalent in

[해석] 24행에 언급된 "dominated"와 의미상 가장 가까운 것은 무엇인가?
    (A) 위협했다
    (B) 대체했다
    (C) 개발하고 있었다
    (D) 널리 퍼져 있었다

[어휘] **prevalent** 널리 퍼진

Sample Test Sections Answer Key

#	Section 1	Section 2	Section 3
1	C	D	A
2	D	B	D
3	C	D	A
4	A	B	C
5	C	A	C
6	A	C	B
7	A	B	D
8	A	A	D
9	B	B	B
10	A	D	C
11	A	C	D
12	C	C	B
13	D	B	C
14	D	D	D
15	D	D	A
16	B	A	D
17	C	B	B
18	D	C	D
19	D	C	C
20	C	D	C
21	D	A	A
22	A	A	C
23	A	D	A
24	C	B	A
25	A	B	A
26	D	C	B
27	B	B	B
28	C	C	C
29	C	C	D
30	D	A	A
31	A	B	C
32	C	D	A
33	D	C	C
34	A	C	D
35	C	A	A
36	D	D	D
37	D	A	C
38	D	A	B
39	A	C	A
40	C	A	B
41	D		A
42	B		C
43	B		B
44	D		C
45	C		D
46	C		C
47	B		C
48	B		B
49	A		C
50	C		B

Complete *TOEFL ITP* Practice Test Answer Key

#	Section 1	Section 2	Section 3
1	C	A	C
2	B	A	D
3	A	B	C
4	A	B	B
5	A	B	C
6	A	C	D
7	C	D	A
8	A	A	A
9	C	C	C
10	B	D	B
11	A	D	A
12	B	D	D
13	B	D	D
14	A	D	B
15	A	A	D
16	B	C	D
17	D	B	A
18	D	B	B
19	C	A	B
20	B	C	D
21	C	D	D
22	D	D	B
23	D	D	B
24	C	C	D
25	D	A	B
26	C	C	B
27	C	D	D
28	A	B	B
29	C	D	A
30	D	D	A
31	A	A	B
32	B	D	C
33	D	A	D
34	B	C	A
35	B	B	D
36	D	A	D
37	C	C	A
38	C	B	C
39	B	A	B
40	A	C	B
41	A		B
42	C		B
43	D		A
44	C		B
45	B		C
46	A		A
47	D		A
48	B		C
49	C		C
50	B		D